# My Terminal Life

*Cancer Habitation and Other Life Adventures*

Amy Lyn Schnitzler

My Terminal Life
*Cancer Habitation and Other Life Adventures*

Amy Lyn Schnitzler

**For audio and video recordings referenced in this book, as well
as copies of the author's original paintings, or to purchase
copies of the book, visit myterminallife.org.**

## Tributes to the author and this book

"There are people who have come and gone during my time at the Breast Cancer Coalition and each one has left their imprint, but none as deeply set as Amy's. I will never forget the strength that she showed—her spirit and determination in the face of a tremendously difficult journey. I will especially remember the early days after her initial diagnosis of breast cancer when she came to Brown Bag at the Coalition, always the youngest survivor in the room and, later, to Common Ground, our group for those living with advanced breast or gynecologic cancer. She exuded warmth and empathy, always, towards others and was beloved by our group members.

Many people find themselves diminished by their terminal illness. They withdraw from the world and into themselves as their cancer progresses, and they, understandably, become introspective and contemplative as they face the end of life. But Amy did the opposite. Amy displayed incredible toughness and resilience through her entire trek with breast cancer even though the path was not always clear.

I have always loved how Amy welcomed people into her life, enclosing them into her sacred circle. I have always loved how she continued to be engaged with the world with enormous enthusiasm and incredible hope every moment she was alive with her beautiful mother, her father, her brother Ryan, and Mark. Right up until her last days. I have always loved her sass and spunk and brutal honesty when sharing her story about what living with metastatic breast cancer was like for her. Because she wanted people to understand that she was *living* with metastatic breast cancer, not *dying* with it.

The pages here are filled with Amy—the words, her own, capturing the way in which she lived her one beautiful, glorious, sadly shortened life. A life lived with dignity and grace.

I consider myself blessed to have known Amy and feel genuine gratitude to her for sharing her journey with us. What she has given to us, to each of us, is deep hope about human possibilities, and comfort as we face our own fears of death.

Amy made a difference. She will be remembered."

*—Holly Anderson*
*Executive Director, Breast Cancer Coalition of Rochester*

<>

"In her third year of living with Stage IV Metastatic Breast Cancer, Amy observed my Meaning of Death class at Nazareth College. Her presence in the class made real all that would have been abstract in our academic discussions. She shared, as she does in this book, with honesty and grace the daily details of navigating the clinical, institutional, interpersonal, as well as the physical and psychological aspects of living with a terminal illness, nestling them within the larger contexts of the meaning of acceptance and hope, love and loss, and life and death. Amy's presence in the class changed many lives, including mine, forever. The same presence lives in this book and I wholeheartedly recommend it to anyone seeking to understand what it means to live fully while learning to fully embrace death. The real-life perspective Amy offers is especially valuable for academic courses on death and dying. What she shared in her first email to me makes this abundantly clear:

*Today I am trying to live a meaningful and enjoyable life while simultaneously making room for death and all of its uncertainty and unpredictability, learning to accept its inevitability and allow it to inform my existence in ways it did not, could not, in my life before cancer. In a strange way, this has all been a privilege… to be stretched so far open, to see this life so differently. And it has also been a challenge.*

Every time I think of Amy, my heart is filled with a sweet feeling. My heart is filled with the same feeling reading this book."

*—Bishal Karna*
*Assistant Professor, Religious Studies Department, Nazareth College*

<>

"I was honored to play a small part in Amy's care/team. She had such a presence when she visited the office that she is greatly missed. I have loaned her book out to my daughter's 'hospice' class. It is an elective for high school seniors. Her teacher loves the book and asked to keep it in the school library. I do think for many of the same reasons that the book would be beneficial to medical students. Many of these young adults are just starting on their career paths like Amy was and could connect with Amy's vibrancy and energy. Amy was 'full of life' with a terminal diagnosis."

*—Lesley James, M.D.*
*Integrative Medicine, Pittsford, NY*

<>

"As an oncology nurse for 38 years, you can probably imagine how many amazing people I have met, cared for and loved, but none were like Amy Lyn Schnitzler. Her beauty, intelligence and talents were matched only by her open loving heart and soul. I was fortunate to be able to transcend the nurse/patient boundary with her and was able to call Amy my friend. Our relationship wasn't just about her cancer and treatment—it was about sharing our lives, our confidences, hopes and dreams. We talked often. She told me about Mark and how much she loved him. We laughed. We cried. We spent a wonderful afternoon at Starbucks where, when telling her so much about my life, I was met with her deep compassion, understanding and acceptance. I got to go to her 30th birthday celebration and witness first-hand the loving connections she had with her family and friends. And I must say that the trust she had in me was humbling.

She was taken from us MUCH TOO SOON, and when she died a bright light went out on Earth… but a shining star rose in the sky to look down on us and forever send us her love."

—*Kitty Forbush*
*Infusion Nurse, Pluta Cancer Center*

<>

"Fiercely curious and smart, vibrant, sassy, 'full force ahead' Amy Schnitzler is dealt the blow of her life as she is just coming into her own as a vocalist. The raw and insightful journey of tell-it-like-it-is writing is a gift to us all, defining the fight and spirit we all hope to possess. After reading her journey, you too will come to love the one and only Amy Schnitzler.

I am blown away by her writings, her love, spirit, raw and genuine 'laying it out there' for all of us to feel and see. What a tribute to her! This is an absolute must-read for every person in the medical field. We 'live and die' by the words of our doctors, and they need to know, as do our friends, that words are so powerful—as are Amy's.

I know her book and life will make a difference and open doors."

—*Nancy Pettersen Strelau*
*Associate Professor/Associate Director of the School of Music, Nazareth College*

<>

"Reading the book was like receiving a letter from Amy—so immediate, so real. Amy was so special to me in so many ways. The opera singer connection was something we shared and it put an extra emotional charge into our relationship. She did things her way and I respected her for that. I think of her often and I wish she were still with us.

Breast cancer research is moving at an exponential pace. Our approach to the treatment of breast cancer has changed vastly during the time I have been a practicing oncologist. Our drug arsenal is expanding rapidly as is our understanding of mechanisms which drive cancer growth and spread.

I always felt honored to care for Amy. Working to serve my patients and helping them navigate the complexities of cancer care is why I do what I do. "

*—Michelle Shayne, M.D.*
*Oncologist, Pluta Cancer Center*

<>

"We will remember Amy's courage, poise and good nature as she navigated every challenge that came her way. She was a bright light, and her memory is part of a legacy that inspires us every day to keep working to advance cancer care for our patients."

*—Andrew Brandmaier M.D, Ph.D.*
*Radiation Oncologist, New York-Presbyterian/Weill Cornell Medical Center*

<>

"Amy meant a lot to all of us here… She was a lovely person, but also very strong and determined, and I learned a lot from her. She will forever be in my memory."

*—Leticia Varella M.D.*
*Oncologist, New York-Presbyterian/Weill Cornell Medical Center*

<>

"…Amy made a HUGE impact on me and countless others, and I feel truly honored that I got to meet her, spend time with her, hear that beautiful voice, and that a bit of her story will live on to inspire others as well."

*—Dana Donofree*
*Founder, Survivor, CEO, AnaOno LLC*

*To my mom, who fought wild tigers for me,*
*and to those who are on similar journeys:*
*Never give up!*

# Table of Contents

* *selected writings (Bristol Bookends memoir writing class)*

_* Published by SHARE, June 2019_

It is estimated that there are more than 150,000 women presently living with metastatic breast cancer in the U.S. Called Stage 4, it means the cancer, which started in the breast, has spread to create tumors in other parts of the body, such as the lungs, liver, bones and the brain. Slightly more than 20% of Stage 4 breast cancer patients survive 5 years. It is remarkable how drugs that target parts of the breast cancer cells have resulted in longer survival and, at least in the early stages of the disease, more cures. Medical scientists have learned much about how cancer cells grow and function, and have produced new drugs that target these functions on a cellular level and stop the cells from dividing, stop the cancer from growing. But either these drugs only work on a percentage of the cancer cells, or the cancer mutates and the drug ultimately doesn't eliminate the cancer completely.

Breast cancers don't "come back" after a course of treatment appears to eliminate the tumor. Some part of the cancer remains and continues to grow. Then scientists have to develop new drugs to destroy the part that wasn't eliminated with the first treatment.

For patients with metastatic breast cancer the result is that they live longer, but they are not cured. We don't cure metastatic breast cancer and annually more than 40,000 women will die from Stage 4 breast cancer.

<>

I first met Amy on April 18, 2016. My note says "a previously healthy 26-year-old." 26-year-old!! She had a mass in her right breast and a mass in her right armpit. Biopsies showed they were both invasive ductal carcinoma—the most common type of breast cancer. Breast cancers also differ in their molecular biology. Some are more likely to be cured, others less so. Her cancer's bio markers indicated that it was estrogen receptor positive and HER 2 negative. This identifies what is usually a less aggressive type.

Other than the two masses, Amy looked and felt like any other healthy young woman. She was on the verge of a career in operatic singing. In December she first felt the mass while staying at a hotel in Chicago. She was there to pursue graduate training at the University of Chicago.

On that first day I explained all that we could do to treat breast cancer in a multimodality approach, involving surgery, radiation, chemotherapy and "hormonal" therapy. When I mentioned genetic testing, Amy put up her hands and stopped me cold. She was having difficulty "wrapping her head around all of this" at once. I should have realized that. It can be overwhelming and I needed to slow down. That's when the two-way street of educating each other began.

Ultimately Amy took it all in and we proceeded to perform X-rays and scans to search for any evidence of cancer anywhere else in her body. We found nothing further. She decided to undergo a bilateral mastectomy and reconstruction.

The pathology report from her surgery indicated that she had Stage 3 disease, documented disease limited to the breast and the lymph nodes in her armpit. This meant that there was evidence that the cancer had begun to spread, raising our concern that although the scans looked clean, there could be cancer cells in her body that could not be removed by surgery alone. Again we talked about all the additional things we should do to try to cure this. Amy began to research other non-traditional approaches. At the same time she spoke openly about the devastating effect this already had on her body and body image—this, of course, in addition to its effect on her future plans and a life now put on hold.

I often tell patients as they move past initial breast cancer surgery that at this point they have no evidence of disease, but will be monitored closely for many years. This is a long-term process; somehow, and to my amazement, patients move through it and get on with their lives. How each patient does this has always been somewhat of a mystery to me. I did not realize how little I knew about the process until I began reading Amy's blog.

On November 7, 2016 Amy returned to my office, while still undergoing systemic hormonal therapy, to show me a few tiny red nodules on the skin of her right "breast." Objectively I knew what this meant, but I still hoped it was just a rash. Biopsy was scheduled for the next day. The biopsy showed that these tiny "bumps" were metastatic breast cancer. When this occurs after mastectomy it usually is an indicator that the disease is also elsewhere. Now this cancer was Stage 4 and likely incurable. This began a series of treatments with partial successes, to be followed by setbacks. Some tumors regressed on treatment; new ones popped up.

Amy's search for effective treatments—both standard of care, and non-traditional alternative approaches to diet, exercise and life style—took on a new intensity. We told her this was not a curable cancer, but she never really believed that. She told me she still had hopes of someday having a family.

The disease was unrelenting, but so was Amy's determination to survive. More than just survive—Amy had moved on with her life. She became an advocate for the need for research funding to treat the breast cancer no one likes to talk about: Stage 4 metastatic breast cancer. She talked about it locally and nationally—what this disease is and what it's like to live with it. She did it with her voice, her words and her artwork. She did it as only a true artist with an artist's sensibility can do. As only Amy could do.

This book is not just about metastatic breast cancer. It's about Amy's life with breast cancer. It's about dealing with the treatments; the successes and then the setbacks; the side effects and change in her appearance. It's about the struggle that she went through day after day and could express in words so honestly.

It is very difficult to read. Anyone, physician, family or friend, who is trying to help someone living with a life-threatening chronic illness can learn so much from reading it.

Metastatic breast cancer ultimately silenced that marvelous voice, but not the words, and not the message.

*Joel Yellin, M.D.*
*Surgeon, Rochester General Hospital*

# Introduction*

My name is Amy Schnitzler. I was diagnosed with Metastatic Breast Cancer at 26 years old. Today I am 29, I will be 30 in July. In the 3 years that I have been living with MBC, my life has changed in countless ways, and yet, when sitting down to organize my thoughts for this talk, I realized that in many ways—important ways—my life still looks a lot the same. Yes, I have a lot more Dr.'s appointments these days, and my organs are beginning to feel like Kardashians with the amount of times they've had their picture taken, but if someone were to look at what brought me joy before my diagnosis and compare it to now, they would find a lot of similarity. I live an active life, and a life of love and connection. This was true before cancer, and it's true now, in many ways, more so.

My diagnosis came the same week I received my acceptance letters to graduate school for opera performance in 2016. I am happy to report that after a year and a half of virtual silence, I made an appearance as part of the ensemble in the RPO's semi-staged production of Bizet's "Carmen," under the baton of Ward Stare. This year, I was selected to participate in the small choral ensemble

---

* *Presentation at "Tools for the Journey: Living with Metastatic Breast Cancer"—16th Annual Cindy L. Dertinger Advanced Breast Cancer Seminar organized by the Breast Cancer Coalition of Rochester, Rochester NY, April 5, 2019.*

**Link to video available here: myterminallife.org**

of the opera Cosi Fan Tutte again with the RPO. I am also currently undertaking a fund-raising project to benefit metastatic breast cancer research in collaboration with Nazareth College Orchestra led by Professor Nancy Strelau, featuring many guest artists. I will be performing in the concert, along with a very special part of my care team who also has a passion for opera. Stay tuned!

Supporting MBC research gives meaning and purpose to my life. The lives of those of us living with MBC depends on research and development of life-prolonging treatments. Today, the over-whelming majority of money raised for breast cancer goes toward prevention, and general awareness. Unfortunately, this does very little to help people in my position, whose disease has already traveled beyond the breast.

*MBC research benefits everyone at every stage of the diagnosis. One-third of all people diagnosed with early stage disease will become metastatic months or years after treatment. We need a CURE for ALL, and that cure will only come through funded research.*

This past October, I marched on Capitol Hill to share my story with legislative officials and their correspondents advocating for increased funding for Metastatic Breast Cancer Research. In February, I walked the runway in New York Fashion week in lingerie for breast cancer patients, designed by survivor Dana Donofree of AnaOno Intimates. This year's show featured all metastatic breast cancer patient models, and all money raised went directly toward METAvivor, an organization that exclusively funds MBC research. We brought in over $100,000. I have found a new sense of purpose through advocacy, fundraising, and educating the public on the reality of stage 4 disease, and how it differs from early stage. I am involved in a memoir writing group, and my writing has been published in the Huffington Post, the Underbelly online magazine, and the BCCR February newsletter. I am also an active blogger.

My life with cancer is not without its challenges. I am, after all, part of a community that is truly dying for a cure. In my 3 years of living with cancer, I have lost many friends. With each loss in our community, we lose parts of ourselves, and our hope. I find it nearly impossible to avoid contemplating my own death when someone I know has died from MBC: How will MY death play out? What will be the actual cause? When? How much will I suffer? How much will my loved ones suffer? And then… what if the headache I had yesterday was not just a headache, but a warning from my body that my days within it are numbered? What if the nausea I felt last week wasn't a side effect of new treatment, but something more insidious…

Living with cancer is living with potential threats from every direction, tirelessly searching for a bit of safety. Active-coping is a large part of my life. Coping with anxiety, depression, and fear, yes, but also coping with tremendous grief. I have found that grief and cancer are inextricably linked. Even excluding death, cancer encompasses so much loss. There is the loss of identity with physical changes that accompany aspects of treatment; loss of breasts, loss of hair, rapid and unpredictable weight changes… All of these changes, as difficult as they are on their own, are representative of perhaps the biggest challenge of a cancer diagnosis—the sudden realization that your life is not in your control. To a certain extent, I believe control is an illusion for us all, cancer aside. Cancer violently strips away this illusion and reveals the fragility of the human condition.

Prior to cancer, like most 20-something's, mortality was not in the forefront of my mind. Today death is a part of my life, woven into its fabric. Death can no longer exist in the ever-comfortable, ever-external "someday." Today I am figuring out how the inevitability of death can give meaning to life.

This semester, I am taking part in an undergraduate course entitled, "Meaning of Death" at Nazareth College in pursuit of clarity and peace. I recently gave a talk in class sharing my experience of living with a terminal illness as a young person. Exploring death in a more objective light through academia has felt important to me, especially in this last year, with the discovery of disease in my brain. Spread to the brain usually has a poor prognosis measured in months. I have been living with brain metastasis for almost a year with great quality of life. For this, I am truly grateful. The "Meaning of Death" class has deepened my desire for spiritual growth and transformation. I believe that spiritual healing is possible, even if a cure for my physical body is not at this time.

Physical activity remains my most favored tool in my coping tool-box, and today I celebrate all my body is able to do for me; I engage in high intensity interval training, running with my dog Riley, yoga at Breathe yoga studios, and regular strength training. I was featured in an NBC nightly news story on the benefits of exercise for chemotherapy induced fatigue in 2017, research led by Dr. Karen Mustian of URMC. Movement has always helped me move through all the mental and emotional turbulence involved in living with cancer. Yoga centers and calms me, running helps me diffuse, and strength training makes me feel empowered.

I am fortunate to have a dynamite medical team that supports and empowers me as well. Dr. Michelle Shayne, Dr. Kenneth Usuki, the wonderful nurses at Pluta, and my team at New York Presbyterian/ Weill Cornell: these are my healing co-pilots, and I am beyond grateful to have each and every one of them on board. I am also grateful to have a mother who has more resilience than anyone I've ever known. She is my true Hero, my biggest fan (even if sometimes she wants to karate chop me in the throat). She is my greatest source of support, comfort and love. Judy Schnitzler: you are amazing, and I am so fortunate to have you as my mom. I am also fortunate to have a patient, gentle, and loving partner. I could not ask for a more wise, and kind-hearted man by my side. My dad is always available for a terrible joke, or to fix parts of my car that I find ways to break at fairly regular intervals. I am so lucky to have the support of a close-knit family and many, many dear friends. The Coalition has been instrumental in my ability to cope with this illness as well. The women in the common ground group are sources of tremendous encouragement, validation, and love, who enable me to walk this road in my power.

I take a very active role in my care. This helps me feel powerful too. In a situation that has the potential to leave me feeling pretty powerless, I arm myself with information and knowledge. I do lots of research and ask lots of questions. I search for relevant clinical trials. This is my way of coping and it works for me. It enables me to be an active participant in my healing, and I have found that there's less potential to feel like a victim in this position. Victimhood is a place I visit, but I don't stay for long. I've found through experience in the first year of my diagnosis that it is difficult to live a life from a place of "why me." There is power in acceptance, even if what you are accepting is not desirable.

To the newly diagnosed: Breathe. Be gentle with yourself as you adjust to this new way of orienting yourself in the world. Don't be afraid or ashamed to ask for help, in the form of pharmaceuticals or support from loved ones or therapists. Your mental health is equally as important as your physical health; nurturing both will only help you. Take your time in putting together your care team, and navigating the world of treatment decisions. And don't be afraid to leave "cancer land" for a while to engage in things that have always brought you joy. It may feel foreign at first, but you will find new meaning in those things. Know that your new life is pulling you in seemingly opposing directions: acceptance of the reality of this disease on one end, and hope on the other. Know that finding a balance between those dimensions is imperfect and not easy. You will find new footing on fresh new ground, and as soon as you are comfortable there, you will have to adjust again. Your new life with cancer demands large amounts of flexibility. It may all feel impossible, but know that you do not walk this road alone. Should you find yourself facing this diagnosis, pull up a chair; there's a seat at the table for you at the BCCR.

I think I've found that the "new normal" we often hear about in the context of cancer doesn't really exist: what's "normal" is constantly changing. A very wise man helped me to see that sometimes it's not about the monumental in this life, but about grounding oneself in the simple beauty of ordinary, every-day living.

Thank you.

*Amyhealthyself Blog Posts
and Selected Writings*

## CANCER: LIFE INTERRUPTED…?
MAY 14, 2016

There are moments in a person's life that are forever imprinted in memory. I have a vivid recollection of sitting at my grandmother's kitchen table doing homework after grade school with my same-age cousin Michael, munching on her homemade chocolate chip cookies between hurried scribbles on my papers, because the faster we finished our homework, the faster we could get outside to play, of course—that was the rule! Taking gulps of sweetened iced tea, (the powder-and-water-kind, in our case, mostly powder, very little water), swinging my feet under the table, kicking Michael across from me until one of us would be put in time-out (this happened fairly regularly). Not monumental, but I'll always remember it. Or ripping off the cast I had on my arm for a broken thumb at age 5 because "I had an itch!" and seeing the look of horror on my mother's face as she scooped me up, put me in my car seat, and rushed me back to the hospital, where the doctor replaced my cast and told me I needed to wear the cast an additional three weeks, and suggested my mother find me an "itching tool." A sea of black robes and yellow tassels on my college graduation day and the electric buzzing of chatter as we all lined up in the basement of the Blue Cross Arena in preparation to walk the stage. Scurrying to the mailbox (or obsessively checking my email) every day for weeks in early spring until the large envelopes from the graduate schools I applied to arrived, the nauseating excitement in my stomach as I tore through the envelope and read through the first three lines: "Dear Amy, We are pleased to inform you of your acceptance to the Masters in Vocal Performance Program for the Fall semester of 2016. We are also pleased to inform you that based on your audition score, you have qualified for a scholarship…" and the frantic jumping and screaming and hugging and crying that ensued between my mother and me after I read the letter aloud. I will always remember this.

I will also always remember April 8th, 2016 as one of the most excruciating days of my life.

Prior to this date, I was an active 26-year-old, to my knowledge in overall good health (being diagnosed with cancer has given me the **opportunity** to assess how I've always personally defined health, however...). I had been applying to graduate schools for opera and classical voice performance in the fall of 2015, received invitations to live auditions after vigorous pre-screening recorded auditions, and began the live audition process in January of 2016.

For those of you who are unfamiliar with the life of a classical musician, I will summarize it briefly: It is hard. It is stressful. It is competitive. As a Soprano, the most common voice type for a female, it is especially competitive. There are often hundreds of applicants for programs of six or fewer spots. Not only is there pressure to be at the top of your game vocally, but there is also substantial emphasis on physical appearance, unfortunately. Sadly, it is not all about the voice, as I do believe it should be. Yes, it is about the voice, but it's about the voice in combination with other things like stage presence, personality, and physicality—whether someone *looks* the part, regardless of how well he or she may sing it. There is this strange misconception in our modern world that opera singers are often very overweight (i.e., the use of the phrase "when the fat lady sings" evokes an image of a rotund woman with blonde braids and a viking helmet dramatically warbling at the top of her lungs). **Let me just clear this up right now**. This is *not* the case. Here are a few examples of the modern opera singer (no viking ladies here): Anna Netrebko, Natalie Dessay, Pretty Yende, Denise Graves, Maria Callas (just look at them brows, *girrrrr!*).

There are some opera singers who have a larger stature, and there are some physiological links between larger statures and larger voice types. Opera is an evolutionary art form, however. There are different styles and periods within opera. Generally speaking, those larger voice types (with sometimes larger-built singers) are found in Wagnerian opera. Wagner composed for extremely large orchestras, and very dense harmonic sonorities, so it required a particular vocal richness, color, and power to be heard above all of the instrumental activity. And to be clear: I'm not saying big ain't beautiful—it is. So is small. So is asymmetrical. So is scarred. Our western world is a particularly troubling brand of ass-backwards in terms of priorities and conceptions, and I frustrate the shit out of myself when I find that I'm buying into the very social constructs that I detest, for example, spending hours in front of the mirror painting my face attempting to cover up every scar, every blemish, in the hopes that I may prove my worth to the world... like what?... Why is there such a push to be validated by someone or something outside of ourselves? (A post for another time...)

Ultimately, the point of my rant here is to highlight untruths about opera—I'm not sure why this "singing fat lady" image has come to define pop-culture's conception of opera, but I digress. In any case, there is a ton of pressure to look a certain way. And obviously, based on the images I provided, that certain way is "beautiful." Young, ingenue, leading-lady opera roles are typically slender, very feminine, and classically attractive. So as you can imagine, the opera world is filled with tons of vanity, and ego (which I have learned to equate with fear... but that's another post for another time). In other words: **high stress**. Especially to a highly sensitive empath like me.

So, it came as no surprise that during this audition process of arduous travel through the winter that I was feeling slightly under the weather. It also was not surprising to me that at this time, I had some swelling under my right armpit. This happened from time to time, with stress, with illness, with infection. And at that time, I could check off all of those things. Stress, check. Under the weather, check. I was on antibiotics for a stupid skin infection, so, check. To be safe, however, I went to Urgent Care mid-January to have it looked at. (Yes, Urgent Care, and not my Primary Care Physician, because at 26 I had just aged out of my pediatrician. Stop laughing at me.) They told me that given my age, and the fact that I am not overweight, and that I do not have family history of breast cancer, this was most likely nothing to worry about. They sent me on my way, but told me to keep an eye on it, and if it didn't go away in a few weeks, or if it got bigger, I should get some imaging done.

So this lymph node swelling really did not concern me at first. I went about my business, continued to travel from city to city for auditions, and essentially forgot about it until March, after I had received acceptance letters to three out of the five graduate programs I applied to, including Peabody Institute, part of Johns Hopkins University (WAHOO!). I realized one day that the lump in my lymph node was still there, and also noticed that my breast possibly felt a little harder than normal, but admittedly I wasn't sure because 1) I am inclined to paranoia, and 2) I had not paid that much attention to my breasts because they were not that fascinating to me, and 3) at 26, who is thinking about lumps and bumps being anything serious? I agonized over whether or not to make an appointment for weeks, and after persistent nagging from my mother, I ended up making an appointment with Rochester General Breast Center where I was certain I would receive a clean bill of health before starting my new life in Chicago at the Chicago College of Performing Arts through Roosevelt University.

I went to the appointment, not nervous at all. The doctor performed an exam, and as her cold hands were palpating my breasts, I asked her, sort of jokingly, "Do you think it's cancer?" to which she replied, "No, I don't. You're at the right age for developing fibroadenomas, but the lymph node is a little suspicious, so I'm going to order an ultrasound. And if they offer to do a biopsy in that appointment, I suggest you have them do it." Okay, fibro-ada-whaddas?? Well, not quite the answer I wanted to hear, but I still believed that my lymph node was just a result of stress and the under-the-weather-ness from all the travel for auditions. This was April 6th. My ultrasound was scheduled for April 8th, which was a Friday.

I was a little nervous, so I asked my mother to come with me. And thank God I did. Initially, I had my mom stay out in the waiting room. I got undressed and put my robe on backwards (rookie mistake, I'm a *pro* at that shit now). The tech came in and kindly asked me to turn it around with the opening in the front so that they could easily access my breasts and armpit, and now that I think about it, I'm sure she had probably said that in the beginning, based on the fact that every appointment since the diagnosis, they still tell me how to adorn the beautiful pale blue spotted gown, but I think I was probably just in a hurry to get on with my day, and it most likely took a fast trip between my ears...

The tech, a young girl who looked to be about my age, was very sweet. She told me to just try to relax, and breathe through the moment. I believed her sweetness to be sincere, but as she began the ultrasound, her eyes seemed to get bigger, and it almost registered to me as either surprise, or fear, neither of which seemed good in my present situation. I scanned the faces of the doctors (both male, go figure), but I couldn't read their expressions at all. Which also concerned me. They were speaking in hushed tones about the features of my ultrasound, which frankly pissed me off. And furthermore, no one was answering my "Do you think it's cancer" question in a way that was satisfactory to me. "We are not able to say anything at this point, but we are recommending that you get a biopsy. We should probably biopsy the breast first, and then the lymph node. We just have some paperwork for you to fill out giving your consent to perform the biopsies today. We will be back in a few minutes."

The tech came back in the room with the paperwork, and asked me if I needed some water. At this point, she was no longer sweet, and I was calling her a tight-lipped rotten bitch in my head, because I was convinced that she knew EVERYTHING and just wasn't telling me. Needless to say, I was reeling. Thank God I had my phone in my hand. I texted my mom:

ME: *Mom somethings wrong I can tell, they're making me f******* scared, they want to do a biopsy I think something's wrong can you come back here?*

MOM: *I will be right there.*

That text exchange basically encapsulates the relationship I have with my mother. Yes, there's some codependence, yes, there's some conflict, yes, we bicker like an old couple. But the bottom line is that she is absolutely hands-down the most loyal person in my whole world. From the time I was small, she always said, "I'd fight wild tigers for you." And I believe it. (My mother's a wimp. She doesn't do blood or guts, or scary movies, or violent tv shows. So for her to say that she would go face to face with a wild carnivorous beast and for me to actually **believe** it is saying something.)

32

In about 18 seconds, my mom was in the room with me, holding my hand, telling me to breathe, to think of Riley, my 3-year-old black lab-daughter. The doctors came back in, and spoke briefly to my mother about the biopsy procedure, while my head was conjuring up a decent sized cyclone of worst-case-scenario-panic. They numbed my breast, stabbed me, and placed a surgical clip inside the lump in my breast because "either way, it will need to come out." I will never forget the way this resident doctor struggled to insert the clip; I could literally see the beads of sweat rolling down his forehead as he raised his free arm to wipe his brow before catching the droplets in his eye. (Yes, please do, Dr. McSweaty. I would like you to be able to see what you're doing while you're inserting titanium and needles into my body.) After that was all over, they decided, given my emotional state, to leave the lymph node for another time. They bandaged me up, disappeared momentarily, and then came back in to summarize.

"So, we are concerned. You have about a 1.6 cm lump in your breast and your lymph node is enlarged. You've felt it, we've felt it. At this point, we do not know if it's cancer. The lab will run tests and we will hopefully have a definitive answer for you by Tuesday at the earliest, Wednesday at the latest. But even if it's not cancer, the road won't end here for you. You will likely need this removed."

Well, aren't you just the beacon of light and hope and good tidings, Dr. So and So. This guy was **really** on my shitlist. I wanted to kick him in the groin with one of my thinnest stilettos. And after that, kick Dr. McSweaty for dripping his rookie doctor anxiety all over me. (Who am I kidding, I hate stilettos, I'm a wedge girl…) Over the last two months, I've definitely lowered my expectations for the medical field in terms of warmth and bedside manner. But at the time, I was not yet desensitized, and had the hopes that every doctor I interacted with would treat me like a daughter—not necessarily *their* daughter, but **someone's** daughter, a person with a life, a story, a dream… I've had to let that go. Harsh lesson to learn, but I learned it relatively quickly.

Oh. To add to the fun, this all took place on a Friday. So I had the weekend until potentially WEDNESDAY to sit with the anxiety and sheer terror over what was to come. It's as if part of me knew it was cancer. I was devastated, but also, surprisingly proactive given my state of desperation. I researched food and nutrition for cancer to learn how to best support my immune system, in the event of the worst case scenario. I began juicing vegetables and small amounts of fruit, cut out all animal products (which I wasn't really eating much of anyway), cut out all grain (aside from quinoa!), and researched supplements. I also did a lot of anxious google searching of symptoms and treatment for cancer, which just made me *more* anxious... so anxious that my mom had to take my phone away. Dr. Google is a horrible horrible rude jerkface asshole. I learned this lesson pretty quickly, though I am still tempted to consult with him from time to time...

On Monday, to my surprise, I got the phone call. As you can guess, my worst case scenario suddenly became my reality.

"Hi, Amy. The lab results came back. I'm so sorry to tell you this, but it's cancer..."

If I was not already sitting down, I'm certain my knees would have given out. I began to cry the ugliest loudest cry of my whole life. (I'm talking shrieking, snotting, boogering, mascara evrrrywhere-ing), and I immediately handed the phone off to my mother and darted to the bathroom where I dry-heaved (empty stomach) until I felt numb.

So, I have Stage II grade 2/3 Breast Cancer. Invasive Ductal Carcinoma. Basically, this means that it began in the milk duct of the breast. It is ER/PR+, HER2-. This means my cancer is hormone responsive (estrogen and progesterone are necessary in order for it to live), and does not have receptors for the Human Epidermal Growth Factor. Invasive Ductal Carcinoma is the most common type of breast cancer—80% of all breast cancers are this type. Because of this fact, the medical field has more of an understanding of it than some less common breast cancers.

**I never thought I'd be thankful that my cancer was widely understood... mostly because I never thought I'd have cancer.** And not in actual registered committed thought like, "I will never have cancer"—it just never occupied any space in my mind. Until now...

One of the biggest things I'm beginning to take away from all of this is that in any situation, there is room for gratitude. Prior to my diagnosis, gratitude was something I struggled with. I have always been a bit of an Eeyore type, prone to melancholy—and tantrums. So like, Eeyore mixed with Angelica from the Rugrats. Now, gratitude is the very thing that keeps me going. Gratitude for the incredible people I'm meeting along this nightmarish journey. Gratitude for phone calls from my doctor telling me my bone-scans and CT scans are clean, that my genetic testing came back unanimously negative, so I don't need to worry about removing my ovaries or getting a hysterectomy as a preventative measure. Gratitude for the way a cancer diagnosis is able to illuminate the truth around relationships—you learn who is able to show up and be with you in your darkest hour, and who never was able to truly be present. And if there's one thing I need right now, it's true, wholehearted, sincere presence. I am thankful for the people in my world who have truly stepped up to the plate to support me emotionally (and eventually, physically, after surgery next week). And I am also thankful to those who are unable to support me at this time, because they have helped me to do something I've struggled with for a long time: Ask for what I need, and if I cannot get what I need from them, find it elsewhere (as opposed to trying to shut off that need... Newsflash, that doesn't work).

Since the diagnosis, a lot has changed in my world. Actually, practically everything. For one, my diet. I am no longer concerned with calories for the vain purpose of shedding pounds. Everything I put into my body has a nutritional value and purpose. My future plans have also changed. I am not able to begin school in August as I was supposed to, but fortunately, Roosevelt is allowing me to defer my enrollment and keeping all of my scholarships. I am beyond thankful for this.

When I applied for a decision extension to the three schools after my grandmother had passed, and before I knew it was cancer, some of the programs were not as compassionate, to say the least (I will not name names). Roosevelt made the decision **extremely** easy for me. They treated my situation like there was a person attached, not like a routine business transaction (ahem...).

So this next year will be completely different from the way I had envisioned it. For one, I won't be in Chicago learning more about what I love. I will be at home in Rochester, New York, going through surgery and recovery from this rat-bastard-asshole disease. But, in a funny way, there is a part of me that seems to be emerging calmly from all of this. If you ask my friends or my mother, there is no calmness in sight... But I do feel an internal shift occurring very steadily. It's like a bubbling in the pit of my stomach, an excitement founded in truth. You know how truth has a way of sort of settling into your body, landing in your bones... that kind of visceral stirring. (No, not gas.) It's as if there is a part of me (a wiser, more grounded, less anxious part) that knows that this is all a part of my journey. I know somehow that I will emerge from this experience with twice the strength I have now, with an ability to trust in my intuition like never before. I believe this detour will force me to assess what's truly important to me (in fact, it already has), and enable me to create the world I've desired for myself for so long that has always felt somewhat out of reach for one reason or another. But, again, that's another post for another time...

This piece* is a recording I made for the pre-screening rounds of grad school auditions. It's called Fleurs, from Fiançailles Pour Rire, poetry by Louise de Vilmorin, music by Francis Poulenc. Just a brief clip of me singing one of my favorite pieces to conclude my first post.

---

* *Link available here: myterminallife.org*

Also:

EFF YOU,
CANCER.

But thank you for the opportunity to learn how to love and care for myself.

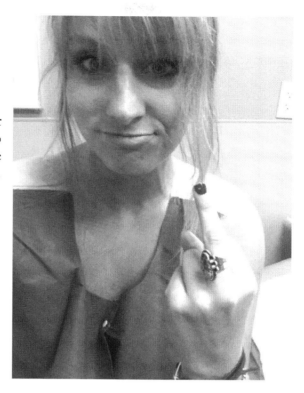

Namaste.

(This is foreshadowing future posts about the transformational power of yoga.)

# JOELLEN MANCARI
MAY 15, 2016

Ten days before I was diagnosed with breast cancer, my grandmother JoEllen passed away unexpectedly. This is another one of those moments I talked about in my first post—a moment that will forever be imprinted in my mind. And maybe not so much in an image, though I will always remember exactly where I was when we got the phone call, and how the greyness of the clouds outside our 22nd floor hotel room window at the Hilton had shifted from neutral to heavy and foreboding in a matter of seconds. My mother and I were in Chicago that week—I was able to schedule a voice lesson with my assigned voice teacher at Roosevelt, the incredible Kurt Link, and I was super excited. My voice lesson was on Tuesday, March 29th, and we were flying home the following morning. I left my lesson beaming. Kurt told me that he heard a warmer, more lyric quality in my sound, which excited me, especially because I was tired of trying to get my voice to sing the chirpy-bird runny stuff (that's the way I describe what is known to the vocal world as "coloratura repertoire"). I have always felt more personally connected to the music of larger roles like Mimi from La Bohème, Pamina from Die Zauberflöte, Violetta from La Traviata—although that role is like a coloratura in the first half and a full lyric in the rest so… I guess it's important to be able to do both. Sigh. It also just occurred to me that all of the characters I'm drawn to in opera are the ones who are depressed, and/or end up dying… Good thing therapy is on deck this week—and probably for the next 20 years… In any case, I was happy to hear that he heard my voice heading in that direction.

After the lesson, my mom and I went to lunch at a vegan café/grocery store called "Kramers," which was going to be my new grocery store come fall 2016 (unfortunately the rat bastard in my breast is keeping me from my new grocery store for another year… Thank god for Lori's Natural Foods right here at home, though).

After our delicious lunch of Indian inspired tofu and green juice, we went back to our hotel room and napped. I kept getting bouts of vertigo and ringing in my ears, which had never happened to me before.

That evening, my grandmother called my mom, and her voice sounded weathered and tired. She was in a lot of pain, and she asked my mom if we were home yet, to which my mom replied, "No Ma, we'll be home tomorrow night." "Oh, okay." I could almost hear the guilt in my mother's voice when she told her we weren't home yet. I knew it was hard for my mom to be away and hear her mother's tired voice obviously in pain on the other end of the phone. They chit-chatted (is that a word?) some more, and she asked about how my lesson went. The ache and fatigue were audible in her voice as she spoke to my mother, which made me feel sad. The conversation ended shortly after "Well, call me when you land tomorrow." (Still bein' a mother till the very end!) If I had known that this night was to be her last night on earth, I would have asked to talk to her. I am still sick about this.

We went to bed early that night. But strangely, both my mom and I were wide awake and restless at around 3 a.m. To this day, I believe that we were awake then because we knew on some spiritual level that she was passing. When we arrived at home, we found out that we hadn't been the only ones in the family tossing and turning around 3 a.m... In all of the sadness, this was somehow comforting; it was as if our souls were all with her as she crossed over from our dimension to the next.

My grandmother was extremely selfless, almost to a fault. Always there to lend a hand or an ear (you just had to make sure it was her good ear). She wanted nothing more than to see me continuing my schooling in my passion, and she was planning on supporting me throughout the process through unlimited encouragement as well as financial support. One of the last moments I had with her, I was preparing to leave for another audition at Bard outside of New York City. I came by one afternoon to visit. I felt compelled to sing one of my audition pieces for her. It was in French, and it was an art song, which basically means it tells a story. Before I sang it, I explained the story to her. She looked at me with her eyes so wide,

"I had no idea there was so much to singing! I thought you just sang words. I had no idea you knew what they meant!" I walked over to her and kissed her cheek after she said that. It was just so damn cute. I said, "Well, yes, Gram, in order to really move people, you have to know what you're singing about!" and she said, "Oh, well, yes, that makes sense." That's another one of those memories I will keep forever. That moment evoked an image in my head of my grandma as a young girl... She was just so innocent and precious and child-like to me then. I felt so close to her that day. And of course after I sang for her, she was smiling so big WITHOUT her hand in front of her mouth, despite her chipped front tooth. That chipped tooth was a tremendous source of embarrassment and shame to her. She was getting it repaired—root canal galore—because "THERE'S NO WAY IN HELL I'M GETTING DENTURES. I'M LEAVING THIS EARTH WITH MY OWN TEETH," despite her dentist's recommendation. I loved that smile, missing teeth or not. And she did leave this earth with her own teeth. God bless her fierce and fiery, warm and loving, innocent and precious soul.

I don't really want to talk about getting the phone call on March 30th, the way time was elastic and slippery and still all at once, my mother and I, numb, schlepping our heavy luggage and heavier hearts from hotel to shuttle, from shuttle to airport, trying to find an earlier flight home, to no avail.

What I *do* want to share is that I have absolutely felt her presence since my diagnosis. **I am 100% certain that she is walking this journey with me.** The first thing I'll share is that my original breast doctor was not my cup of tea. We will call this person Doctor Voldemort. I promptly switched from Doctor Voldemort's care after having two appointments. Sidenote: If you or anyone you know is going through a tricky medical situation, I cannot emphasize *enough* how important it is to have a medical team that you are completely comfortable with. I am beyond glad that I made the switch. Doctor Joel Yellin (sounds a lot like JoEllen, huh?) is one of the most compassionate people I have ever met in my whole life. He calls me personally to inform me of my test results, spends over two hours with me in appointments, has given me his personal cell phone number... And in this shitty situation, warmth and compassion are extremely important to me. They're actually quite important to me, shit-storm or not.

The week following my diagnosis, I decided to leave my house (for something other than a doctor's appointment). That was a monumentally huge sign of progress. I was choosing life, as opposed to choosing existence (if you could even call it that) in my nest of blankets and snotty tissues on the couch. My mom and I went to the Breast Cancer Coalition on University Ave downtown. I spoke with some amazing women there. This place is incredible. It provides so many services to the patients and families of people with breast cancer like yoga, meditation, lunch sessions, lecture series, information seminars, and the list goes on. I feel lucky to live so close to such a valuable support system in my recovery, surrounded by so many strong women who have walked their own version of this cancer journey. (That's another thing I'm learning— no two women's experience with breast cancer is exactly the same, though there are many foundational similarities).

After my first visit, I went home with a gigantic gift bag filled with several books on breast cancer and resources to consult on the journey, a beautiful new journal, an assortment of teas, a Wegmans gift card (and I know I'm still forgetting things). Conveniently, right next door to the Coalition is a juice bar (nope, not steroids, the raw fruit and vegetable kind) where I've met some beautiful and inspiring women who in fact all work behind the counter. The owner is one of the most warm and friendly people I've EVER encountered, always there to share a laugh, suggest a recipe book, give a hug. One of the other workers sent me home with a beautiful salt lamp, a raw vegan recipe bible, and a salad spinner. Actually, all of the women at Just Juice 4 Life are kindhearted and in a word, wonderful. Since the diagnosis, I've cried and sobbed and cursed and dripped snotty tears all over this place (not quite literally), and all of these women have unflinchingly wrapped their arms around me. I am so in awe of the kindness I'm surrounded by every time I walk in the door. Two of these women at the juice bar have had/are currently having their own intimate experiences with cancer. One of the juice-makers is a 19-year-old girl with a rare form of liver cancer (diagnosed at age 16), and the other is a 27-year-old woman who was diagnosed with stage IV tongue cancer (never smoked a day in her life) and beat it holistically (with surgery). Talk about inspiring. These two women have given me so much hope. When I first met them, it was shocking for me to see that they were both still living their lives "normally." They had jobs, they had social lives, they were active, they made juice, they smiled, they laughed. Given the place of despair I had been in, witnessing this was something that almost made me have to rub my eyes and pinch myself to be sure that what I was seeing was real. They were happy. They expressed gratitude. It was not a mistake that I met these women.

Initially, in my appointments where chemotherapy was discussed, my whole body would tense, and I would feel physical pain in my abdomen. I had several nightmares where I was all "hooked up" and ready to start chemo, and then multiple tornadoes would appear from all corners of the sky, making a direct path for the hospital. Needless to say, the idea of chemotherapy has felt like a violation to my spirit from the beginning. Everything in my whole being has been telling me no from the get-go. So these next couple of events really gave me a lot of hope in my situation. And I'm holding onto that hope. Every. Single. Day.

The 27-year-old tongue cancer THRIVER introduced me to one of her friends who had healed herself from breast cancer with surgery and a holistic approach, and she has been ten years cancer-free. When we first met (at the juice bar, my new Turf), this remarkable woman greeted me with a gigantic hug and a gift. She handed the bag to me and said, "I don't know why I was compelled to bring this to you today, but I was. I was getting ready for church and something just told me that I needed to give this to you, in particular. This was given to me by someone very close to me when I was first diagnosed with breast cancer, and for some reason, I felt like I needed to bring it to you. And you will pass it along to someone else someday. I know you will." Before I even opened the bag, my mother and I were already teary and then I just about lost it when I pulled the gift out. It was a beautiful angel. Not anything too crazy, right? Unless you knew my grandma. JoEllen had angel decor EVERYWHERE. Precious Moments Angels, Willow Tree Angels, Lenox Angels, No-Name Angels. You name the angel, JoEllen probably had it. And the fact that this wonderful cancer-surviving woman went the route I envisioned for myself from the beginning and has been cancer-free for ten years was a HUGE source of hope for me. Oh yeah, and her cancer's pathology breakdown was the same as mine: ER/PR+, HER2-.

To top that all off, later that week, at my cousin Mark's house, he suggested I pick some oracle cards (cards by Doreen Virtue). The cards I chose that night were: Guardian Angel, Transformation, Spiritual Growth, and Emerging.

The cards came with a book that further explained the meaning of each card. First, my Guardian Angels were guiding me through my OWN intuition, and that they would not steer me wrong. Second, my current situation is going to be a source of a significant trans-formation within me. Third, through my struggle, I will obtain a tremendous amount of spiritual growth and my faith will be strengthened, and Fourth, my experiences will help me to emerge into my most authentic, wisest self, and my wisest self is destined to help others.

I'm going to let all of that digest.

Bottom line: Grandma Jo, I know you're with me. (And you better make sure they give me some fun drugs before surgery on Friday!) I love you forever. And I thank you for all of the ways you have blessed and continue to bless my world. I know you'll be with me (and Joel Yellin!) in surgery this Friday.

## MY ANGELS ARE WITH ME TODAY...
MAY 16, 2016

I was walking in my neighborhood with a friend today. When we got to my house, I approached the front door... I don't know why I did that, I *always* go through the garage. But as I was walking up the stone walkway, I saw something fluttering in the grass from the corner of my eye on my right hand side. It was a feather.

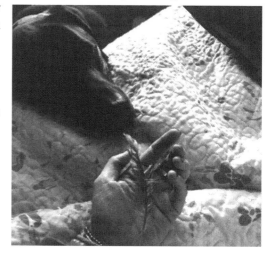

I think my angels are with me today.

## THINGS I LOVE
MAY 17, 2016

As a recovering pessimist, I've been trying to focus more of my energy toward the things I'd like to manifest in my life, as opposed to the things I don't have. I'm becoming ready to release my furry Eeyore tail to the universe because it's gotten me stuck in places I'd rather not be. It's a subtle difference, I suppose, to focus on the things you want and what they mean to you, as opposed to the thousands of things you are lacking. I see the former as desiring things for yourself from a place of worthiness, where the latter is essentially whining or falling into the victim trap—sometimes all too easy to do. And I am *Ohhhh-so-very-good* at whining. And when I was first diagnosed, boy oh *boy* was I the victim. And in a sense, that was appropriate. The week of the diagnosis spent in hospitals and doctors' offices where they were talking to me about my options for surgery: "We may recommend a hysterectomy as a preventive measure based on how your results come back in the genetic testing, but you can meet with a fertility specialist to discuss your options, and actually we recommend you do that regardless because chemotherapy can affect fertility." *Oh, okay*—"We will get you started on chemotherapy as early as next week. You will lose your hair but don't worry—it grows back! I suggest you go out and get your wig made before so they can match your current hair as closely as possible." —*Oh, alright, is that all, Doctor Voldemort? Just remove all my lady parts and watch my hair fall out in clumps to top it off? Get a port sewn into my clavicle to flood my body with toxic chemicals that make me feel weak and drained and lifeless and sick to my stomach? Decide RIGHT NOW if I wanna freeze my eggs in case having a family is important to me? Alright, bro, nbd.* **NOT**. It was my own personal hell. *Waaaaayyy* too much information for my body, mind and spirit to process. (And I know it's wrong to shoot the messenger, but in this situation, I felt a kneeing in Doctor Voldemort's groin would have been both appropriate and reasonable…)

This *is* unfair. And I needed to experience that anger and devastation and complete despair in the first few weeks following diagnosis in order to come to know that I DO want this crazy, absurd, messed-up, beautiful, wonderful life. (For those of you who aren't close to me, there was a period where I wasn't so sure). Yes, this process has been uglier than I've wanted it to be so far.

***And also:*** I needed to work through that place of despair, dangling from the edge in order for these little golden nuggets of insight and positivity to begin to emerge. But, as you can imagine, being diagnosed with cancer in your 20s is not a predictable or stable path emotionally. Everything is moment to moment. ***Everything.*** Some moments I'm fine and I'm at peace, some moments I forget I even have cancer (two seconds max), some moments I feel like I need to cry, most moments I feel like I need to be eating. But I am realizing that my thoughts are a very powerful place for transformation to begin. Louise Hay, author and speaker and healthy-living guru, talks about self-hatred as simply hating a thought that you have about yourself. **WHAM**. And your thoughts can be changed. KA-*BOOM.* When I first read that, I felt like somebody clobbered me upside the head. With several baseball bats. That was a tough one for me to read because it made me realize how accountable I have been for all of the unhappiness in my life. On some very real level, I have been *choosing* that unhappiness by not caring for myself. How completely insane! Every time I've been unhappy in the past (and admittedly sometimes now) it's always been somebody else's fault, if you were to ask me—and even if you didn't ask, I probably would have told you anyway: This person was mean, that person is selfish, this person didn't *deserve* the recognition—I DID, DAMMIT.

But this concept of taking responsibility for your life in such an active way, and owning your contribution to your own frustration (as well as your happiness!!) has also been liberating. It's very easy to point fingers at people that have hurt us and blame them for our bad feelings in the situation. And it's not always easy or pleasant to channel inward and ask ourselves how we've participated in the dynamic of the relationship or situation that is the source of our frustration. This concept has given me the opportunity to really take some personal moral inventory. It's time for me to dig deep…

Since I am coming to know the power of my own thoughts, I am beginning to focus more of my attention on the things in this life that excite me, move me, make me feel alive. So I thought I'd share a few images of some of my favorite things with you!

Outdoor yoga has become my new favorite solo activity since the weather has started to shift.

Delicious and nutritious vegan food and juice makes me feel like I am taking my health into my own hands (actually my mom's hands since she's been doing the cooking), which is empowering, to say the least.

My. Dog.
That FACE.

Quinoaaaaaaaaaaaa! Avocado banana cacao powder mousse. No sugar. Just that and coconut water and coconut flakes in a blender.

Teaching the little boys yoga...

More food…

And more yoga:

Namaste

# POWER IN VULNERABILITY
MAY 18, 2016

* Myself, accompanied by Roland Martin in "Sure on this shining night" by Samuel Barber, poetry by James Agee

*"Sure on this shining night*
*Of star made shadows round,*
*Kindness must watch for me*
*This side the ground.*
*The late year lies down the north.*
*All is healed, all is health.*
*High summer holds the earth.*
*Hearts all whole.*

*Sure on this shining night*
*I weep for wonder wand'ring far alone*
*Of shadows on the stars"*                    –James Agee

Typically I hate singing in English for a few reasons. One, English is not a vowel-friendly language for singing. We singers spend countless hours learning how to physically modify our vowel shapes (by engaging our lips, closing or opening our mouths, dropping our jaws, and the list goes on) to get optimum resonance and "shimmer" in our sounds, and those modification techniques change depending on 1) what vowel we are singing and 2) where we are range-wise in our voices. (I won't bore you with the details of "the singer's formant" because this would require me to take out my vocal pedagogy and anatomy and physiology text books, and I think they look better collecting dust on my dresser right now, but the basic concept is that all vowel sounds have inherent pitch or frequency. The voice is the only instrument that uses vowel sounds, and that's what enables us to be heard over gigantic orchestras without amplification. It's that mysterious glorious "ring" unique to singers).

---

* *Link available here: myterminallife.org*

Another reason I hate singing in English is because it's my native language and I don't find it aesthetically beautiful. It's inconsistent. Some words are mellifluous and fluid, but for a whole sentence to sound beautiful and smooth... that just doesn't really happen in English. We also have a lot of ugly diphthongs (and they are especially ugly in Rochester, New York, where every sound is manufactured in the nose). Pure vowel sounds are a rarity in the language. I guess I'm a purist. A snooty, English-hating purist.

Another reason that I dislike singing in English that I've probably never admitted to anyone aside from myself is the fact that it's more vulnerable, in a world where pretty much everyone knows English. I don't like that people know what I'm saying!! I'm insane, I'm well aware. I have spent my whole life trying to be "understood." Except when I'm doing the very thing that I love most... that's when I feel I need the most protection. Singing is *scary!* Its *vulnerable!* But I believe in that vulnerability lies the potential to move people. That level of opening oneself up, and offering something that is so universally human... that level of emotional authenticity—there's real *power* in that.

I shared my recording of "Sure on this shining night" with you (and it's beautiful poetry, in English—yes, I'm half-eating my words) because this is the first English art song I've truly gotten intimate with poetically. (I'm usually all about the French impressionist stuff, and hardly ever felt compelled to do the in-depth poetic analysis in undergrad even though it was a requirement). That enabled me to immerse myself in the beautiful marriage of the notes on the page and my interpretation of the text. It's not a flawless recording by any means (there are parts where I literally cringe when I hear them) but I have kept it because it was the first real time I truly showed up with my whole self present. And that's where the power is.

This entry is a little bit jumbled so I apologize. I've got my mind on a lot with surgery in two days. But this was therapeutic! Thanks for listening/reading.

## TA-TA, TA-TA'S
MAY 19, 2016

So, today is the last day on earth living with my own breasts. Since the ones I was born with are trying to kill me, I'm trading these suckers in for a better, less lethal pair. They are OUTTA HERE.

This decision has been a surprisingly easy one for me to make. As someone who has never particularly liked her breasts (that's putting it lightly—I HATED them), and given the fact that my spirit is not on board with chemotherapy, a bilateral mastectomy with reconstruction seemed to make the most sense to me. I know that this is a difficult decision for some women to make, but I can honestly say as I sit here, looking down at my cleavage for one of the last times, I feel very much at peace.

I do anticipate that I may experience some grief post-surgery. Grief for the loss of my own flesh, symbols of my "femininity." But this whole crazy experience has given me the opportunity to look at some of my beliefs about the world and about who I am. I've become aware of my understanding of myself as a woman being inextricably linked to my physical appearance. This isn't the truth—the "who" in all of us is so much greater and more monumental than our packaging, but I know I'm not alone in this. And frankly, it is a belief I've subconsciously carried for so long without question that has not ever served me, and I don't think it serves any of us. It is a belief that has caused me a tremendous amount of pain and suffering—periods of starving myself, skipping meals and smoking cigarettes instead (in undergrad, while studying opera. Yes, I thought I was *reeeeaalllly* edgy and cool), punishing myself at the gym in the hopes of beating my unruly flesh into submission, obsessing over scars on my face, not leaving the house some days because I felt so ugly and so unworthy—of what, I'm not sure. I'm saying this not to whine or evoke pity, but to highlight the pervasiveness of these thoughts and behaviors, because I know I'm not alone. If you are a woman, or you have women in your life, I'm sure you've seen some of what I'm talking about. And this isn't just a female issue. We have a societal epidemic of self-hatred on our hands.

I've been forced to acknowledge my own vanity, and I am truly grateful for this. Because I believe my vanity has always served as a layer of insulation or protection, based on this core belief that who I am underneath my outer existence is somehow bad, or less than, or not worthy, or fundamentally flawed. So I have always put tremendous stock into my physical appearance for fear that the truth of my existence was actually rotten and needed covering up— with makeup and special clothes and accessories—identities to be put on and taken off like sweaters.

It has taken a cancer diagnosis for me to finally be willing to release this harmful belief.

I feel privileged being able to sit in my comfy bed, on my nice new laptop, pondering my existence with no real or immediate threat to my survival (aside from the pesky-rat-bastard-asshole currently residing in my breast and lymph node). I realize that my thoughts are indicative of my privilege because I have the freedom to consider these things, as opposed to where my next meal is coming from. It's ironic that out of a cancer diagnosis, I am coming to know gratitude.

So, yes, I may be sad about my breasts being gone in the future. I may encounter fear around meeting someone special and what their reaction to my fake breast situation might be. But if that's what's important to that person, then they're not the special one for me...

So actually, I am coming to know cancer as a hellishly beautiful liberator. I may be sad later on, but I am at peace right now. And what could be better than that? All we have is right now, after all...

## TODAY IS THE DAY!
MAY 20, 2016

Last night's outdoor yoga session with a few friends was exactly what I needed. This was one of the last times I'll be able to do yoga for a while, so I wanted to have a meditative and intimate experience, and it was *exactly* that.

I am nervous about the surgery today. It's considered a "major surgery," which is terrifying. So is the name of my procedure. Modified radical bilateral mastectomy. The "radical" part is what's scary. But actually that just means they're taking out the cancer from the breast and the involved lymph node(s)... Which is a good thing. So maybe I'll just have to picture a hippie California surfer man saying "radical, *duuuuuuude*" and then I will feel more at ease with the verbiage.

Because I'm a worrier, I have a fear that I won't make it off the operating table. I know the chances of that are extremely low, especially because I am young and healthy, my heart is great, so is my blood pressure—basically without the cancer, I'm in tip-top shape. I'm vegan. 60% of what I eat is raw. I feel strong. I can imagine that I'm walking into today's procedure in better overall health than most in my shoes.

I also know in my gut that that fear is there to remind me of how much I love this life. I love it more now post-diagnosis than I *ever* did before. Everything tastes sweeter. And the despair and pain I felt initially in all of this craziness was actually a very real wake-up call to me. Because the darkness helped me come to know my desire for life, my own inner light.

The life of my breasts might be close to over, but *my* life is just beginning. And I have so much life to live and even more love to share.

Oh, and also:
I'm gunna be a Godmother!!!!!
I am beyond honored and thrilled. Thank you Mark and Marci. I promise I won't teach him *too* many swear words.

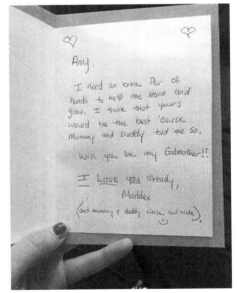

I have nothing but positivity with me today. And I'm bringing Grandma's angel ornament with me into surgery!
(Thanks, Michael.)

In 24 hours, I will be drugged up and cancer free!

Thank you to everyone for your support. I appreciate it more than you know.

## <u>CANCER FREE!</u>
MAY 21, 2016

Drugged up and cancer free!

I am in a tremendous amount of pain. But, I'm alive and kickin'.

Thank you to all my friends and family who came last night to be with me and my misery after surgery. I'm sure I bit everyone's head off at least once. In my defense, the pain is like your entire thoracic area is being squished on both top and bottom by thousand-pound freight trains. Last night was particularly bad because it hurt like hell to inhale. Which made me anxious. And of course, my go-to method of self-soothing in times of anxiety is deep breathing, which as you can guess, was not available to me which only perpetuated more anxiety…

They gave me Dilaudid in an iv, and apparently I was saying some very insightful things… I remember *none* of them. "Dentures are like glasses for your teeth," "I can eat candy apples with both my dentures in and my dentures out, because I have strong gums" (I do not have dentures; nor have I eaten a candy apple since I was about 6), "I feel that if I could tickle myself, I wouldn't be so needy," "Ellen can probably tickle herself, because she can do anything," "I wish we were all self-sufficient ticklers" (yeah, no idea)… And the list goes on. Thank goodness my mom and aunt Janet were there to witness and document it…

I'm on Flexerol now, and it's helping, but I am still extremely sore. One of the doctors told me that today will probably be the most painful day, and then it will improve from here. So I'm keeping my fingers crossed…

I cannot wait to get home to my pup. I'll be here at the hospital all day today, and then part of tomorrow.

Thanks again for all of the support.

## FLOWERS AND FLEXEROL
MAY 22, 2016

I have a whole garden in my room! Thank you all so much for all of your love and support. I feel like a celebrity! Depending on my pain level, I may be able to go home today. This has its pros and cons. Obviously I'd rather be at home healing in my own bed. But at the same time, I still feel like I need assistance and supervision with getting up and around and controlling pain meds etc. Also, the drains that are attached to me thoroughly gross me out, so I'm not sure that I'm quite ready to be emptying them on my own. So, I'm just trying to take today moment by moment without putting pressure or expectation on myself. That's hard for me—getting rid of the "shoulds." Especially because I'm used to being able to do what I want to, when I want to do it. This is definitely giving me a greater appreciation for what my body is normally capable of. I cannot wait to be healed enough to be able to do some yoga! That first session after all of this nonsense is going to be so much more appreciated, because I will be so thankful for all that my body is able to do.

Also, I have the largest room in the hospital, and I was told by the nursing staff that it's a VIP room. It's basically like a hotel suite!

I've been on and off pain meds and muscle relaxers for the last two days, so I don't feel as eloquent as usual…

Thank you all so much for all of your support.

## <u>HOME SWEET HOME!</u>
MAY 23, 2016

After three whole days at Rochester General, I am finally home. I came home this morning around 10 a.m., sufficiently drugged and a little groggy, but I was happy to be heading home. Today has been a somewhat tough day emotionally, mostly because I have to be separated from my dog—we don't want to take the chance of her jumping on me and potentially hurting me.

For those of you that don't know, my dog is like my child. Actually, she *is* my child. Riley is my best friend on the whole planet. So it's been hard for both of us to be separated from one another. I'm hoping that we can resume our normal bonding relatively quickly, because it feels like torture to have her so close and yet so far. She has been whining in her crate too, which just breaks my heart.

The pain from the surgery is becoming more manageable, but it's still pretty uncomfortable, especially getting in and out of bed. It's amazing how much we use our arm and chest muscles for simple tasks like this and we don't even realize it until those muscles have been compromised in some way. I wish the road to recovery was quicker and that I could resume normal activity like… yesterday, but if nothing else, this experience is a great opportunity to develop my patience and gratitude "muscles," while my physical muscles heal.

Thank you all so much for your love and support. I know I could not get through this trying time if I didn't have your kindness. I feel very blessed. A special thank you to my friends and family who took the time out of their busy lives to be with me at the hospital, and/or sent me beautiful flowers, made special juice and magazine deliveries, and distracted me from my discomfort and pain. I love you all tremendously.

Also, my mother is the most kick-ass woman I've ever known. Judith Kim Schnitzler, you're my hero. Thank you for walking this hellish journey with me. I know this is taking its toll on you, and I appreciate your undying support, day after grueling day. I love you more than anything.

I expect to be feeling more like myself in the next week or so, but until then, you will have to just deal with my not-so-eloquent writing. Healing the body takes physical and mental energy, and I'm certainly low on both right now…

Thank you all again for your presence in my life.

## CREATING A NEW NORMAL (UPDATED VERSION WITH LESS OXY INFLUENCE)
MAY 24, 2016

I'm sitting on my couch, trying to ignore the numbness in my right shoulder, the constriction in my calves from the lovely hospital-provided compression socks, the pain from my incisions. I know that all of this discomfort is temporary, but I do believe there is some permanent change to come from my cancer experience. And in many ways, I am thankful for this.

Health and wellness have always been things I have desperately desired for myself. If you know me at all, you've probably seen the various health "phases" I've been through with diet and exercise, with spirituality and mental approaches to healthy living. You've also probably seen me struggle implementing any lasting changes in many of these areas. I would eat tremendously well one week, and I would be enthusiastically engaged in my gym routine, and then when the weekend came I would put away whole bottles of wine (followed by whole pizzas) on evenings with friends. Or I'd smoke myself into oblivion (yes, I was an opera singing student with a significant pot habit) and eat the entire contents of my fridge. And the aftermath was always the same: I felt so terribly guilty and disgusted for allowing myself to behave so loosely around "temptation," and would kick into MAJOR self-loathing mode. My self-loathing mode looked a lot like military style punishment. My inner self-talk was insulting *("pig," "filthy pig,"* and other niceties), and I would beat myself to a pulp with exercise, followed by starvation and the occasional purging because I truly felt so repulsive, disgusting, and at times, unfit for living. Most of my thoughts began with "You don't deserve…" After I felt I had been sufficiently punished for my sins, I would try to resume my "healthy lifestyle," always anxious and on edge, waiting for my inevitable failure, my inability to stick to anything (that's what I thought it was), for the next time I stepped out of line and needed punishment again—that was my pattern with diet and exercise until very recently.

I realize now that my black and white thinking around food and health was extremely rigid, founded on punishment rather than kindness, which made the whole thing very unsustainable—nobody can maintain that yo-yo lifestyle and be truly healthy. It's madness. You might look like the picture of health on paper—I certainly did!—but if your thoughts look anything like what I just mentioned, you may want to gently ask yourself some questions. My inner dialogue was a reflection of a core belief that I was fundamentally flawed, that the essence of who I was was inherently bad and unlovable. This core belief is what prevented me from taking on self-care in a compassionate and loving way.

I think I mentioned in my first post that I've experienced a radical shift in my mentality around food and weight and exercise. It took a cancer diagnosis for me to begin the process of learning to love myself, and to make choices for my body out of this love. In some ways, that saddens me. It saddens me because it's evidence of how deeply seeded these harmful beliefs were. It took something so awful and extreme for me to even begin to recognize my inner light, my compassion, my kindness, my lovability—all of these wonderful things that reside in each and every one of us. It's quite tragic that it's taken the horror of these last few months of hospitals and doctors' offices, of dizzying blood work and MRI's, of bone scans and major surgery for me to see some of the truth about my value on this earth. But in another sense, it's quite beautiful that out of something so terrible, something so solid and strong and trusting is emerging. I am embracing this part of my life for all of the huge lessons I'm learning—lessons that I don't believe I could have learned any other way. Not because I wasn't trying… I absolutely was. Health and wellness were always so important to me, but they were blocked by my own self-hatred. I truly see my cancer experience as a gift because it's allowed me to start to gently move aside my feelings of unworthiness to make room for **the truth.** I've come to see my cancer diagnosis as an almighty tap on the shoulder from God/Source/Spirit telling me, "Hey lady, you've got some big learnin' ahead, and some things in your life have gotta change in order for you to be your truest highest self. And *I'm with you…*"

People have been asking me if I will ever go back to eating the way I did prior to all of this. Don't get me wrong, my diet was never *horrible,* but it certainly was not what it is now—today, I consume a mostly raw, vegan, no grain or flour or dairy, nothing that comes in a package, plant-based diet. At this point, I highly doubt I'll ever go back to my pre-diagnosis diet. Today, I eat for health. My diet is one of the biggest areas of influence I have over my own health, so I believe doing everything I absolutely can in order to support my immune system is a necessity, especially now. I *soooo* wish I was doing these things as a preventative measure as opposed to after-the-fact, but that is all the more reason for me to continue on my path of health-and-wellness-centered living.

I believe my body had been crying out to me for a very long time, and for whatever reason—there were probably many—I was unable to hear it. Probably because my inner Regina George (the name I've given to my inner mean girl, my super ego, the voice of my self-hatred) was squawking away in my ear. I believe my immune system had been suppressed for years due to diet, frequent antibiotic use, anxiety, depression, and overall self-loathing. Although I do not understand the exact science behind this belief, something inside of me knows that all of these factors in combination provided an environment for disease to flourish.

We are all constantly creating cancer and mutated cells in our bodies. In healthy immune systems, these cells are taken care of and discarded appropriately before any issue comes out of it. For some reason (and I'm beginning to come to some pretty profound realizations around this), **my body was unable to do what it was *made* to do**. I believe my cancer developed as a result of an unhealthy immune system, and I am doing everything in my power to rebuild my health from the ground up.

I'm in a bit of a pain killer-induced haze right now, but I will definitely be writing more on this topic, because I have a lot more to say.

Also: I have been happily reunited with my pup. She has been such a sweet little healer.

I'm scratching her sweet spot on her chin— makes her left rear leg twitch like Thumper from Bambi…

Until next time…

## THE NOT SO PRETTY AFTERMATH—FYI: LOTS OF EXPLETIVES
MAY 28, 2016

So, it's been eight days since my surgery. I've been sort of reluctant to write—mostly because I am processing a lot on an emotional level, and that's a full-time job in and of itself. It also hasn't been super comfortable to sit up (or lie down), so sitting myself in front of the computer for the length of time to write one of these things hasn't seemed too inviting at this time. I also haven't been emotionally ready to write about all of this, because, frankly, I feel bad that I don't have more positive things to say at this point. I think I may be afraid that I'm disappointing other people or letting them down when I'm unable to see this shitty situation through rose-colored glasses. This does not mean that my previous posts that were more uplifting and lighter than this one are any less authentic or real. Breast cancer is a fucking roller-coaster. There are a lot of beautiful shifts occurring within me as a result of this cancer b.s. But I will be honest in saying that this part of the process has been the most challenging thus far.

It is strange to look in the mirror and see big purple incisions and flat, lifeless-looking mounds where there once was nipples and buoyant flesh. It is difficult to embrace this look, considering that breasts are so caught up in our cultural understanding of what it means to be a woman. My drains from surgery were removed at my doctor's appointment on Thursday, and I was given the o.k. to shower the following day. Seeing myself in the mirror after stepping out of the shower was one of the more horrifying experiences I've had in my life. (I could probably consider myself lucky for this, but I'm emotionally not there yet. I'm having a more difficult time accessing gratitude post-surgery than prior.) I screamed and sobbed, "I LOOK LIKE A FUCKING LINEBACKER JESUS FUCKING CHRIST I WISH I HAD NEVER DONE IT."

The process of healing is hard. I definitely had my fit yesterday. Several, actually. I cried a lot. And I think that was necessary, just like working through the despair after the initial diagnosis was necessary. This cancer shit isn't linear. At least for me it hasn't been.

I probably can't speak for everyone else that's ever been dealt this fucked up hand, but it doesn't seem like any aspect of this follows a steady course—emotionally, mentally, physically, spiritually… none of it is neat and tidy. There are lots of ups, and a shit ton of downs too. The positive aspect in all of this is that the way my body looks currently is not the way it will look forever—I will begin the reconstruction process as early as next week. And nothing in this life is permanent. It seems like incorporating the Buddhist principle of "non-attachment" might be helpful here. But it's really hard to eradicate feelings of inadequacy that occur after traumatic body events, as my friend pointed out to me in a conversation earlier this week. And it's even more challenging when you already believed you were inadequate to begin with… and that belief is what I'm forced to address through all of this.

So maybe I'm not quite ready for the Buddhist approach. Maybe I'm not ready to be zen about this. Maybe I need to have my shit-fit and cry and feel sorry for myself a little longer. This is a lot to deal with. Being 26 and kissing your breasts goodbye. Not to mention the physical pain and temporary impairment as a result of surgery. Or the fact that my life has taken a hugely inconvenient turn and I'm not starting grad school this August like I was supposed to. Somehow not having breasts seems to have made everything else more real. I'm actually pretty fucking PISSED about this whole situation.

(And I've heard from many people that "that anger will *help* you!", and every time I've heard it, I've kinda been tempted to punch them in the throat. Just because.)

Clearly I've got a lot of anger that needs processing and dealing with, and I'm determined to work through it, just like I have been determined to work through everything else. So I'm just going to say that my inner mean girl (Regina George) is responsible for this post.

To be clear, I don't regret my mastectomy decision. I still believe it was the right thing for me in my situation. I was aware that I may confront some grief around my new virtually chestless (for now) body, but that grief is not something I could really prepare for, aside from being open to the fact that it may occur.

This is a process, and I know I will be on the other side of all of this someday, but I have to accept myself where I am right now. Foul-mouthed and pissy. And still hopeful.

Namas-motherfucking-te.

## GETTING INTIMATE WITH ROCK BOTTOM
JUNE 1, 2016

I had my post-op appointment yesterday, which I was rather optimistic about. I'm finding that that's my biggest mistake, and my biggest weapon in all of this, and apparently I haven't gotten the timing quite right.

On the bright side, my incisions look great, and my mobility is coming back nicely. On the not bright side, they officially staged my cancer as Stage 3 Grade 3, as opposed to their original Stage 2 Grade 2-3. The lump in my breast measured smaller than what they originally thought… But, this kills me, it went from looking like less than 2 cm in the ultrasound, then inconclusive in the MRI because my tissue is dense, but they thought it was around 5-6 cm based on that particular test, then at my last appointment, my doctor noticed that they both (lymph node and breast) felt smaller from the last exam three weeks prior, and when it was all out of me, it measured 3 cm. They changed the staging because of the number of lymph nodes involved. Post-surgery, my doctor said he removed a couple of lymph nodes, but he didn't know an exact number because they are small, and they're also encased in fat, which makes it difficult to discern how many are actually there. Every person has a different number of lymph nodes in their body. It ended up that he actually removed 13 on my right side (in the underarm area) and of those

13, 8 tested positive with cancer, 5 were negative. In surgery, they insert a radioactive dye that follows the path of the cancer, so I suppose it's good that 5 of them tested negative for cancer.

Now that I've had to get rid of my fucking breasts, there's still a concern that this isn't over. They do believe that they got it all in surgery, but they're also unable to test for micrometastases that could be in other lymph nodes that their technology cannot see or test for. So they'd like me to do chemotherapy "just to be sure."

I'm not okay with this.

I'm not okay with flooding my body with poison and destroying my already weakened immune system. I'm not okay with the side effects of chemotherapy, like chemo brain, or decreased sex drive and energy levels, neutropenia and the illnesses that can result, having a fucking port sewn into my clavicle. No, thank you. I'm hormone receptor positive. I will explore the avenue of hormone therapy.

I realize that my beliefs about chemo might be radical and possibly offensive to some. Obviously that isn't my intention, but I'm speaking from a place of what I believe in FOR ME. I understand chemotherapy in cases where there is actually cancer to treat. But my cancer has all been removed. The doctors believe this. So to go through the hell of it "just in case" is not something I'm willing to do. There are too many unknowns for me in my current situation to just jump on board with a smile on my face.

We are all creating cancer in our cells all the time. The difference between a person who has cancer and a person who does not is in the immune system. The immune system in a normal person is able to shut down haywire cell growth before any problems arise. The immune system in someone like me was not able to suppress the angiogenesis (the process through which new blood vessels are formed from pre-existing blood vessels—crucial for reproduction of these mutated cells). So it doesn't seem right to poison this same immune system that was already damaged to begin with just to knock it on its ass further… while *hopefully* wiping out the pesky rogue cells that may or may not be present.

It makes far more sense to me to focus on strengthening my immune system through extremely focused nutrition (RAW and juiced vegetables, very minimal fruit as sugar feeds cancer, no animal products) and proper supplementation (I'm on about 50 supplements per day, split up at breakfast, lunch and dinner, as prescribed by my integrative MD—yes, she is a Western Medicine Doctor), as well as healthy stress management. This involves emotional healing too, to a large degree, and I'm finding that I have a lot of that to do… Basically self-care is the number 1 priority. I believe it should have always been number 1 for me, cancer or no cancer, but my poor self-value and self-worth made this challenging… and I believe there is a strong mind-body connection which I will write about at some point.

I was given a statistic yesterday that there's a 30% increase in survival at the 10-year mark when chemotherapy is combined with hormone therapy, as opposed to hormone therapy alone. I'm not a statistics person. Nor does that number seem substantial enough for me to just jump on board with something that has felt like a violation to my whole self from the very beginning of this fucking god-awful nightmare. (Obviously I'm fucking angry right now and unapologetically so.)

I realize that everyone is different. I know that my treatment will not work if I'm not behind it. That "positive attitude" that everyone is so adamant on preaching to me WILL NOT be there if I do something that I am not at peace with.

Right now, I need support. My mom and I both do. We do not need to be told what to do or how to proceed in terms of treatment OR in day-to-day life. Comments beginning with "You need to…" are comments we have no time or space for. We do not need interrogation or criticism or judgment. We are still gathering all of our information before we make any decisions.

I will define support as being present with us. Regardless of whether you agree with our approach or beliefs at this time or not. Regardless of how uncomfortable and scared this makes YOU. (You better fucking believe we're scared too!) Regardless of how much you are inclined to "fix things." Just be here. And if you can't, then don't.


## I AM NOT AN OLYMPIC FIGURE SKATER, AND THAT'S OKAY
JUNE 6, 2016

I will never forget the time a few years ago, when I was high on marijuana, that it occurred to me with a deep and crushing sadness that I would, in fact, never be an Olympic figure skater.

Yes. You read that correctly. To be clear, this was during my stoner phase.

At that moment, in my state of silly stupor, I was extremely overwhelmed and bothered by this fact. If you know me at all, you know that I am an anxious person, and my mind moves very quickly. I'm not exactly sure how I arrived at the thought in the first place, but I do know that I perseverated on it for a long time (and by long time, I mean somewhere roughly between three minutes and three hours—time always evaded me when I smoked the giggle bush).

Of all things to be sad about, my mind chose to agonize over the fact that I was not an Olympic skater. Worse than that, I wasn't even a competitive skater! And worse than that, I wasn't even sure if I could skate! How do I go on living my life knowing that I am a pillar of mediocrity?

I remember having that thought, getting out my journal, and writing it down to revisit the concept later, because it seemed alarming to me. Even in my high state I was so acutely aware of my own fear of not being "The Best" at something.

It's also quite funny that I was not thinking things like "I will never be a star at the Met" or something more relevant to me. Instead, my mind chose to agonize over this extremely unattainable non-goal of mine. (Or maybe it was subconsciously a goal of mine?? I'm gonna go with no, it was just the pot...)

I'm sharing this with you because I had a moment that reminded me of that time today. I was looking in the "mirror" after I got out of the shower. I say "mirror" because I've taken the liberty of covering up the majority of my bathroom mirror with my newly created vision board to make the breast reconstruction process more emotionally bearable.

So anyway, I was looking in the 3-inch sliver of mirror on the far right-hand side that isn't covered by my vision board and I found myself thinking not-so-nice-thoughts about my physical appearance. *My boobs look weird, I hate my scar, my eyebrows aren't right, my eyes look asymmetrical, yadda yadda bullshit yadda.* And for whatever reason, my mind flashed to that high time at my old apartment sitting in my bed and being suddenly jolted with sadness over my figure skating status.

It occurred to me today that my obsessive thoughts around my looks are just like my ruminative thoughts about my non-skating. They both are unimportant. (And unattainable non-goals).

In the wake of a cancer diagnosis, it is almost comforting for me to get lost in the melodrama of my 20-something culturally inspired vanity, because it makes me feel more normal. Strangely, it reminded me that I'm still me.

It is also comforting to feel myself having more and more of these "ah-ha!" moments around what's truly important to me in my life. A year ago, I would have given anything for a scarless forehead. Today, I accept my scars and wounds. They are perfectly imperfect proof that I am alive, and I have lived.

## TODAY I SING
JUNE 8, 2016

I have the dreaded oncology appointment today, wherein I will be fed statistics and survival rates and other comforting information.

*And also*, I cannot describe the amount of inner peace I feel regarding my decision for treatment. I feel more in touch now with my life's purpose to serve others than I ever have. There are some things in life that cannot be explained. This is one of them. Through this diagnosis, I have come to recognize my own strength, and the amount of love for my fellow human that has always resided under layers of blubber and fear. Something in me has softened through all of this (aside from my muscle tone...). But really, though, my tummy has never been squishier. Actually maybe the beginning of college when I was chasing beer with pizza on the daily... Can't wait to start running and power-vinyasa-ing again!

I was having anxiety earlier in the week regarding this appointment. And then today, something miraculous happened.

I sang.*

It was ultra phlegmy, and under-supported. (These tissue expanders have made deep, diaphragmatic breathing a whole new experience...) I nearly choked on my own throat-goobers so hard that I had to stop the phrase. But I sang.

I have not opened my mouth to sing since the diagnosis in April. The last time I sang was the day we buried my grandmother. Getting through the Ave Maria was one of the hardest things I've ever had to do in my entire life. And then being diagnosed with cancer less than two weeks later pummeled me to the ground so hard that getting out of my nest of tissues and blankets on the couch became my goal for the day; tackling repertoire study, vocal technique, coloratura, etc., seemed a bit irrelevant.

Today I sing for hope. I sing today in celebration of the inner peace I feel in this moment. I sing because life is beautiful. I sing for love and I sing for fear (and I believe we fear only *because* we love, so all there really is is love). I sing for surrender and I sing for release.

Namaste

---

* *Link available here: myterminallife.org*

## BOOBS AND OTHER THINGS
JUNE 11, 2016

Three weeks post-op and I'm officially out and about *at night* with some semblance of breasts! How *exciting!* (Note my water in the picture. Hydration is the sensation.)

I have to laugh at the combination of words around my breasts and actually this whole situation, because they are words I never thought I'd be combining, let alone exclaiming in a celebratory manner.

Last night, my cousins and I were at Lovin' Cup and the band "sophistafunk" was playing. It was super enjoyable. I appreciated them lyrically and their keyboardist was unreal. I get inspired when I see people tapping into the transformative power of music, when it bleeds over into areas of social justice and equality, dismantling the differential stratification our dysfunctional system depends on... Ahem.

What was even more enjoyable was when the lead singer/rapper said, "Put your hands in the air," and I squealed to my cousins "I CAN DO THAT!!"... Because three weeks ago I could not. I could not even get out of bed without assistance. It's amazing to me how quickly my body is recovering from **major surgery.** There's something to be said for all my dietary changes and supplement-ation. All of my doctors are super impressed and tell me every appointment, "You're a fast little healer," to which I reply, "Damn straight I am."

So lately I've been getting lost in the joy of the little things in life. Spending hours in the grass searching for four leaf clovers, going for walks and feeling the sun on my face, drinking nourishing juices and visualizing them getting to work and oxygenating my cells. (Visualization has become quite meditative for me.) And of course, it wouldn't be right if I didn't mention that I'm also playing a butt load of Spyro the dragon (a highly addictive PlayStation game that when played elicits a euphoric response in all the lobes of the brain. Probably the ear lobes too.)

I feel gratitude. I think about how I used to live my life before canSer (Kris Carr suggests spelling it wrong every opportunity you get to take back your power and I like that a lot) and compare it to how I'm living now. Facing my own mortality has made me more willing to let go of my mistakes of the past and reclaim my truth, the fundamental part of me who has been there all along, but has hidden under fear or shame or whatever other bullshit my superego loved to hold onto and torment me with. I feel that this experience has brought about a death in me. That careless "it will never happen to me" way of living is gone. In some ways I'm grieving this loss. In other ways I'm super ready to start tackling the mother fucking shit out of this life. And in that way, I feel blessed. I'll write more about this later, but I'm off to hyperbaric oxygen therapy...

Namaste

# I THINK IT'S GONNA BE A GREAT DAY
JUNE 15, 2016

Good morning! Lately I have been so happy and grateful for the abundance of love and support in my life. Things have a funny way of coming together, sometimes in ways you least expect… I never expected my own cancer diagnosis to become a catalyst for my own happiness, and strangely, that's what's happening.

On Monday, I went to a lecture called "Diet and Cancer: Does nutrition matter?" It was hosted by the Rochester Area Vegan Society and the speaker was Thomas Campbell, MD, son of T. Colin Campbell (featured in Forks Over Knives), and co-author of The China Study, a fascinating study of nutrition and disease throughout the globe.

The short answer is yes, diet ***absolutely*** matters.

The Standard American Diet, also known as SAD (for good reason, our insides get SAD when we eat that way…) is one filled with animal protein, dairy, and lots of processed, packaged crap. We've been told from day 1 that milk makes us strong, and we need meat to build muscle. I don't know how this became the mainstream consciousness around food, but this is where we're at.

For those of you who have seen Forks Over Knives, you may remember T. Colin Campbell talking about his accidental findings on Casein, the main protein in milk. If you haven't watched this documentary, I suggest you check it out pronto. It explains the findings in this slide much better than I could…

I am certain that my diet is playing a huge role in my healing. I am eliminating inflammation in my body and lowering the level of acidity through food (cancer thrives in inflamed, acidic, oxygen-starved environments).

Good-morning juice! (And a random fly-away chunk of hair…) Dandelion root, Swiss chard, ginger, lemon, lime, and turmeric.

About to head out on my morning power walk!

Namaste

## A SHOWER OF ABUNDANCE / FEELIN' GOOD
JUNE 26, 2016

Lately, I'm just a happy dreamer enjoying moments with my head in the clouds. (Total photo fail, but I tried…)

I feel like my life before BC was some kind of strange dream. In hindsight, I was a disembodied zombie in some strange land where up was down, and self-love was an interesting concept to read about, but not something I believed I was capable or worthy of experiencing.

Most of the time, I was bordering suicidal, not necessarily actively wishing I was dead, but often wanting to "disappear" in some ambiguous and painless way. I would never have killed myself because I was too afraid, and my depression monster, we'll call him "Hank," would often twist and contort that very normal fear of death into an excuse to hate myself more... The taunting and teasing voice looped in my head over and over, "You're a Fucking baby, you can't do anything right. You should just die, but you won't, because you're a coward." Exemplary self-talk, obviously. Depression is a boa constrictor that coils itself around your body and soul, crushing bones and dreams, dissolving hope into its scaly skin. It wraps itself around your throat, rendering you paralyzed in fear and voiceless.

Three months post breast cancer diagnosis, I can happily say that "Hank," as I always knew him, is a fairly infrequent visitor.

The remnants of a familiar and fatally toxic love affair evoke electric and nauseating pulsing and throbbing in my abdomen. Do I sometimes find pieces of Hank's shed snake skin lying around? Sure. But dealing with a layer of dead flaky skin is a lot more manageable than trying to singlehandedly fight off a bone-crunching, soul-crushing, blood-thirsty beast.

I believe my diagnosis was a gift of renewal. It has shown me how much I love life. Even with all of the good in my life prior to diagnosis like getting into top grad schools for opera, having this huge outer validation of my internal truth (that I am in fact a gifted singer, and an intelligent person) was not enough for me to begin to see myself as worthy. Only from beginning to unbury myself and climb out of the depths of Rock Bottom (with emphasis on the capitalization) have I been able to see the glinting glimmering sunlight peering directly at me through the cracks.

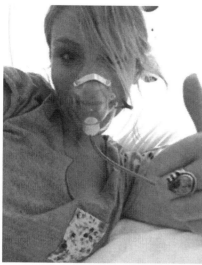

Also, guess who ran her first whole cancer-free mile in the blistering heat just one month post-op? This girl. And then I power-walked / jogged two more. And then lifted my 3-lb weights.

The goodness, in the way of beautiful people with hearts of gold and stories of infinite hope, just keeps pouring into my life. Today I feel so blessed. Happy Sunday.

# BATTERY RE-CHARGED
## JULY 15, 2016

I haven't written in a while because I've been so busy living my life, which feels really great to say. I just came home from NAVS Summerfest (a 5-day health and wellness conference) held at the University of Pittsburgh at Johnstown.

This conference came at the perfect time for me, because prior to it, I was experiencing a bit of the "birthday blues". I've never not had the birthday blues; I remember turning 16 and crying on my birthday because I was halfway to 32 (yeah, I've always been nutty). In anticipation of July 13th, I was feeling a lot of intense emotion. My mind kept wandering to my potentially shortened life expectancy (cancer at 26 may take off 33 years of my life… but there are a lot of factors in a statistic like this, so in my more positive state, I can honestly say "we'll see about that" because I know I'm more powerful than a number, and I'm feeling healthier, stronger, and more grounded every single day). I was feeling pretty sad in the few days before the conference.

And then I went to the conference, and my passion for living was reignited. Being around like-minded people with similar struggles and a similar approach was incredibly healing to me. I also had the opportunity to discuss my situation with Dr. Michael Greger (author of "How Not to Die"), Dr. Michael Klaper, George Eisman (RD), Keri Saunders (RD), and health guru John Pierre, all of whom offered their recommendation and insight free of charge. I had five days to soak in all of this light and positivity from those around me, and I'm realizing how important it is for me to keep reaching out to those who support me, to recreate that sense of peace now that I'm home.

Wednesday was my birthday, and it was hands-down the best birthday I've ever had. I've never really enjoyed my birthday but this year was different. I woke up that day with an appreciation for the breath in my lungs, and the sun in the sky, and my ability to go out and enjoy the day with all my limbs, with my sight, with all my senses. This was the first year I've ever wanted to celebrate my birthday. My mom made wonderfully delicious vegan food, and I was surrounded by friends from all stages of my life—high school, college and after, and my family. It was a beautiful day.

Also, I'm GODMOM. My Godson Maddex was born July 6th, just one week before my birthday. Seven pounds of joy and wonder. I'm so happy to be a part of his world.

I started my hormone therapy drug today (Tamoxifen). So far, aside from a minor tummy ache in the beginning of the day, I don't have any real complaints. I'm feeling pretty great these days, and in the moments where I'm feeling vulnerable, I know exactly who to reach out to. I am so thankful to be in this space of positivity and light. I'm becoming who I really am. And I am so thankful for this.

## "OPPORTUNITIES FOR GROWTH"
JULY 28, 2016

Lately I've been trying to see my challenges (large and small) as "opportunities for growth." I put that in quotes because that very positive spin on things still seems a bit hokey to me. But sometimes I personally need to embrace the hokey and set aside my cynicism. I don't think it would hurt me to do so. I wonder sometimes why I cling so hard to my dark and somewhat pretentious beliefs, especially when these beliefs inform my behavior, and sometimes my behavior is that of an ass-clown. Somewhere along the way I learned that smart people are cynical and critical, and since so much of who I want to be (and who I fear I'm not) is rooted in intellectual aptitude, I don't allow myself to be happy. Sounds absolutely insane as I'm typing this.

This whole life is one big-ass opportunity for growth. I am not who I was five years ago, or even five months ago. Cancer has transplanted me from one world into a drastically different one. I find myself uncomfortably vacillating between the two, only to come to the same conclusion over and over again—I am no longer who I was. Standing in front of the mirror obsessing over my scars—this is a way that I notice myself grieving the death of my former self. I yearn for the person I used to be before all of this, because even though I wasn't happy, in some ways the familiar self-torture is more manageable than acknowledging my mortality—which is what cancer has brought me right up against. And then I realize hours have gone by, I haven't left my house, or even my room, and it occurs to me that I'm not dead yet (and I don't plan on being dead for a long while), but engaging myself in front of the mirror (or worse, inside my head) isn't exactly living either.

The Tamoxifen caused serious visual disturbances, which is a rare side effect of the drug, so I'm no longer taking it. All I can say is that I believe my grandma was with me on the ride home from Canandaigua where I had visited an acquaintance. My eyes started to feel a little tired and heavy, and my vision was slightly blurry when I was driving home on the thruway. Within three minutes of setting my purse on the counter at home, my vision went BLACK with small flashes of light. I couldn't make out faces. I sat down on the couch for a second and tried to breathe through it, and I stared blankly ahead at the tv which was airing a commercial for Mazzola insurance. One second I was staring at a woman with long brown hair talking about insurance with green frogs at the lower corner of the screen, the next second, I saw black with patches of green where the frogs used to be. This lasted for about ten minutes before I called the oncology nurse, who told me to stop taking the drug and that they'd find me something else. The effect carried on for a solid 25 minutes or so.

In order to be sure that it was the effects of the drug before calling it quits, I went to the eye doctor for an exam. My eyes are good, I have 20/20 vision. Aside from the visual disturbances, I was pretty miserable on the drug. Anxious, weepy, ready to fight with anyone (mostly my mom), and lots of stomach upsets. Lots of night sweats too. All in all, my experience on the drug was pretty lousy. I believe there's a reason my vision didn't go completely black while I was still behind the wheel on a busy expressway at lunchtime. It's because I've got shit to do in this life.

Last night, I went to a memoir writing class at Writers and Books on University Ave downtown. I missed the first class last week because I was too busy feeling almost-suicidal, thanks in large part to good ole' Tamoxifen. When asked to introduce myself to the class of 9 people, I found myself stuttering and babbling all over the place. After my flop of an introduction was finished, I shriveled up, and existed inside of my head for the remainder of the class. I couldn't even get through the exercise the teacher was leading us through because I wasn't able to hear past my super-ego who was kindly telling me I was worthless and stupid and that everyone else in the class now knows how stupid I am. It probably seemed like I was frustrated with the class itself (actually, I know it did because I received a compassionate but concerned email from the instructor this morning), but in actuality, I was pretty pissed at my own thoughts, my own reactions, at the skeletal and beautiful bitch hissing in my ear, reminding me of all the things I am not. I felt like a closed circuit; the more I existed inside my head, the more my behavior sucked, which just kept the bad thoughts going, and so on and so on. (I literally sighed—more like HUFFED—loudly. About 4 times. Like a child. I'm so charming.)

I wonder what it would have been like if I had been able to extend just one crumb of compassion toward myself in the beginning of class after the self-deemed inarticulate and less-than-stellar introduction. I am, after all, going through a whole fucking lot. I wanted to drop out of the class right then and there, and I drove the whole way home in tears.

When I got home I was angsty and pissed so I decided to jump on my mini trampoline in my backyard under the stars, listening to some Red Hot Chili Peppers—a much healthier coping mechanism than I would have chosen just five months ago. When I first started jumping, I was looking directly at the light from Pandora on my phone, because I was afraid that if I looked anywhere else, I'd fall directly on my ass and break it—the whole ass. And I was thinking as I was jumping that my choice to focus on the light of my phone is like any other choice of perspective I'm making at any given time at life. I chose to stare at the light of my phone because it felt safe and comfortable, but in doing so, I was missing the view of the stars overhead, the warm golden glow of the neighbors' porchlight, the breezes brushing my face and bare arms, the fresh green smells of summer air on a humid night.

I decided to carefully shift the direction of my bounce, so that I was facing the neighbors' porchlight. As I began to transition my gaze toward the new focal point, I felt extremely uncomfortable and wobbly, like I was going to collapse any second. But I didn't. And before I realized it, my mind was in awe of the stars above me, the sounds of night all around me, the whispering leaves in the bushes and trees, the faint buzzing of insects all around, the soothing yellowy glow of the lamp above my neighbors' deck. I pictured myself breathing in this warm yellow light while I was jumping and I started to get blissfully lost in that, but then Tom Petty came on Pandora and I had to start laughing at myself. A good friend said to me recently, "What doesn't kill you makes you funnier," so there's that. I don't know if I'm funnier, but I'm most certainly looking for the humor in things these days, because the bleak does not serve me.

Sometimes all that's needed is a bit of perspective, and some green tea (for the polyphenols).

I've realized that for most of my life, I've been sleeping. I haven't been living authentically. Not with others, and most certainly not with myself. I have lots of "opportunities for growth". My cancer journey has been a powerful illuminator of these opportunities. And as it evolves, I'm sure more opportunities for growth, adjustment, reflection, moral inventory, change, and shifting will reveal themselves...

## <u>MOM</u>
AUGUST 16, 2016

Below is the writing exercise we did in my writing class that I referred to in my post entitled "Opportunities for growth." I thought it would be good for me to share something that I really struggled in creating at that particular class, just to teach my ego to sit its ass down and shut up...

*It strikes me how you always say there's something in your eye when I catch you crying. Even as a child, after long arguments you had with Dad in person or over the phone, I'd see tears. I'd feel the heaviness expanding in the air around me, and before I was even able to ask what happened or what was happening, you would say, reflex-like, theatrically, "There's something in my eye!" Your eyes: hazel and mysterious, with deep brown borders and yellowy green around the pupil; the longer I'd look, the more light-green and gold they'd become, but you never let anyone look very long.*

*You stand, shoulders slumped, with a heavy sadness, apologizing for the space you take up, as if your existence is a shameful sin of sorts, and I wonder what has happened to you long before you pushed me out of you.*

*You are a bird with a hurt wing. You flit about the kitchen, throwing this and that into one of our two juicers, slicing and dicing, mixing and fixing, as if standing still might actually hurt.*

*And I suppose maybe it does hurt. I am frozen, and I burn.*

*I hug you.*

*These days, your shirts smell like garlic and warm earthy spices from your labors in the kitchen, cooking me mushrooms and green leafy things to keep my health. NED—"No Evidence of Disease"— is what's written on my chart, this status a relief and a threat to us both, and I realize that you've had cancer too, right alongside me, and yet you never tire of chop-chop-chopping my vegetables and pressing them into our juicers to keep me healthy. 64 ounces of carrot juice a day. You take 2 sips for yourself.*

*I wish there was someone around to take care of you the way you've been taking care of me since April 11th, the day my ears went numb from the voice on the phone and you grabbed life's steering wheel from my fragile shaking hands. If I could bring Grandma back for you, I would; I know she'd be chop-chop-chopping away with you to lighten our load, your load, everything to do with me lately. I'll admit, I'm not used to being the needy one. And yet lately, I come ill-equipped for the tasks of the day on most days. The energy supply that I would channel toward, making you and others believe I was well, has vanished without a trace. In its place, a rawness like oozing flesh. I want to tell you I'm sorry, but it seems my voice has vanished too.*

*You grind the bitter green dandelion root in the slow masticating juicer, sweat hanging in the hair by your neck that has fallen out of your ponytail. The kitchen shrouded in the familiar smells of the sweet and bitter earth, and the whirring sound of the Breville juicer.*

*My mom, chopping and grinding away, does all of this with one wing. For me. I stand in sad and still silence, in awe of you. I want to tell you so many things, but the persistent lump in my throat makes me oddly quiet, cold, and sterile in moments of potential vulnerability. I can scream and shout in our moments of shared pent up anger over naïveté and innocence lost, both past and present. But I do not like to cry in front of you.*

*Like mother, like daughter. I find myself using your "something-in-my-eye" line more and more these days.*

*It appears my wing is in need of repair, too.*

## ADVICE*
## LATE SUMMER 2016

After a series of particularly frustrating conversations with family and friends regarding my situation, I am compelled to write about my needs in a very clear way.

The array of ridiculous things I've heard since my diagnosis is astounding. Anything from "Well, at least you get perky new boobs!" to "Well, you're lucky! You'll probably lose weight from treatment!" to "Oh, should I try that alternative therapy to prevent cancer?"… to criticism of my ability to proceed with my life in a "normal" fashion.

1) Breast cancer surgery is not a boob job. I don't have nipples anymore, I have long pink scars in their place now. They don't look like boobs outside of clothing, and they certainly don't feel like boobs, either—try sleeping with these impostors… they don't move or shift with you like the old ones. I understand that comments like "New Boobs, YAY!" are people's way of trying to help you find the positive in the situation, but let's be real here. There is nothing

---

* **Editor's note:** *This important post was not included in Amy's original blog.*

fucking positive about kissing your tits goodbye at 26 years old—especially in this hyper-sexualized culture where breasts are all caught up in our traditional views of femininity. Feeling like a fraud in your own skin is not sexy; it's confusing, and emotionally loaded. And if eventually, the cancer survivor finds the positive in her new rack, then GREAT! It'll mean something because it came from HER, not because of other people's expectation that she hit the ground running all smiles and butterflies and kittens and rainbows.

2) The comments about weight loss and treatment are appalling on a number of levels. First of all, what if I personally was not concerned with my weight to begin with? What if I, unlike the majority of women in this fucked up culture, was actually happy with my current weight, shape, and size? And then someone makes a comment that would imply that weight loss in my situation is a desirable thing. The FUCK? Cancer patients are dealing with a lot—like the threat to their survival, maybe?? They don't need your projection of body image added to the mix. Sadly to say, I'm part of the majority of women who has a list of body-woes a mile long. But I make an effort every single day to accept the skin I'm in. So when someone says, "Lucky you, you'll probably lose all kinds of weight from treatment," it's kind of like saying you have all kinds of weight to lose, and that weight loss is a good thing—never mind the fact that you're going head to head with a disease that claims the lives of thousands of women every year. You'll be thin, that's what matters, right? That's evidence of our patriarchal world culture—the one that devalues women and encourages women to devalue themselves. And contrary to what most people believe, the treatment for breast cancer often makes women GAIN weight.

3) The "Oh, wow, should *I* do that?" comments are aggravating. I get that people are affected by your health crisis, and maybe your situation is encouraging them to get more serious about their overall health and wellness, which is a great thing. But I'm sorry, I'm not your fucking doctor. I don't know what you need. Just because I've been forced to enter this world where health and wellness occupies so much of my focus, out of a diagnosis that indicates that I am not healthy or well, I don't know what's best

for you. And also, there's a part of me that's like.... UMM HI I JUST GOT DIAGNOSED WITH CANCER CAN YOU PLEASE SEE *ME* RIGHT NOW? ME. Be here for *me*. With *me*. My entire world just got blown up and I'm still finding shattered pieces of myself amidst the rubble. We can absolutely focus on your health if something comes up, but I'm processing a fucking trauma like nothing I've ever experienced in my entire life; I'm unable to answer your questions about what you should do about your health since I'm trying to wrap my head around my own.

4) The "Be Grateful! This is a second shot at life" bullshit is beyond irritating. Especially coming from someone who has not been forced to face their own mortality from a cancer diagnosis. Yes, gratitude is important, and it's powerful in manifesting goodness in your life. But you know what else is important? Being REAL. Feeling the feelings, regardless of how painful and unpleasant they are. Because feeling them allows you to move through them. And guess what? Once those feelings are worked through, TRUE gratitude is possible, and so is acceptance of this experience as a "second chance," or whatever Hallmark greeting card phrase people want to shove in your face. But it will be absolutely meaningless if I'm feeling forced to present this image of stability and optimism to please those around me, so that *they* feel better. Would you feel overwhelmed with gratitude just months after serious trauma? Maybe, but it would take a process to get to that place. A lot of anger. A lot of grief. A lot of thick emotion to get through. So please don't project expectation... leading nicely to my next point:

5) "You just need to..." or "You should..." or "You've got to..." Stop the FUCK right there. Comments of this nature are *not helpful*. At all. When the person is ready and able, they will do what they can. I've personally received several of these well-meaning "recommendations"—my personal favorites are, "You have got to start living your life and stop worrying about what life is going to be in the future. It is making you withdraw from life. Be Amy as Amy used to be." K. I know this person meant well. But telling someone in this situation what to do is just never helpful. You don't

think that they'd like to just go back to the way things were? The expectation for me to "be Amy as Amy used to be" is completely unfair. I will never be who I was, ever again. And maybe that isn't a bad thing. But this is a process. It's MY process. This is an isolating experience. And it isn't something people just snap out of and move on from like it's nothing. It's a process that requires a lot, mentally and emotionally. Telling me what I should be doing is pretty much a criticism of where I'm at, and implies that I'm failing on some level, in your eyes.

Why does this culture have such a hard time just being PRESENT with someone in need? We are so uncomfortable with things that aren't pleasant, even when they are honest and real. Why does the truth scare us so much? I personally think that my situation has triggered a lot of fear in those close to me, yes, because they're afraid of losing me, but also because they're afraid of their own mortality. And that's fine, but maybe work that out on your own, instead of projecting your shit onto me. I've got enough of my own to deal with right now. I would appreciate it if people would just be here for me and accept me as I am, where I am with all of this. Without expectation of where you think I "should" be, or how you think I "should" be handling it.

This morning I got a text from a well-meaning person asking me if I'd like to shop. When I declined, her response was "Okay, but do NOT stay in the house today, you need to get out. I know you don't want to hear it, but it's the best natural medicine for you." When I told her, "Please don't tell me what to do. I can't handle that right now. I'll do what I can when I can," I got a clearly angered response: "Ya know what Amy, that's rude and disrespectful. I am only trying to help you see things in a different view. Sorry for caring that you are going through this. But you are now cancer-free and a cancer survivor. Start telling yourself that! Have a nice day!"

First of all. Maybe waking up and getting out of bed every day is the best that I can do right now. Maybe some days I'm happy to leave the house. And maybe other days, I feel like the world is scary and heavy and overwhelming and would prefer the comfort of my living room, my blankets, my dog to the outside world. And all of that is okay. Maybe consider that getting devastating news about my close friend, who has been dealing with the same fucking disease I was diagnosed with, is hitting pretty close to home and has knocked the wind out of me, and ripped the floor from underneath me. Maybe consider that the medical field will not consider me "Cancer Free" until I'm 5 years out from diagnosis. It seems that it's pretty easy for people on the outside to prescribe EXACTLY what I need. Try living it. Calling me rude and disrespectful for expressing what I need and don't need? This isn't the first time I've expressed my distaste for the "Shoulds," particularly to this person. My advocating for myself is not rude or disrespectful, it's honest. I'm telling you that the brand of support you're trying to give me is not helpful or what I need in the moment. If my telling you what I need and don't need is striking that kind of chord with you, it seems as though this is more about you than it is about supporting me, no? People do what they think is right, always. Fine. But when I'm making it clear that what you're doing or saying isn't helpful, please try to empathize as best you can with the situation I'm in. I'm not attacking *you* or telling you that you're wrong or bad.

The expectation that I just gobble up any brand of "support" people want to give, regardless of whether or not that brand of support feels toxic or oppressive or hurtful to me. is just bullshit. Bottom line: Quit telling me what to do, and trust that I'm figuring out how I need to proceed. I can do that with you or without you. And if I'm telling you what I need and don't need and you're unable to hear me, then maybe that's an indication for a need for space at this time.

6) This should be common sense, but I've been surprised too many times that it just needs to be said. Please don't tell me about your dad's sister's husband's mother who died of breast cancer. Or the young girl you knew who "had really aggressive BRCA cancer" who just died. First of all, do you think it's comforting for me to hear about these people who are dying from the same thing I was diagnosed with? Yes, I know it happens. Do I want to fucking hear about it? No. I don't. Second of all, if you're saying things like "She

had BRCA cancer," you obviously don't know very much about the disease. Which is fine, I know it's a lot for people to understand. But at the same time, it's like you could at least have the courtesy to maybe brush up on your shit for me if you decide you're going to have a conversation with me about it. There's a part of me that's bitter and resentful toward the amount of knowledge I have about this thief of a disease, because it's yet another way that cancer has changed me, and sets me apart from the normal 27-year-old. This is something I need to work through, and it has very little to do with other people. But I'm being honest in saying that the constant need to explain the jargon of this disease and its processes to friends and family around me makes me feel pretty alone. Like, just because it isn't happening directly to YOU, you could still educate yourself a bit—that's one way you could support me, and it would mean a lot. I don't think that's asking too much.

In general, my advice would be to just use common sense, but common sense doesn't appear to be all that common, from my view these days.

## TAMOXIFEN: ROUND NUMBER DOSE
SEPTEMBER 14, 2016

So, because I'm not really a reckless person, or a *complete* fool (jury is still out on that but just go with it), I've decided to try Tamoxifen again, but at a lower dose. Clearly the 20 mg dose was too high for my sensitive little body to handle, as it caused severe visual disturbances. The more that I read, the more that I believe in the use of hormone therapy for me, considering my age and my naturally high estrogen production because of where I am biologically on that front (my cancer had strong receptors for estrogen). I do believe that my integrative approach to healing is best for me. I had my breasts amputated. My entire lifestyle is different—no more booze, no more weed, no more dairy, no more meat, mostly raw, running daily, a gajillion cups of matcha green tea daily, high dose vitamin C, acupuncture, too many supplements to mention, iscador therapy, and most importantly, facing my demons and inviting them for tea and crumpets, even if they sling poo at me for giggles. (My demons are 4-year-old monkeys.)

Bernie Siegel's book *Love, Medicine & Miracles* has been pretty transformational for me so far. The author is a surgeon who has worked with many cancer patients, and he discusses what he's observed consistently in "exceptional cancer patients" throughout his 40 years of practice. He defines exceptional cancer patients as patients who defy the odds, and he highlights the thread of commonality among them all: outlook, attitude, a somewhat defiant personality, and overall life perspective rooted in solid self-esteem, and feelings of control in their treatment. I'm encountering, yet again, the importance of the mind in the healing process. Honestly, that's my biggest weapon, as well as my biggest challenge in all of this. I find myself resisting things like meditation, mindfulness, anything that resembles stillness—even yoga. At this time, running feels better to me, so that's what I'm doing, but I'm allowing myself to be curious about what that resistance is all about for me. Perhaps it's fear. Fear of what might come up if I sit still. I find it challenging to take a really deep diaphragmatic breath lately. It seems I exist in a state of tension for most of my waking day—my breathing is always pretty shallow. And when I consciously choose to breathe low and deep, it feels foreign to me; I almost feel a lump in my throat, like I might cry.

My fragility makes sense, given the circumstances. And even if the circumstances were different, fragility would make sense because of the fact that I am human. We are all fragile. Life is tough stuff for all of us.

I want my life, no matter how long it is, to be a reflection of what's important to me. So far, what's important to me is love, expression, empathy, compassion, understanding, music, and truth.

Today I feel a bit scared, but excited for what the future has to offer, because I'm hopeful that this next chapter of my life will be better than the last.

# THANKFUL THURSDAY
SEPTEMBER 18, 2016

I have some background information to give you before my thankfulness for today makes sense.

So, it is common knowledge among breast cancer patients that breast cancers like to travel to the bone, lung, liver and brain. My oncologist mentioned to me that estrogen receptor positive cancers tend to like to nestle themselves in the bones, and since she mentioned this in my follow-up appointment after my mastectomy, the fear has been in the back of my head. Actually, not even the back of my head. It's been in the front of my mind. Terror. Fear. Every ache and pain, my first thought is "Oh my god, it's cancer." Never mind the fact that I'm running daily. Never mind the fact that sometimes "normal," non-diagnosed-with-cancer-people, past or present, sometimes feel twinges or aches or twitches or muscle spasms. I ended up texting my surgeon a couple weeks ago because I was having pain in my chest/shoulder area. If I were not in my current situation, I would have chalked it up to a pulled muscle from running my dog, who sometimes gets overeager and drags me whichever direction her nose leads her. But because of my circumstances presently, my mind went to the dark side. The "oh-my-god-it's-cancer-and-I'm-going-to-drop-dead-tomorrow" side. So my surgeon, being the wonderful person he is, squeezed me into his schedule. I had an ultrasound (holy fucking PTSD Batman— I was in tears and shaking the entire time). Everything looked fine. It was determined that it was just a pulled muscle, and that I'm okay. And it would be unlikely for me to be presenting symptoms at this point after having just had a clean bone scan in April. I was also told that most women in my position are like this—terrified of absolutely EVERY sensation they notice in their bodies—for the first year. So good news, I'm normal?

At my pre-op appointment for my most recent surgery (8/18, surgery on 8/26), it was determined that my white blood cell count dropped a little bit from where it was in May after my first surgery. The workup from two days after my mastectomy recorded my white blood cell count at 4.5. Normal range is between 4.0 and 11.0.

94

The pre-op appointment recorded my white blood cell count at 3.9. Not really alarming, but of course, because I'm me, I was terrified. Because cancer that invades the bone interferes with white blood cell production. So after receiving those results, my mind went to the dark side, yet again. I was told that it didn't appear significant, but my surgeon ordered a differential the day of surgery just to keep an eye on it. So, after I got out of surgery, in my horrendous anesthesia-bitch-monster-fog, I was given the results of the differential: 3.6. I was inconsolable. Part of my inconsolable state was most likely due to anesthesia, as it tends to make me extremely volatile and reactive and emotionally all over the place. But the other part was legitimate fear, I think.

The anesthesiologist came back to visit me after surgery in the recovery unit to tell me I looked like a young Barbara Streisand, but found me in tears. He told me that my "low" count was not really that low, and to try not to worry, and to trust that if the doctors thought there was something wrong with it, they would have ordered more tests, which sort of calmed me down. I reached out to my integrative doctor to tell her my "horrible news," and she just told me to take a deep breath, that differentials are essentially just a picture of your cells in a moment in time, and that white counts (and other counts) can dip for many reasons (one of them being a vegan diet, another, running). She told me we would watch the trend, and mailed out lab papers to have this followed up. Told me to breathe. So I did. But only after I looked at my blood work records from the last five years. In general, it appears that I tend to run on the lower side of normal. There were lots of 3.6's, some 3.9's, some 4.2's, one or two "highs," which aren't even considered high, just higher for me. This did make me feel a little better, but still not completely settled.

I had bloodwork done last week, and today I had a follow-up appointment. My white blood cells were back up! 3.8. While just under the normal range, it made me relieved to know that my counts weren't steadily falling. Also, my thyroid function is good, my vitamin D levels are now GREAT (they were extremely low when they were checked just after diagnosis in April), and so are my insulin and glucose levels as well as my selenium level (which also was pretty low around my diagnosis). My B-12 is a little low, which is typical for vegans. At this point it isn't a concern, and not something to supplement because folic acid can stimulate cancer activity in some cases.

Today I am thankful that my bloodwork reflects vitality. I am here, and I am very much alive, with scars to prove it.

Also, day 2 on low-dose Tamoxifen, and I feel NOTHING in terms of side effects. We shall see what tomorrow brings. But today I am thankful for my body. Because even though it betrayed me a little bit with the whole cancer thing, it seems like it's adapting quite well to my new lifestyle. And I'm thankful for that.

## I HATE PINK
SEPTEMBER 18, 2016

Okay, I don't hate all pink. For example, I love my salmon-colored shirt. But I do not like pink in relation to breast cancer.

With October right around the corner, I thought it would be a good time to share my hatred for the pink movement. Breast cancer has become so publicized with pink ribbons on the labels of pretty much anything one can think of that it gives people this false sense that something is being done on the front lines to end this terrible disease. But the truth is, the majority of the money that is raised by charities like Susan G. Komen's is not used toward research, but instead, lining their CEOs' pockets. And overall cancer mortality has not changed a whole lot since the 1950s. We are being fed serious lies every day in the form of pink propaganda.

The following quotes can be found on this site:
https://www.chrisbeatcancer.com

*"Only 21% of money that Susan G. Komen for the Cure raises goes to cancer research 'for the cure'. Simple math tells us that 79% of the money they raise isn't going to anything that could produce a cure. As if that wasn't bad enough, donating to cancer research is essentially giving free money to drug companies who make billions in profit every year, and don't need your money, and are only interested in research that can lead to patentable, highly profitable drugs that they can sell back to you."*

Pretty sickening.

*"In 2010, Susan G. Komen for the Cure partnered with KFC who sold pink buckets of chicken 'for the cure'. Apparently the folks at Komen don't know that fast food consumption is directly linked to obesity, and that obesity is the 2nd leading cause of cancer."*

DISGUSTING. It also sort of reminds me of the picture at my oncologist's office of "Healthy eating" through breast cancer treatment. In the middle of this picture, a big ass carcinogenic piece of meat, a couple of peas on the side, a glass of frothy hormone filled milk, and a potato. And this is somehow supposed to help our odds? It's fucking disgusting. We are fed lies literally every single day. The medical profession has no knowledge of nutrition and its ability to help the body access its own powers. It only knows drugs. And drugs bring in profits to the pharmaceutical companies who are funding many of our top medical institutions, so of course that money is going toward DRUG research, not NUTRITION research.

*"In 2011, Susan G. Komen for the Cure created and sold a perfume called 'Promise Me' containing potentially cancer-causing toxic ingredients coumarin, oxybenzone, and toluene. After criticism they pulled it from the market."*

Clearly, our best interests are not what's important. Komen is interested in profit only, not in our health.

*"In 2012, Komen Founder/CEO Nancy Brinker was paid $684,717, a 64% increase from her $417,000 salary in 2011. And this was AFTER a big drop in donations and half their 3-Day races were canceled."*

What I could do with that kind of money. Infuriating.

*"In 2012, Komen drew criticism from the medical community for using misleading statements and deceptive statistics in their ads promoting mammograms. Komen uses donation money to provide mammograms to women who can't afford them, which seems good, until you learn that a 25-year study of 90,000 women proved that mammograms don't save lives, and that what early detection campaigns are actually doing is overdiagnosing and funneling women into an industry of harmful overtreatment, resulting in unnecessary surgery, chemo, radiotherapy and hormone therapies."*

. . . .

**"In 2013, Susan G. Komen for the Cure partnered with Real Water to sell pink water bottles, even though disposable plastic water bottles contain BPA, which is linked to breast cancer tumor growth."**

It would be hard to believe that someone so involved in the world of breast cancer would be unaware of the link between BPA found in plastics and breast cancer. So hard to believe, that I do not believe it, and think Komen represents a particularly sickening brand of capitalist-pig-evil.

*"In 2014, Komen partnered with Baker Hughes who produced 1,000 pink drill bits to be used in their fracking operations with the cutesy slogan 'Doing their bit for the cure'. Fracking involves the use of 700 different chemicals, some of which, like benzene and formaldehyde, are linked to cancer."*

More on Komen's partnership with an oil fracking company to 'fight for the cure' in this article. Un-fucking-believable: "Komen is supposed to be curing breast cancer. So why is its pink ribbon on so many carcinogenic products?" (Washington Post 10/21/2014)

An excerpt from the piece "I survived breast cancer but I hate Breast Cancer Awareness Month" in the Washington Post (10/10/2014) sums it up nicely:

*"So, I hate October. I think pinkwashing the NFL or running sales promotions designed to earn corporations more money or refurbish their brands all around other people's pain is sick and twisted. The color of baby blankets, fluffy cotton candy and your favorite Laffy Taffy does not represent the pain breast cancer patients have endured. Make it gray, make it black — or better yet, stop participating in the self-serving Cult of Pink and help make the switch from 'Awareness' to 'Action.' How? Instead of buying pretty pink things where the **majority of the profits do not go to research,** donate directly to organizations that help women deal with the devastating diagnosis of cancer. Or, go see your friend and let her talk about what it's like to lose her breasts and live with the constant fear of it sneaking up and making her endure it again. If you want to reflect on breast cancer and its true toll, visit and give to the SCAR Project. That is the real face of breast cancer and survivorship. Just like the confusing and contradictory cacophony of life, survivorship is ugly, hard, beautiful and joyous all at once."*

"Think Before you Pink" is a great consumer resource, with guides and questions to ask before you contribute to a charity or purchase a product. I.e., "How much of the money from this product/donation is going toward breast cancer research?" http://thinkbeforeyoupink.org

If you know someone with breast cancer (or any cancer) ask them how they'd like you to support them. They may have a favorite charity or organization they believe in. Or they may just want your physical and emotional presence. Maybe even a delicious juice or homemade vegan meal! I have more to say, but it felt good to get this information out.

## MOODS
SEPTEMBER 21, 2016

I upped my Tamoxifen dose because I was tolerating the low dose rather well, aside from extensive hot flashes and night sweats. I read somewhere that women who experience these side effects tend to have lower recurrence rates, so even though I'm not a huge fan of sweating my ass off, I'd take a little sweat to the alternative any day.

The Tamoxifen has also made me extremely moody. Moodier than I already am. And if you can't tell from my previous posts, emotions pretty much run my world, and emotions are particularly intense right now. Even before the Tamoxifen, the diagnosis alone made me feel a bit bi-polar. Sometimes I actually wonder if bi-polar is something worth investigating for me, particularly because I know there's family history on my dad's side, and because anti-depressants never really did much for me in the past, aside from make me zombie-like. Something to think about. But I do think this situation would make any person swing violently back and forth between hope and despair. Adding Tamoxifen to the mix has made the despair side particularly intense for me these last couple of days, but being able to step back and observe this in myself, and acknowledge that it's likely drug-related has made it a bit easier. It's the remembering to exercise my "observer muscle," as opposed to getting lost in my overwhelming thoughts and hopping on the anxiety train that is the challenge. The anxiety train appears to want to run me into the ground. The fact that I'm working hard at just existing is proof to myself that even through the struggles, I'm still hopeful. Even when I want to roll over and give up, there's something in me that keeps waking up every day and doing this "life" thing. I might not be smiling, but I'm here.

Thank god for running. I don't know why it took me so long to get into it, but I'm thankful I discovered it. I run every day now. And it ALWAYS makes me feel better. So on days when I'm feeling particularly rotten, I'll rack up around 7-8 miles, but most days I'm running between 3 and 5. I'm thankful for what my body can do. Despite its act of betrayal and confusion, this body is still a miracle. I am thankful for what it does for me.

Feelin' sweaty and good after my 4.6 mile run today! I'm officially back in the 120s again, weight-wise. Hoping it stays that way—I know some women report weight gain on Tamoxifen.

I think the running along with my constant green leafy veggie consumption should keep me fit and healthy, though.

Just sharing a picture of my dog, the contortionist. Riley is truly my best friend. She's my running partner. When I cry, she comes over and licks my tears away. When I'm happy, she wants to play. When I sing, she barks—and I'm choosing to believe that that's because she wants to join

me in song, not because she thinks I sound bad. When I'm mad, she puts herself in her kennel, which just breaks my heart because she internalizes my anger—so perceptive! So usually when I notice she's in the kennel donning her "sad eyes," I have to stop being angry and comfort her, and that actually helps me. She is so beyond perfect. She might not be the smartest dog, but holy crap is she lovable.

So, in summary:
I am thankful for modern medicine.
I am thankful for my side effects because of what they imply.
I am thankful for my body.
I am thankful for my dog.
Also… I am beyond thankful for my mom.

That is all.

# HELL IS OTHER PEOPLE
SEPTEMBER 23, 2016

Jean Paul Sartre was right. Hell is other people.

I woke up today and immediately wanted to punch things. So obviously the day was off to a good start.

I had two appointments on deck: neurological mind-body balancing, and mistletoe injection number 2 at my integrative md's office where I was to prove to my doctor that I could administer the injection to myself after my tutorial injection on Wednesday. (I found this interesting article on the Johns Hopkins Magazine website—spring 2014: "Are mistletoe extract injections the next big thing in cancer therapy?")

Last night I made frozen "treats" for my doctor and the people I've gotten to know through the vitamin C infusions. I made chocolate with raw cacao powder, coconut oil, cinnamon, agave, and vanilla extract. And then I dipped banana slices in the chocolate, and also made "blobs" of chocolate covered sunflower seeds and chocolate covered coconut flakes and stuck them all in the freezer. One of my favorite treats when I'm feeling like I want something that isn't a green leaf. So this morning I was rushing around trying to find a way to keep the frozen treats cold because they would be sitting in my car while I was in my first appointment. I packed one of those insulated hot/cold bags with a bunch of ice packs and frozen juice boxes, put the treats in a glass Pyrex container and hoped for the best, and got in my car, happy that I was running about 15 minutes early for once in my life. I even had the idea that I might actually have time to stop at Lori's Natural Foods to get myself a salad since I neglected to eat a substantial breakfast.

Except about 10 minutes into the drive I realized that I left my mistletoe ampules in the refrigerator, and since that appointment was directly after my first appointment, I had to turn around. So I went back, grabbed my mistletoe and rushed out the door, realizing that I'd likely be about 11 minutes late— you know, my usual timing.

I'll talk about the neuro mind-body balancing appointments in another post because there's a lot of interesting stuff I'm learning in these sessions—essentially it's all about finding other ways to release trauma aside from talking about the trauma. But for now I'm going to fast forward to being in the car on the way to my mistletoe injection, treats in tow, hitting every other red light, and getting stuck behind every possible bus. School bus, RTS bus, magic school bus, etc. Growing angrier by the second. So what should have been a 7-minute drive took more like 18 minutes. COOL.

So I get there, and I'm running with my big-ass tote bag of treats, and I see one of my vitamin C iv buddies in her infusion chair. I offer her a treat, and she says, somewhat disappointedly, "Oh, it's dark chocolate..."

And THAT set me off. YES it's dark chocolate. So sorry. Because MILK chocolate has HORMONES which are not ideal for people with CANCER (or anyone). So sorry to disappoint. I was just trying to bring some cheer to the office, apparently I failed. (Did I mention I upped my Tamoxifen dose?) I wasn't sure if I wanted to scream or cry or eat or do all at once.

So then I went back to try to show the nurse that I could do the subcutaneous mistletoe injection myself. Only, too bad I couldn't. First of all, insulin needles are way too fucking small and delicate. Worse than holding a baby. I was shaking and couldn't figure out how to draw up the liquid without contorting my entire hand in some monkey-witch awkward manner, and I was terrified I was going to drop it. You have to be careful not to hit the needle to the glass when you're drawing the solution, otherwise you might dull the needle. This is not something I'm cut out for. I don't have the patience. Also, I was mentally preparing for the self-stabbing, and that part wasn't going well either. So finally, almost in tears (hello Tamoxifen, I see you), I told her, "I'm not doing this. Can you just do it today? There's no way I'm going to do this today." She told me to be patient, that I was doing really well, and I'm thinking, "Yeah, okay, but just stab me please, because I'm not working any longer at this." So she stabbed me in my belly. And it hurt more than it did on Wednesday. Probably because I was all wound up.

I got in my car muttering every single swear word to myself, gritting my teeth and looking like an angry animal. So naturally, I decided I needed to buy some food.

There are people who, regardless of how good their intentions might be, just annoy the piss out of me. On a good day. And today was not a good day. (Am I the only awful person out there?) I walked into the store and this person came over to me in his usual annoyingly cheerful manner, talking to me about "healing frequencies" and his music—what he talks to me about literally EVERY TIME he sees me.

He walked away after that conversation and I thought I was in the clear. I was in no mood to interact with other humans, since that didn't seem to be going so well today. But then he came back over to tell me more about his healing frequencies. He probably doesn't know he's talking to a music major and I was in no mood to really converse about the healing power of music at the "cellular level"— yes I believe in the power of music, but I don't believe in people talking about things that they clearly don't really understand... Or maybe he does and I'm just an asshole, but I'm gunna go with, no. Mostly because he doesn't use musical terminology correctly... And then tells me, "Hey, guess what? You're wonderful!!" with his hands on my shoulders (please don't fucking touch me!) and "Have a blessed day!!" (This also happens every time I see him.) Today, I was NOT in the mood. First of all, the touching thing needs to stop. (And yet every time it happens, I find myself unable to say, "Yo, stop touching me, bro," and I don't know why, it's like I'm more worried about offending him than taking care of MY needs... Which in this case is to not be touched. I have to work on that.) And then he pops back over one more time to tell me that some of the other workers were there so I could go say hi. And I just said, "Okay, thanks," took my food, got in line, and left.

His seemingly incessant "popping over" reminded me of the game of whack-a-mole. I wanted the hammer.

So then I came home and I sulked for a while, because I really didn't even know what I was mad about. I numbed out with an episode of Narcos, drank some green tea, obsessed over my droopy eye/forehead scar. And then decided, "This is stupid and I hate everything today," so I put on my running clothes and I went for a run in the rain. I passed a dead raccoon and nearly started crying. His insides were on the outside, but his face looked peaceful and I wondered how this was possible. (Okay, I didn't nearly start crying, I actually had tears running down my face as I ran past him, and yes, I decided it was a him, though it could have been female...)

Today is just one of those days, but I am so thankful I am able to use my legs. I ran 5.18 miles today at an easy 9:22 pace. Running creates some space between me and my problems. And sometimes that's very necessary. Hoping I wake up not wanting to kick in doors or people's faces tomorrow.

Happy October. Let the pink washing begin. From perfumes (filled with harmful chemicals), to t-shirts, to Campbell's soup and BPA-laden water bottles with delicate and beautifully feminine pink ribbons on them. I want nothing to do with it. Fuck your pink ribbons. There are still too many of us dying. It's not a pretty pink disease. It's full of scars and disfigurement and destroyed body image, infertility due to the barbaric methods of treatment,

isolation, depression, anxiety, indescribable fear. But sure, KFC, slap a fucking pink ribbon on your buckets. Cuz hormone-filled fried chicken is really good for breast cancer.

I've HAD IT with this place. This is the insane asylum of the universe.

This week has felt incredibly heavy for a number of reasons. I feel like the universe is doing some crazy shit across the board, and I'm just standing here confused and hurt, feeling incredibly alone.

This breast cancer experience has brought some incredible people into my world, and I'm certain I never would have met them if it hadn't been for my diagnosis. I don't have the right words to express my gratitude and appreciation for that aspect of this tremendously difficult time in my life. I know that without these women, I would certainly not be able to face the day with the willingness to view this experience as a teacher.

Early on in the diagnostic process, I was led to a friendship that has provided me with hope when I've been overcome with doubt, strength when I've felt cripplingly weak, and courage when I've wanted to run away and hide instead of facing the day's itinerary. I was at Breathe yoga in Pittsford getting a juice with a friend when one of my instructors who I hadn't seen in about a month (because I was a little busy trying to pick up the pieces of myself that were shattered by the "You have cancer" phone call on April 11th) came over to say hi, and asked how my decision making for grad school programs was going. I told her through my tears what was happening in my world, and she offered her sincerest apologies, and told me that she has a cousin who is around my age who has been dealing with breast cancer since she was 21 years old, and offered to connect us. At this point, I had not met another 20-something diagnosed with breast cancer, so I was extremely grateful for her offer. She gave me her email address, and I emailed her that same night. The following day, I received an email from someone I now consider a sister and dear friend. We have both expressed several times (including the first time we heard each other's voices on the phone) that it feels like the universe wanted us to meet—there are just too many similarities, aside from the shitty diagnosis of cancer. Our ways of thinking, our views on disease in relation to emotional trauma, spirituality, the fact that we are both black lab lovers and owners… This is an excerpt of the very first email I received from her:

*Amy, I am so sorry you are dealing with this! Although it is really refreshing to come across someone else with such a similar mindset about all of it. It sounds like you are doing all the right things. My first go around, at 21, I was scared and my doctors scared me more, and therefore I fell victim to conventional treatment, when I believe it was against my best interest. I think chemo is a crock of shit, it weakens the immune system, the strongest defense our bodies have against cancer, weakens the mind, and weakens the spirit- It is an outdated treatment, and quite barbaric at that. During that time I had sought out all sorts of alternative treatments, I found a holistic doctor, Dr. Mary Wise, who was a Yale graduate and studied with Dr. Andrew Weil, who conveniently was located right in Henrietta. She unfortunately has retired this spring, otherwise I would be recommending you see her!*

*My second go around at age 23, I was pissed. I refused all treatments until I was comfortable and did my homework. I flew to Chicago to see Dr. Keith Block who is in my opinion the most educated, realistic, forward thinking doctor in the country on integrative medicine and cancer- he wrote the book Life over Cancer, and I highly recommend you read it. I also flew to see Dr. Donald Abrams at the Osher Institute in San Francisco who is very forward moving with AIDS and cancer and has done extensive research on the benefits that marijuana has on fighting immune related diseases. I went to the university of Miami and met with one of the doctors who created the test for HER2 to learn more about HER2 + cancer, because initially my cancer was ER/PR + and HER2- and the second time it was triple positive. I wasn't very keen on a mutating cancer and needed to understand what exactly was happening before accepting any drug treatments like Herceptin. During all of these visits and travel I learned a lot about what cancer is, how it works, and what we can do to fight it. Supplements, exercise, and eating well can only take us so far. Before I was even diagnosed I was a vegetarian for 5 years, I was a 3 sport athlete, and was raised on organic food. It took reading Mind over Medicine to really hone in on what the greatest defense of disease was for me. We are all different- and you nailed it, the one size fits all treatment is bullshit. It comes down to following your gut. You're the one that has to fight this battle. What feels good, what feels like it is curing you, is. Whether it's the mushroom complex (I've even gone so far to start a shiitake mushroom farm), whether it's the yoga or exercise (I run 5+ miles a day, completed my first half and full marathon in the past two years and am 100 percent positive it has helped keep my cancer at bay), whether it's meditation, or reading, or being around people that make you feel alive- those are the things that are the best medicine. Honestly. I've never felt healthier, more alive, more strong than in the past few years since taking my health into my own hands.*

Reading her email was eerie in a way, because I almost felt like I was having a conversation with myself, even down to her writing style. Her words were reinforcing so much of what my gut had been telling me all along, that the "one-size-fits-all-protocol" is garbage, that I'm the one who needs to feel comfortable with the decisions I'm making. That my happiness and emotional well-being play a role in the healing process. Her email felt like a gift from some higher power. Later that evening, we talked for several hours on the phone about everything from cancer to our dogs. She came to my birthday party in July, we participated in a writing class together at Writers and Books, we've gone for runs, we've shared meals, laughs, and love together. I am so tremendously grateful for her presence in my world.

This past Thursday, I got a text message from her saying "Welp— I'm no longer a good role model for ya :/", with a picture of results from a CT scan. She went in Thursday morning for chest pain, and they found 3 large masses in her lungs—"Findings are worrisome for a neoplastic process." Fuck. Shit. Piss. Fuck. For those of you that don't know, once breast cancer moves beyond the breast and regional lymph nodes, survival statistics are not very good.

Later in the conversation, I expressed my frustration with the fact that we aren't scanned regularly. This was our exchange:

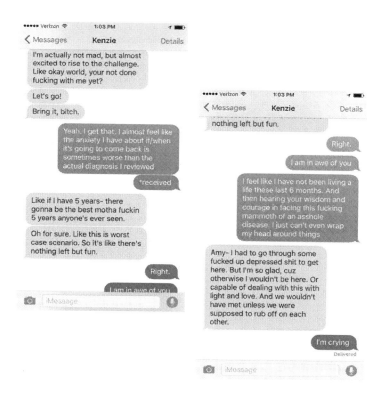

Awe is an understatement. I cannot begin to express the amount of gratitude I feel for her presence in my world. Her being is an inspiration to me.

Another friend of mine, a 19-year-old with liver cancer with more spunk and energy than I've ever seen in one human being, was rushed into emergency brain surgery this week when it was discovered that there was a tumor on her brain. Her spirit is beautiful and wonderful and I have no doubt that she will recover well. As of right now, speech is a bit difficult, but I know she's a trooper. In a text conversation with her this afternoon, I asked how she was feeling and she said, in typical Willow fashion, "Doin better every day. I've still got lots to do here hehe." And she's not kidding. The world needs her spirit.

With all of that being said, I'm fucking angry. I'm angry that anybody has to go through this. I'm angry at the number of young people dealing with cancer in our world. I'm angry with the fact that the barbaric treatment they're putting us through is still not enough to stop this fucking trainwreck of a disease. Why are there so many of us? This wasn't always the case. And yet it seems like it's everywhere I turn. There are so many toxic aspects of our modern lifestyle… and I'm furious that people are dying every single fucking day, and the medical community is still scratching its head in confusion. There are so many truths regarding our health that are hidden from public consciousness, it seems. Dairy, for starters, is something I've mentioned before, and I don't have the energy to go into detail about it now. But hormones from another BEING mimic the effects of hormones in our own bodies when we consume them. Even if you're buying the "hormone-free" milk— just because it doesn't have ADDED hormones doesn't mean it's risk free. I'm planning on writing something about the dairy industry when I have more energy…

I'm emotionally spent. I have cried more this weekend than I have in a long time. I didn't run yesterday or today. I'm just not myself right now.

Seeing these horrible things happening to people close to me is also bringing up a lot of fear around my own situation, wondering if every sensation I experience is cancer trying to take over my body. There's a part of me that seems to intrinsically know that I will not die of cancer. I don't know how, or where that part of me comes from, but it's been present from the beginning, and it's something I continue to try to hold a space for, even when my fears challenge it. This week's events have definitely triggered lots of fear, which has muted that inner voice, and I am questioning it. Honestly, I'm not really afraid to die. Am I ready to? Do I want to? No. And actually that's pretty significant for me to even be able to say considering my struggles with depression: I don't want to die. I'm also not particularly afraid of it—it's the one thing we're all guaranteed to do at some point upon entering this world. I am afraid of suffering. I'm afraid to leave my mom and other loved ones behind. I'm afraid that I'll never experience healthy romantic love and true intimacy and sharing with a man. I'm not ready to leave this place, I feel like I still have lots of work to do. And so do both of my friends. And nobody knows what's going to happen— to any of us. I am continuing to try to foster hope in the face of challenge… I don't think there's anything wrong with having hope.

This post is dedicated to Mackenzie and Willow, two of my personal heroes. I love you both and believe in your strength. Please keep them in your thoughts, prayers, meditations, etc.

## MY MENTAL HEALTH DEFICIT
OCTOBER 8, 2016

I am not in a good place these days. I've gotten so that I don't want to leave the house. I'm beyond depressed. I don't know if it's the Tamoxifen exacerbating my already shitty feelings or what… But I'm definitely not living a life. And I'm losing the desire to, which is scary.

I'm finding it hard to be grateful for anything and I'm experiencing so much self-loathing and heaviness—I can feel it in my chest and my abdomen every single day. I wake up on edge and everything just feels so off. I don't want to leave the house because I'm obsessing over my stupid fucking forehead. I don't want to see people because I'm afraid they'll notice my facial asymmetry and my wonky eye/eyebrow. WHY DOES THIS EVEN MATTER TO ME is a question I ask myself a hundred times a day, and I come up short on answers. I know it has a lot to do with the culture we live in. But that seems like a cop-out because this feels way too heavy and complex and deeply personal. I just have yet to dissect and unpack everything around it, probably because I find it so overwhelming.

I'm terrified of everything. I don't know how to help myself when all I want to do is sleep. And I'm encountering a sense of shame like no other right now, and I'm not sure what exactly it's about, but at least I've identified the emotion... Shame is thick and difficult to work through.

On a more positive note, my friend Mackenzie went for a biopsy on the masses in her lungs today... Turns out they don't look like breast cancer... Which is actually EXCELLENT news. They believe it's lymphoma at this point, but won't know for sure 'til next week sometime. Lymphoma has a much better prognosis than metastatic breast cancer. YAY LYMPHOMA!! Probably not words one hears together very often... But in the cancer world where up is down, a secondary cancer is arguably better news than a Stage 4 recurrence. Unfortunately, this secondary cancer was likely caused by the treatment she underwent for breast cancer in 2011 and 2012. It's sad that our methods of treatment can have such devastating effects on the body, both short and long term.

I know in my heart of hearts that there is another way. I firmly believe there is a cure for every disease on this planet supplied by the earth. I mean... the breast cancer chemotherapy agent Taxotere was derived from the Yew tree. A PLANT. And so many of our

112

cancers are linked to diet. We've gotten so far away from our connection to the earth.

Not knowing what I need is difficult for me. Or maybe I do know exactly what I need (like to get out of my house) and I'm resisting the fuck out of it for whatever reason, which just further entrenches me in my hole of misery. Praying this passes. Before I decide to flush the fucking Tamoxifen down the toilet.

## NEWS INTERVIEW, DOGS, MENOPAUSE
OCTOBER 11, 2016

Tomorrow, my friend Mackenzie and I will be interviewed by News Channel 13's Ginny Ryan on our experiences with breast cancer as young women—thanks to Holly Anderson from the Breast Cancer Coalition for setting this up! I'm looking forward to it because I'm hoping it can inspire young women to become more in touch with their bodies and more in tune with all aspects of their health.

With Breast Cancer Awareness month in full swing, I'm getting pretty sick of the "get your mammogram!" crap, because that only applies to women 40 and older... What about those of us in our 20s? Mammograms don't do jack-shit for us. I went to Urgent Care for a lump in my arm pit in JANUARY, and was essentially told that because I'm not overweight, not a smoker, and don't have a strong family history, this lump was unlikely anything to be concerned with, but was instructed to "keep an eye on it"... That was in JANUARY. I was diagnosed with aggressive invasive breast cancer in April. My story is not unique. I know so many young women who were essentially told that because of their age, their "little problem" was probably nothing. Yes, breast cancer in young women is rare, but it's becoming more and more common, probably due to the fact that our environment is full of xenoestrogens, garbage food that is so widely available and harmful chemicals that are in everything from plastic containers to the shampoos we use, that wreak havoc on our developing bodies… So, yes, it's rare, but it seems as though everywhere I turn, younger and younger women are being diagnosed with this disease. So. I am looking forward to the interview. I'm going to have to be really conscious of my language, though, since my inclination to swear like a sailor on the subject of all things breast-related is pretty strong these days.

I am so grateful Mackenzie and I crossed paths, and I don't think it's a coincidence either.

After a lengthy discussion with my oncologist yesterday, I decided to begin Lupron injections to create a true menopausal environment in my body, so that I can eventually take an aromatase inhibitor instead of the Tamoxifen. This might be TMI, but the last period I had on the Tamoxifen was the most miserable experience I've had in a long time—I'm pretty sure my ovaries had box cutters in their hands and were trying to slice their way out of my body. I was essentially crawling around the house on all fours for about four hours, in tears from the pain. Finally I decided, fuck this shit, I'm taking a hydrocodone from my surgery.

In general, Tamoxifen seems to make me pretty miserable. And I'm sure menopause at 27 won't make me shit rainbows and see the world through rose-colored glasses either, but I'm willing to try a different drug to treat the hormonal aspect of the disease. So. I'll be doing Lupron injections once every 28 days. (Mackenzie said she used to turn her injection day into her "treatyoself" day, so I might just do the same.) Once my FSH (follicle stimulating hormone) levels get to a certain place, I'll be able to switch to an aromatase inhibitor. (Aromatase inhibitors are only available to post-menopausal women, hence the need for the Lupron injections to put me in menopause so that I can take the aromatase inhibitor.) So, Lupron, then aromatase inhibitor, and then a bone density pill to counteract bone density loss. I'm not thrilled with the idea of all this. But I'm willing to give it a try for the time being.

Puppy love makes it all better.

## NEWS STORY
## OCTOBER 14, 2016

Mackenzie and I had our interview with channel 13's Ginny Ryan on Wednesday evening. I think it went pretty well, but I definitely felt I was speaking much more fluidly and articulately when the camera WASN'T on, go figure. I also had no idea where to look because the camera was directly ahead, and Ginny was across from us diagonally, so I'm curious as to how spastic I actually looked between my glances at Ginny, Mackenzie to my right, and the camera. I might as well have been doing some exorcist style neck rolls. After Ginny left, Mackenzie and I both talked about how we literally didn't remember anything that she asked or how we responded exactly, but we both felt like we were sitting extremely hunched over. Like little trolls. "Cancer trolls," we joked.

Originally we thought the story was going to air today (Friday), but Ginny emailed me and said they want to do more promoting of the story, so they will be airing it on Wednesday. She also asked me for a clip of myself singing… So I spent today looking through recordings and cringing at some of the sounds I was making. I sent her a couple of options, but the first two were extremely poor visual quality, and the last one was better quality visually, but not the greatest singing on my part. So I compromised and told her in the last piece, she could use anything from minute 4:18 onward because the stuff before that point was not good.* Nice to know I still have a bit of my inner diva. As I said, 4:18 onward. Don't watch the stuff before that.

---

*Link available here: myterminallife.org*

I bet if I tried to really sing now I would actually sound like a dying animal. Actually, I know I would because I caught myself singing the other day and it was rough…

Sifting through all of those recordings from this last year made me realize I've lost a bit of weight. Probably around 15 lbs or so. I don't really look the same anymore. It was odd watching these recordings and remembering what my life was like then, before I knew that my body had committed the ultimate act of betrayal… I almost felt myself softening as I was watching. I looked so pure and innocent, and it made me sad. It was an odd experience—remembering what exactly my life was like then, what was important to me (vanity, grad school auditions, getting the fuck out of Rochester, feeling validated by male attention, weed…). Watching myself singing, I felt a part of me break. I had no idea what was about to happen and looked so innocent then. Because in a way, I was. Dare I say that I was feeling a bit of compassion for the girl I was watching (no matter how intensely some of her singing made me cringe…). I think that's a step in the right direction. I think I might be moving ahead. Even if it's at a snail's pace.

## I THINK I'M TURNING A CORNER
OCTOBER 18, 2016

I don't have much else to say aside from the fact that I'm noticing small subtle shifts every day. For the better. And I'm thankful for this.

I'm also thankful for my friends because they say things like this:

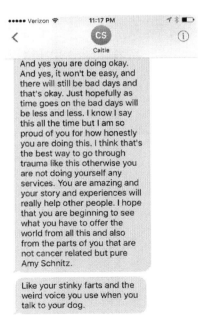

And yes you are doing okay. And yes, it won't be easy, and there will still be bad days and that's okay. Just hopefully as time goes on the bad days will be less and less. I know I say this all the time but I am so proud of you for how honestly you are doing this. I think that's the best way to go through trauma like this otherwise you are not doing yourself any services. You are amazing and your story and experiences will really help other people. I hope that you are beginning to see what you have to offer the world from all this and also from the parts of you that are not cancer related but pure Amy Schnitz.

Like your stinky farts and the weird voice you use when you talk to your dog.

My stinky farts and my baby talk voice define me more than this unproliferated cell growth nonsense does. Thank GOD for that. Truly. I'm still me. (And still gassy. I blame the increased broccoli intake.)

I had a follow-up appointment with my surgeon today, who also had a traumatic health experience… he tore his carotid changing a light bulb years ago. Most people drop dead. He did not. And I am so incredibly thankful for this. He has given me more hope than I can even say. He's truly a remarkable person, and I feel lucky to have him as part of my medical team. In the appointment, we were having a conversation about adjusting to life after traumatizing experiences, and he said something along the lines of "For a while, the small stuff stopped bothering me. Like delayed flights or missing a plane—those things were suddenly less important in comparison. And then eventually, I became the same old jerk I always was."

I'm curious if I will ever become the same old jerk I always was. Cancer has opened my eyes to things I never dreamed of. First of all, for someone without a medical degree or any real scientific knowledge aside from high school chemistry and bio, I know far more than I ever thought I'd know about this disease. It's opened my eyes to the power of nutrition, and the health crisis we have on our hands in this modern world, which is directly related to larger social and political systems in very complex ways…

Cancer has highlighted what it means to be a friend. My ability to be a friend to others has been challenged in this process, because I find it harder to connect with the worries and concerns of my non-cancer friends. But at the same time, isolation isn't good for me. And I have a lot of great people in my life. And my ability to connect to others on an emotional level is one of my biggest strengths, I think. So cancer or no cancer, I am still able to be a friend. Regardless of if my friends' biggest concern is with the complications of dating, and not with trying to wrap their head around their mortality. Everyone's got their shit, the c-word just happens to have a cameo role in my life right now. But I will not let it steal the show. This life is mine to lead. And I'm leading it. Every day that I wake up and make myself a healthy meal. Take my supplements. Run my 5 miles. Give myself my mistletoe injections. Read feminist literature. Research. Think critically about things related to health. The health of the planet. Contemplate the meaning of my existence, and how cancer fits into it. Wonder what the actual fuck my dog is thinking when she decides to attack her pillow, or when she looks at me. (Is she looking at me lovingly? Or does she think I'm a straight up imbecile?) Listen to opera arias and sometimes find myself thinking somewhat arrogantly, "Yeah, I know my technique is bad/ non-existent, but I like the tone quality of my voice better than hers…"

So maybe there are parts of me that are "the same old jerk I always was" (as evidenced by the last sentence in that long litany). And maybe there are other parts that are emerging. We shall see.

## FOOD, GLORIOUS FOOD
OCTOBER 19, 2016

The news story is airing today! I've seen about 20 promos between yesterday and right now, and I look like a dweeb in every single one of them, but oh well! At least we are getting the word out there that young people are taking their health into their own hands, and that nutrition matters…

On that subject: I'm inserting a link for those of you who aren't familiar with Dr. Michael

**Michael Greger M.D. FACLM**

Dr. Greger is a physician, New York Times bestselling author, and internationally recognized speaker on nutrition, food safety, and public health issues. A founding member and Fellow of the American College of Lifestyle Medicine, Dr. Greger is licensed as a general practitioner specializing in clinical nutrition. He is a graduate of the Cornell University School of Agriculture and Tufts University School of Medicine.

Greger's work. He is the founder of nutritionfacts.org, the largest data-base of nutritional research. I had the privilege of meeting him this summer and discussing my breast cancer situation with him. His insight was great; he believed because of my age, hormone therapy intervention was absolutely necessary (which I was reluctant to hear at first), but he also told me that what I put in my body every single day could have dramatic impact on my overall survival. Which was absolutely empowering. His website is so great and informative. I find myself watching video after video, unaware that over an hour has gone by… I hope you find his website (https://nutritionfacts.org) as valuable and informative as I do!

The video "How not to die from cancer" cites the body's ability to slow and stop cancer progression through a whole-food plant-based diet in men with prostate cancer and women with breast cancer.

Another video "The role of bovine leukemia virus in breast cancer" is about the bovine leukemia virus in cattle and its link to breast cancer development in women.

There is also a video of the industry's response to the bovine leukemia virus and breast cancer link.

"Zeranol use in meat and breast cancer" is a video on the use of chemicals in meat production and its link to breast cancer. It's a scary world we live in… but the good news is we have choices in how we navigate this world once we are informed…

I hope you all enjoy these videos and feel empowered to take your health into your own hands more and more every day! And now I'm off to eat some kale for breakfast.

*Ps. Can someone tell me if any of my links are working because I'm tech illiterate; I should know how to insert a hyperlink but I'm in the wrong generation…*

# WE JUST GOT PINKED
## OCTOBER 19, 2016

So. Our news story aired tonight, and it will be airing again tonight at 10 p.m. I was excited to see it. Unfortunately, it was not what I expected at all. Instead of it being a piece about two women who had to learn how to be their own advocates in this scary health system, it was a cutesy story about our friendship. Not that our friendship isn't valuable. It is. But that wasn't the whole point of the interview. I was hoping this interview was going to be a place for us to express how important it is for all women, regardless of age, to be in touch with their own bodies, foster self awareness, self care, self advocacy in medical situations (should they ever find themselves in one)…

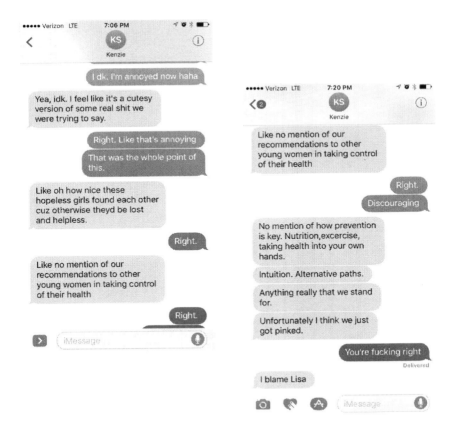

Oh, and to clarify, "Lisa" was the name the reporter gave me in the opening of the story. Oops. My name's Amy.

That's the "story."* I'm pretty upset, to be honest. Because it doesn't convey our TRUTH. And I believe our truth is what has the power to help people. Not some bogus pink-washed version of reality. Ugh. It appears we are operating within a system that doesn't really want to hear what we have to say unless it's happy! And smiley! And sweet! And cute! And optimistic! This disease is none of those things.


## I'M NOT SICK, THIS SYSTEM IS
OCTOBER 21, 2016

I'm becoming increasingly aware that we humans don't like the truth unless the truth is butterflies, sunshine, rainbows, baby pandas, etc. This is fact across the board, regardless of the issue. We are actually very relational and empathetic creatures, and because this world is so painful for so many, it's easier for us in this world full of endless distraction to exist in a comfortable state of denial about the sometimes ugly reality of living. We may be aware, to some surface degree, of the struggles of those in poverty, of racial disparities, of the hardships women face across the globe—we know these issues exist, but "thankfully" for us, we have the Kardashians and puppets like Trump to distract us from our discomfort regarding the bitch of living.

My concern is this: how is any real progress going to be made in any aspect of social justice when we insist on anesthetizing over accepting the truth?

I believe the truth is more workable than some fluffed up version of reality. But we must accept truth in order to really move forward.

---

*Link available here: myterminallife.org*

As you know from my previous post, the airing of the news story was a bit of a disappointment. The story was "cute," but failed to express the unique challenges young women with breast cancer face. We are dealing with a different disease. The research indicates that breast cancer in women under 40 is often more aggressive, and our survival statistics are much worse than women over 40. We are more likely to be diagnosed at a later stage, and the treatments for us tend to be more aggressive, aka, more harmful.

So, Mackenzie and I decided to write to the reporter to express our feelings about the story:

*Hi (keeping the name anonymous),*

*Unfortunately, I was still "Lisa" in the second airing. I'm a little disappointed in that.*

*While it was fun to see ourselves on tv in a nice portrayal of our friendship, Mackenzie and I are also slightly disappointed with the fact that the story didn't emphasize our message to young women—self awareness, knowing your own body, self care, health and wellness—everything we have both come to stand for through this experience. We were truly hoping this was going to highlight the unique complexities of dealing with this disease as a young person. Instead, it seemed to depict a very "cutesy" version of some very real things we were trying to say, and I'm afraid if we had known that was going to be the case, we would not have participated in the interview. We were hoping this would provide the opportunity to inspire young women to better care for themselves, but instead, this was a dolled-up version of something that breast cancer isn't. Breast cancer is not pleasant, or lighthearted, or happy. Yes, the bond that Mackenzie and I have is very special, and we are tremendously grateful for each other's presence, and we are happy that people were able to see the power of friendship in tough times. But breast cancer is not cute, or fluffy, or lighthearted. It is a devastating disease of forced confrontation with mortality, shattered body image due to invasive surgery, awful and debilitating side effects from medical intervention, and overwhelming uncertainty for what the future may bring—regardless of the aggressiveness of the treatment you receive. And when you are facing it in your 20's, when you are just really beginning your life, the disfigurement from surgery, the implications on fertility from chemotherapy and hormone therapy, and the psychological toll it takes on your entire existence feels unbearable. The closing remark discussing mammography was frustrating to Mackenzie and I as well— it seemed to imply that our odds as young people would somehow be better if we had mammograms earlier, when we both clearly voiced that even with cancer being seen on other screenings, mammograms didn't detect it for either of us. There was just a lot of disregard to what we said and some inaccuracies too, for example: Mackenzie did not discover her own lump, her husband did. I realize that you aren't responsible for the way the story was presented, but Mackenzie and I both agreed upon the importance of expressing our overall feeling. I think it's important to emphasize that the Breast Cancer we see in the media, especially during breast cancer awareness month is not an entirely accurate picture. It's often watered down, "pinkified", and inauthentic. I think progress we make on the front lines in ALL aspects of this disease depends on our willingness to get honest about what this disease actually is—and isn't.*

*Sincerely,*
*Amy and Mackenzie*

Writing this felt empowering and necessary. This was the response we received:

*Amy and MacKenzie,*

*Thank you for your note. I was, to say the least, disheartened to read it.*

*It was clearly never my intention to misrepresent you or your wishes, or paint breast cancer as something "lighthearted or happy". I've met far too many women to ever consider that, nor do I think that was done.*

*The story did initially have a section in which you spoke about issues unique to women in their 20's and self-care.*

*The length was 2:30 at the point and it needed to be 2:00, as our average story runs between 1:20-1:40.*

*It is an important message and not including it was in no way an effort to minimize it.*

*The relationship aspect of your story was/is unique to you and for that reason, a story that had never been told. It is also one in which I thought people could relate and find inspiration.*

*I also believe featuring two women in their 20's with breast cancer is, in itself, awareness raising.*

*Time is always the enemy in presenting a story and in this case, I requested and did get more time, but it still wasn't enough. Choosing a focus can also be a subjective process.*

*Having said that, I have requested and was granted a follow up to your story during our 5:30pm half hour today about the importance of knowing yourself in regard to your personal thoughts.*

*In taking to heart your note, I realize this may not suffice, but it is a way of trying to answer your concern and show my sincerity in sharing your story.*

*I wish you both the best and admire your courage and strength.*


Her response was kind and compassionate and very much appreciated. This is what they aired after all that:[*]

(Forgive the quality of the video.)

We appreciated her trying to capture more of our message to young women. Unfortunately, the clip she used was one where I was channeling my inner valley girl… oh well. But it's very clear that nobody wants the truth.

---

*** Link available here: myterminallife.org**

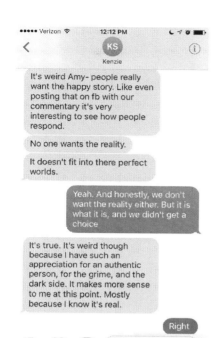

It's weird Amy- people really want the happy story. Like even posting that on fb with our commentary it's very interesting to see how people respond.

No one wants the reality.

It doesn't fit into there perfect worlds.

Yeah. And honestly, we don't want the reality either. But it is what it is, and we didn't get a choice

It's true. It's weird though because I have such an appreciation for an authentic person, for the grime, and the dark side. It makes more sense to me at this point. Mostly because I know it's real.

Right

iMessage

And then yesterday, Mackenzie's doctor called to give her the results from the 28 (twenty-eight) biopsies they performed on her lung masses on Tuesday. Turns out it was breast cancer all along. This has been a fucking exhausting week. Mackenzie's attitude never ceases to amaze and inspire me.

Please keep her in your thoughts as she figures out how she wants to proceed.

*November 6, 2016*

# IT'S CANCER
## NOVEMBER 11, 2016

I received a phone call from my surgeon last night. "I don't have good news."

It's cancer. Same pathology as before. ER/PR+, HER2-. Tumor cells were found in my lymphatic tissue which typically indicates extensive disease. Not necessarily always the case, but typically, is what I was told.

Next week I have scans to capture the extent of disease. I have lots of questions. There has been a pea-sized bump near my incision since I had the tissue expanders. Every doctor I've had look at it has told me it's "probably nothing," "a cyst," or something completely benign. But with the sudden outburst of this cancerous rash, I'm not so sure anymore, especially considering that there's documentation of skin metastasis taking this particular shape and form. I believe the current cancer outbreak is a result of leftover cancer cells from surgery, and not actually a "recurrence." It's also interesting timing-wise in relation to the Lupron injection. Lupron shuts down the ovaries, and it says on the sheet the oncologists gave me following my first injection that Lupron can cause "tumor flare-up" when it's being used to treat active disease. I'm wondering if that dot by my mastectomy scar that's been there all along was cancer, and this caused it to flare up...

I will know more next week. Strangely I'm calm. Because things can't get too much worse.

To my friends and family, thank you for being here for me. I'm sorry for being impossible to deal with at times. I do think the proper psychiatric diagnosis and its treatment is helping me to handle all this with a bit more grace. I feel like I'm handling this new chapter a bit differently than the first. This time, I don't want to isolate. I want to enjoy this life however long I have left, with you all by my side. Xo.

## DEAR AMY: HOW TO FACE YOUR FEAR OF DEATH AND THE UNKNOWN
NOVEMBER 13, 2016

Cry.

Run.

Paint.

Read about your mental illness(es), or anything else aside from your potentially lethal condition. Quit lookin' that shit up. It won't change a damn thang, sweetheart.

Eat.

Eat.

One mo'gen: eat. Eat healthy food. Eat food that you would not normally eat—treat choself to some desserts sweetened with agave (gasp).

Watch shows. Laugh at the stupidity of humans exemplified in masterpieces like The Office, Parks and Rec, Shameless, etc.

Listen to music. Or don't if it's too painful right now.

Research weed in relation to your current predicament. And fantasize about laughing while smoking that shit once again.

Talk to friends.

Laugh.

Hug your dog.

Hug your family.

Punch shit.

Scream.

Cry.

Swear.

Tell God he's full of shit and the joke can be over now.

Acknowledge your fear. Say, "sup?"

Allow yourself to need the support of others.

Brace yourself. A bumpy ride is behind you. And a bumpy ride is ahead.

Love,
Your (maybe) wiser self.

## METASTATIC BREAST CANCER
NOVEMBER 21, 2016

On Friday, I found out the cancer spread to my lungs. Several little spots of disease are on both lungs, though it's difficult to tell how many exactly, because some of these spots appear to be blood vessels—the size makes it difficult for the doctors to discern. I have at least one 1 cm mass in each lung. It's odd, because I don't feel anything with their presence. I found out Friday afternoon, and shortly after that phone call from the oncologist ("There's disease in your lungs, and no, there isn't time to harvest your eggs, having a child isn't an option for you since you'll be in treatment for the rest of your life") went on a 3.5 mile jog with my feelers out, so to speak, to see if I could sense my new little insidious friends' presence. Nothin'. That's what's so bizarre. It's an odd thing to be told that you're essentially dying, and to not really resonate with that because physically you feel great.

This is excruciating. To be told that treatment won't end 'til the day I die, that that day is coming sooner rather than later most likely, that childbirth is no longer an option for me—at any age, this is a lot to swallow. But at 27, this feels like my life has been stolen from me.

128

I know people want the feel-good, "but-I-turned-it-around-with-my-positive-attitude!" story, but I'm not there. Who knows if I ever will be. But one thing has become abundantly clear through these experiences: This culture really has no idea what to do with death, with illness, with darkness. We want a comforting story of how someone persevered and made it through the "other side," because the alternative unsettles us to the core and brings us face to face with our own mortality.

People have told me to "just try to live out the time you have and enjoy it." I know people mean well when they offer their advice, but this is really difficult to hear. It's hurtful to hear from friends, because it's dismissive of where I am presently in this process of trying to accept that I've got more years behind me than ahead of me. At 27 years old. This isn't easy news to swallow. There's no "just" in any of this—as if I can snap my fingers and will myself to accept that the worst case scenario is now my reality. Wish I could, but I'm human—like you, I have a normal fear of death, it's just that mine is a bit more pronounced and center-stage right now. The advice is a bit cold… as if my impending death is something you're able to easily accept, therefore I should be able to as well, with no problems. I just was told this news on FRIDAY. That's pretty insensitive given the magnitude of the situation. But that's our culture. We deny the darkness even though it's just as real as the light.

I hope this changes someday. I hope that message is something I can instill in others before I go. We do ourselves (and others) no favors by evading the truth of our experiences—especially if that truth is dark. We all have darkness within us. It isn't bad. What's bad is that we are shamed for being in touch with and aware of its presence in this culture. We keep the darkness in the dark, which just allows it to consume us and isolate us. But darkness wouldn't have such a grip on us if we allowed in light, in the form of human connection. So, no, we don't need to dwell in the darkness, but acknowledging its presence within us is honest and authentic—I trust it more than the Pollyannas of the world. We walk around like desensitized zombies in a world of distraction. We need so many distractions because so much of this existence IS incredibly painful.

Or we are trained to be "Miss Mary Sunshines" on the outside because that's what people want, regardless of how we feel on the inside. Denial denial *denial*. The truth is what interests me.

It's likely that I was actually metastatic at original diagnosis. There was a 2 mm spec in the upper left lobe of my left lung in April. In the same location, there is now a 1 cm mass. Nobody followed up on this when there was even a note that said "should be watched for metastatic disease given patient's history of breast cancer"…

When I brought this up to one of my doctors, he said it wouldn't have really made a difference prognostically, because once you're metastatic, regardless of the degree, the prognosis is generally the same. I suppose I can agree with that, though if I knew it was metastatic at diagnosis, I probably would have started chemo right away, and there would have been fewer spots to treat than there are now…

They've recommended a really aggressive chemo treatment to try to knock down the lung metastasis. They seem confident that this will be successful. I still am not so sure. They had me scheduled to begin chemo TODAY, and I said hang on, guys, let me get my bearings and enjoy the gluttony of Thanksgiving without a barf bag.

They also hadn't addressed the fact that my veins are horrible (they always require an iv tech for routine blood draws), so I will absolutely need a port. My white blood counts are also pretty low normally, and that's a concern on chemo. I'm not going to just rush into something that has felt like violation to my whole self from the very beginning without these things in place.

Keep me in your thoughts and prayers.

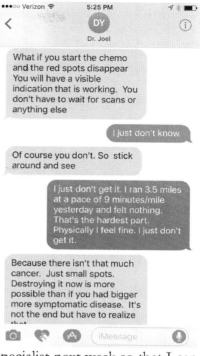

(I have the best surgeon in the world. I don't know that all surgeons converse with their frantic 27-year-old patients via text message on Saturday nights.)

It's been an eventful past two weeks. Waiting for the results of the biopsy from my mastectomy scar "rash" feels like forever ago. I'm making a lot of shifts mentally and proceeding forward with an army of support and love both behind me and at my side. Also, thank God for marijuana. Seeing a palliative care specialist next week so that I can get some state-sanctioned medicinal grade happiness. That's what I'm calling it. Because when I'm stoned, I'm able to view this as "an experience." And right now, attaching myself to any idea of *anything* being completely or definitively good or bad isn't safe. And probably isn't truthful, either. Things aren't all-or-nothing.

This week has been a revolving door of hospital and doctors' offices. It began on Monday morning with my oncologist, and finished yesterday at RGH post port placement surgery.

Monday's appointment was interesting. My oncologist pulled up the images from the chest CT scan onto the computer. For some reason, I was picturing these spots on my lungs to be gigantic and evil looking, perhaps with faces or devil horns and red pitchforks. When I actually saw them on the screen, I was surprised at how small they were, and their constellation-like appearance. They were truly just little specks, a spray of tiny dots, like a misting of stars.

How poetic, I'm the girl with stardust in her lungs! It was almost kind of *pretty*—you know, in a dangerously lethal kinda way. And the entire time I was looking at the screen, I felt as if I was looking at someone else—not because I found it so overwhelming that I detached from the experience somehow, but because it's simply strange to see your insides on a computer screen. Not everyone gets to see their own lungs and lymph nodes and skeleton in this way! Lucky me?

The NP told me to eat as much and as often as possible before chemo and during chemo… Apparently this particular regimen can make people drop weight because of the side effects like nausea and vomiting. Was also told they give you steroids to counteract that, so I might actually gain weight. But I tuned that part out and said well eff that, I'm gunna eat.

I began eating my weight in all kinds of food starting Monday, continuing to this moment, as I sit on my couch eating dried pineapple. I was 125 a week and a half ago. At my appointment at the same office (same scale) this week, I was 130. Five pounds in a week and a half…. apparently we don't have to worry about my appetite right now.

I have breast cells in my lungs. Cells from my boob made their way to my lungs. Regardless of the cancer part, having boob cells in your lungs definitely indicates that your body is confused. I was thinking about that on Thanksgiving and laughing hysterically to myself. I keep picturing cells in the shape of boobs floating around in my lungs, next to lung-shaped lung cells who are all giving the rack cells dirty looks and gossiping about how unwelcome and overweight the boob cells are, behind their backs.

I had my chemo port put in on Friday, which will hopefully make the next 16 weeks much easier. My veins are impossible, and they typically have to try multiple times before they're successful even for routine blood draws… so the port should simplify things. The port surgery was relatively short, and I vaguely remember calling the surgeon "mother hen" before I went under… so all in all, it was a good day.

I keep thinking about how things would have played out if it weren't for the rash. If I hadn't noticed the change in my scar, I wouldn't have known about the cancer in my lungs… at least not until the tumors were so large that they were causing symptoms like pain, wheezing, difficulty breathing, coughing up blood, appetite/weight loss etc. I'm thankful we caught this before that point. There's really not a lot of cancer present. Yes, this is scary. Metastatic disease is the disease everyone fears, with good reason—breast cancer contained in the breast (in situ) rarely hurts anybody; it's when it travels through the lymphatic system to different organs that poses a threat to one's survival. I feel relatively lucky (bear with me). I feel lucky that we caught this at a point where I am not at all symptomatic, where there are not large tumors blocking airways, where I have a visual marker on the outside that I can use to gauge if the chemo is working or not (my rash!!—I don't even have to wait for scans in order to know if my body is responding!!)

I start chemo on Monday. A lovely blend of Adriamycin and Cytoxan. I'm not looking forward to this at all. Not one bit. But I'm doing it. I'll be working out before every chemo session (that's the plan, anyway) to open up my lungs and get my blood flowing there, so the chemo will more effectively get to where it's needed. That's the theory anyway, founded on instinct.

My fate is not sealed. I'm proving this to myself as much as I am to any one of you. I've told my doctors that I don't want to talk statistics or numbers or prognosis, I just want to live MY existence without any worry about what the numbers might say. And you know, statistics haven't really ever been entirely accurate with me when you consider that about 1% of all breast cancer cases occur in women under 30… Fuck the numbers, I'm living my life. It's about damn time I started, too.

So, this "fight" begins, though I really hate the "battle rhetoric" around cancer. But I guess it seems appropriate given my current situation. Being metastatic means there will be a part of me fighting for the breath in my lungs 'til the day I die.

My mom has been by my side always, but in a new way in the last year. From listening to my screaming and crying about cancer, or how much I can't stand my face/body/mind/self, accompanying me to my spa retreat at the psych unit in October, buying every single supportive supplement and fresh nourishing food, to taking me to every appointment, acting as my scribe so that I'm free to absorb and ask questions, to throwing Kleenex boxes, pens, notebooks, pillows at me upon receiving bad news from the most recent biopsy, to holding me like the little girl I still am on the inside while I crumble in her arms...

Mom, this fight is for you.

## I'M DONE
DECEMBER 13, 2016

I'm done being the victim of my life.

Have shitty things happened? Are my anger and hurt justified? Yeah. But holding onto both of those things makes this life pretty un-fun, so I'm trying something new.

I'm not a victim. Will I have bad days? Will I have days ahead where I feel sorry for myself again? Yes probably. And I will feel the feelings, and move on when they've been processed. Move on, as in *live*. Pick up an opera score, watch Joyce Didonato *saaaaaang*, listen to Berlioz, run/walk on the treadmill, hug the dog, hug the mom, laugh with friends, smoke some pot (goes nice with laughing with friends), eat. *Live*.

I am not a victim.

I'm not sad or helpless. I'm PISSED. And I'm going to allow that anger to help me on days where helplessness starts to creep in.

I cut my own hair off this afternoon. It was gathering in delicate handfuls in my hands all morning and I decided, "Not today, cancer." My golden shield of protection is gone now. My mom told me to wait 'til my appointment with the wig woman on Saturday, but I needed to reclaim some power in my life. Two inches now remain on my head.

Not today.

You don't get any more of me, cancer.

I am not what's "happened to me." I am Amy. And I'm figuring out just what that means.

I had a rough rough weekend. Was ready to give up on chemo, was ready to give up on life. Thanks to Ativan and pot, I made it to Monday night, last night, where I had the pinch-me privilege of seeing and hearing Joyce Didonato (operatic legend) sing at Kodak Hall. My mom bought the tickets a couple of weeks ago. And it came at the perfect time. Joyce's dedication to her craft reminded me that music is a part of my core. It's visceral. It's authentic. It's undeniable. My connection to it makes my life richer. And I've been avoiding it for the last several months because I've been afraid to attach myself to this life in any positive way for fear that it will make it more painful when it's actually my time to go. But to deny myself the sheer joy of listening to Stravinsky or Debussy to try to soften the blow of my inevitable passing (not from cancer, just death in general) is actually just crazy and sad.

So today, as I jog/walked on my treadmill, I listened to Berlioz's "Les Nuits d'Été."

And then I cut my hair off.

Today I won.

## ADRIAMYCIN AND CYTOXAN ROUND 2
DECEMBER 15, 2016

That face encapsulates how the day started off. I woke up at 5, about an hour and a half earlier than needed, because I was anxious about what was on deck for the day. My first chemotherapy  experience got off to a very rough start due to difficulty accessing my port... I just had the port placement surgery three days prior to the first treatment, so the area was still extremely swollen and tender. Because of the swelling, there was difficulty with the needle, so the process took a lot more time and tears (on my part, because it fucking HURT) than it "normally does," said the nurses. But with that being my first experience, I was still kind of traumatized and pretty terrified that things would be just as difficult today... but we'll get to that.

I tried to calm myself down at 5 a.m. by taking a nice relaxing bubble bath. It was going nicely until I realized I was floating in a tub of hair. Even with what little hair remains on my head, as it was falling out in the bathtub it felt like I was suddenly Rapunzel (didn't realize I still had so much fucking hair to spare, but apparently I do...), so the anxiety continued.

I had a serious breakdown following that. And then of course I get out of the bathtub and what do I see? A mirror. Me. My nearly-hairless head and my doughier-than-usual-hips. My scars. All of them. I think my mom anticipated that my mood would be difficult.

136

She quickly medicated me with 2 Ativan to get me to chemo since I'm out of oil for my vape.

Thankfully, this morning's experience was much better than the first treatment. The needle went in like butter. I barely felt a thing. They were able to get my blood work from the port, too, which was convenient considering that my veins are not only microscopic, but also temperamental and bitchy.

So here's a photoshoot from my day today. From the pre-chemo exam to the treatment.

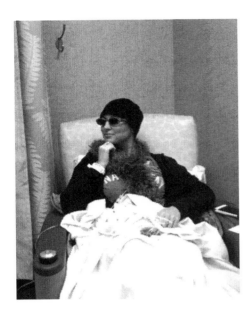

Fabulous Accessories
courtesy of earth-angel,
Michelle Cotturone.

#chemodiva

## <u>BABY, IT'S COLD WITHOUT HAIR</u>
DECEMBER 22, 2016

It never occurred to me how freezing it would be without hair insulating my head. Now that my hair is gone, my temperature is hovering somewhere around -30 degrees Fahrenheit at all times. Thank God for cozy knit caps.

"Fasting-like diet turns the immune system against cancer."
(https://news.usc.edu/103972/)

I have been implementing the water-fasting-like diet into my chemotherapy schedule and I have to say, I really think it's making a difference as far as side effects go… Adriamycin and Cytoxan are known to cause lots of tummy problems, mouth sores, and all kinds of other weird sensations… So far (knock on wood) I've barely had any. It's insane that even with the light eating, I'm still gaining weight. Just a couple pounds, but I don't like it, obviously. It's just one more thing to add to the situation. I would more willingly be hairless and extra cushy at different times as opposed to simultaneously, but I guess I don't have a say in that. Still working out as much as I can. Jog/walking between 20-45 minutes every day on most days. And I find that physical activity DOES help with fatigue, even though that seems counter-intuitive. Sometimes forcing myself to get out of bed and get on the treadmill is exactly what I need to get myself  going. A special thank you to my wonderful family who bought me this treadmill to get me through the winter on chemo. I love you guys so much.

Since chemo on Thursday, I have been feeling fairly decent. Just one bout of nausea, and on Friday, all I did was sleep. But today has been a decent day. I picked up my wig this afternoon, and I'm happy to say that I feel like me, which is exactly what I wanted. Disregard the random hairs in my face… I'm still a newbie to this whole wig-wearing thing…

And check out my fabulous new red hat that was given to me by the shop-owner because I "just looked too cute in it!"

Today I have felt overwhelmingly more hopeful than I have in the last month or so. Abundantly hopeful, actually. The rash on my incision is essentially melting away, which my oncologist is interpreting as an extremely positive sign that what's happening on the outside is also happening on the inside.

Please keep the thoughts and prayers coming.

And **thank you** to *everyone* who has contributed to the Gofundme account set up by my father's work. You have no idea how deeply touched we are by your sincere generosity and loving kindness at this time. I'm brought to tears daily with gratitude. Thank you for supporting this process.

# CHEMO-SOBBY
DECEMBER 24, 2016

This past week or so has been brutal. It's sucked. It's kicked me in the shins, stomach, kneecaps, vagina, and fake boobs repeatedly.

I was fine the first four days after chemo. Walking on my treadmill, feelin' fine. I even had an outing which is a big deal for me since I've recently become mildly agoraphobic. And then I got hit at 1:00 a.m. on Tuesday. I was awakened by nausea. I took a Compazine. 20 minutes later I took an Ativan (aside from its use as an anxiety med, it also can work to alleviate nausea). And then precisely one minute after swallowing the Ativan, I was hovered over the toilet bowl, throwing up the applesauce and ginger juice I had before bed. It burned. (You're welcome.)

After I was done heaving, I went back to bed. I was able to sleep shortly after and slept for about 5 hours. I woke up the next morning feeling vomit creeping its way up my esophagus. Wednesday was miserable. I spent the day rolling around with my knees up to my chest, crying my eyes out, praying for the pukey feeling to pass. We (my mom and I) called my oncologist because I felt so terrible, even though I hadn't thrown up since the night before, I was still completely miserable. Prolonged nausea is just the *best*. They told me to eat bland foods and take Compazine every 6 hours, with an Ativan in between. I have a feeling I'm going to finish chemo with a benzodiazepine problem with the amount I'm taking… if that palliative care doctor would hurry up on my medical marijuana certification!!!

I spent the entire day feeling like I was on the verge of throwing up, including the car ride to acupuncture. I also started to develop my first mouth sore almost immediately after vomiting, most likely due to the acid. For those of you who have not been introduced to the fun of chemo-induced mouth sores, let me tell you, they're a gas. I currently have one along my left back molar, so my right side has been delegated the chewing side. The pain is *awful*.

Anyway, so acupuncture: My integrative doctor recommended an MD who also does acupuncture to support my body through chemotherapy. I went to the appointment with my eyes swollen and bloodshot from crying all day, in a beanie sans wig, in boy baggy sweatpants and a crummy hoody, in other words, I looked really presentable and beautiful, just like Heidi Klum. This appointment was an initial consult so I'm pretty sure the acupuncturist thinks I'm a homeless male child (so, you know, I made it clear to answer his questions about my menstrual cycle extra thoroughly, so he'd believe there was actually a female body underneath all the Hanes garb). In all seriousness, he spent nearly two hours with me, asking me about both my medical and emotional history, and explaining to me how Chinese medicine regards certain physical presentations in the body (like tumors), as well as the balance of heat and cool, yin and yang.

All of this is fascinating to me. It's something that really resonates with my spirit. Yes, I just said that queer-ass sentence. But I mean it. It's a more personalized approach to medicine which is comforting to me on a lot of levels. Chinese medicine sees the human over the ailment. He asked me an interesting question before I got on the table: "What do you think this is about for you?" Startled by the question, "You mean the cancer... like spiritually or whatever?" I asked. "Yes. Some people have a sense, others don't until they spend some time with it..." "Self loathing," I said, with a confidence unparalleled. It was like some deep and almost primal voice from the depths of me answered for the version of me that normally speaks and exists.

Since my acupuncture treatment my nausea has been at bay but I'm extremely emotional. I've been crying and yelling a lot. As I'm typing this, I'm remembering the acupuncturist mentioning that it can free up stagnation, and I'm wondering if I've been emotionally stagnant and the treatment triggered some kind of release, and that's why I've been one effusive bitch lately...

At the end of my session, he gave me a homework assignment. I'm sharing it with you because I found it helpful on a number of levels.

I know the holidays are tough for a lot of people emotionally. If this helps anyone else to facilitate in their own emotional healing, then I'm happy. I'll share the exercises because I'm finding them to be helpful in that I'm cultivating a bit of objectivity through them by stepping aside and observing my thought patterns and where my mind tends to wander.

1. Make a list of your perceived obstacles, barriers or limitations. These can be physical, emotional, intellectual, spiritual, or literal life things. Sit with this for a day or so, spend a little time doing this. Monitor your thoughts for a day or two.

2. Now, make a list of your positive affirmations to counteract each of the perceived limitations in your list. Write them down. Keep them short, to the point, and in the present tense. No "should, could, or would" words. Make sure they don't contain negatives. You may want to carry this list with you until you know it by heart.

3. Look at your list and repeat the affirmations every morning and just before you go to sleep. It's also a good idea to focus on these when you are stressed, worried, or when your mind is busy with non-productive thoughts. You can look at these throughout the day if you wish.

Alright. So. This first part of the exercise was ugly for me. My inner mean girl is vile and vicious and cruel and so incredibly cutting, and this first part of the exercise basically asked that I invite her to tea. To hear her bitch. About me. Dealing with mental illness alongside cancer is certainly challenging. The two antagonize one another and I'm supposed to be the calm collected mediating parent who sends them both to time-out and then gets them to play nice together again. Only in this situation, I've got jack shit in the realm of control over either of these things, it seems. This parent is at her wits' end. And she's got two wildly complicated assholes for children.

Writing out the first list made me realize how fucking mean I am to myself at all times. I realized within the first few minutes of the exercise that I put so much pressure on myself to be a certain way, and convince myself that I'm responding to some external demands of me. Maybe other people do have expectations of me. Maybe they don't. But who the fuck cares?! ESPECIALLY in my present situation. Shit's REAL right now. If people have expectations of me that I'm failing to live up to, too damn bad. But it seems the majority of the pressure I feel is from myself. Like giving myself shit for not being able to really run like I used to while undergoing some of the most aggressive chemotherapy known to breast cancer. Or beating myself up over eating food that isn't low on the glycemic index because MAYBE I AM JUST CRAVING A PIECE OR 3 OF WEGMANS TUSCAN GARLIC BREAD DAMMIT. I am also extremely critical of my imperfections and perceived shortcomings. My sense of self-worth is not super high, that was also apparent in creating this list.

The second exercise was pretty challenging because I had to phrase things in ways that were acceptable to me and also authentic, while also meeting the criteria of the list like "present tense, no shoulds, etc." But I did it, and I'm going to continue expanding on my affirmations. I could use some positivity at this point in my life, and since I don't have much of my own naturally, I have to start planting the seeds for some to grow.

I hope some of you try these exercises. They've been helpful to me so far, if only in the aspect of perspective and beginning to experience the act of observing my "monkey mind," as opposed to latching onto every anxiety ridden thought I have.

I'm off to go eat my third muffin of the day, because Christmas.

Happy holidays, everyone.

*2017*

## TITLES ARE HARD
JANUARY 2, 2017

For those of you who haven't read my most recent post, I talked a bit about the mindfulness work I'm doing with my acupuncturist, who has become a sort of spiritual coach to me in the last three weeks…

As a homework assignment for my first session, I was asked to create a list of my barriers, limitations, shortcomings, obstacles, etc. I was then asked to reverse every statement I made in the first list. So if the first statement was "I have crippling anxiety," the converted statement would be "My nervous system helps me to navigate the world safely," or something along those lines. The goal is to create the space for mental shifts to occur. Affirmations can be extremely helpful in facilitating these shifts, according to every healthy person I know/know of, in "theory." What was especially interesting to me about my list of perceived obstacles and barriers was that my physical health (cancer stuff) only came up twice, out of the mile-long list of "limitations." And both of those things had to do with feeling slightly scared to trust my body again. Which is understandable. I guess I thought cancer would take up more of mental focus since it takes up quite a bit of my every-day life right now (chemo side effects, appointments, etc.).

Like my acupuncturist said, "This isn't about the physical for you," and honestly, that seems to be reflective of my experience. I'm not symptomatic, I have not felt sick from cancer, **I have felt more "sick" from the horrible self-talk in my head than I ever have from cancer**. This was really exciting for me to recognize, because I now know where my healing focus needs to be. Obviously continuing to focus on nourishing my body as best as I can, continuing to exercise as much as chemo-fatigue allows, and resting as much as I need to are all good things. But I believe my real task is to work through, process, and let go of the stuff that I've been carrying with me in my abdomen and chest (that's where my stress-response clenching lies) for a long time. This requires honesty. Compassion. Empathy. Forgiveness.

*Aside:* It seems appropriate that I'm bald right now, with all this new Buddhist-ish stuff I'm getting myself into....

But *really*... Chemo is teaching me a lot. It's teaching me how to be more gentle with myself. It's teaching me just how much I struggle in listening to my body, operating from a place of worthiness, rather than a place of punishment (even on chemo! Clearly I have some beliefs that require some attention). It's teaching me that I am more than my physical identity. I look different. My eyes look dull and vacant to me. My body is not toned in the way that it was before I began this bi-weekly poisoning. My hair is gone. I'm veinier than normal. My physical self is just different, and that's been hard. It's difficult to look like a penis when you're used to looking something like a woman. Chemo is teaching me how much pressure I've always put on myself to look "together," and I've caught myself multiple times getting worked up over how I'm going to look when going out in public, never mind the fact that my "public" is going to the *doctor's office,* and who the HELL cares about how I look there? I'm not planning on meeting my soul mate, let's be honest... And I'm realizing that my soul mate won't give a shit about how I look in comparison to my fundamental truths like my sensitivity, my intelligence, my depth. Because *I'm* beginning to give less and less shits about the way I look. No makeup. No wig. Just caps and my bare face. And that feels incredibly liberating. Detachment from my physical self is probably one of the healthiest lessons I could begin to learn at this time.

It seems there's a part of me that does still trust in my body's innate wisdom—the wisdom that allowed my rash on my mastectomy scar to come to the surface, which triggered all the tests, which led to my most recent diagnosis. I'm working on trusting that my body knows exactly what to do in order to heal itself (that's one of my affirmations).

I feel grateful to be here on the 2nd of January, 2017.

146

## COULD USE SOME MORE PRAYERS
JANUARY 8, 2017

I'm having a really hard time these last couple of days.

I went to a metastatic support group the other day and didn't realize how triggering it actually was until I completely fell apart on Friday, and have continued to do so all day today. It was hard to attend my first group when there was mention of someone who used to attend now being on hospice. That's a harsh reality of the disease I'm facing, and I was not ready at this point in my own personal experience of all of this to be confronted with that. I also don't think support groups are for me, upon further reflecting.

This is an isolation unlike anything I've ever experienced. I have never felt so alone and vulnerable and scared in my life. I keep seeing myself letting go of my willingness to invest in my life and with every round of chemo I lose the energy, both physical and emotional that it requires to just exist. This is excruciating. I don't recognize myself when I look in the mirror, all I see are scars and my fat and my grotesque looking veiny face. I'm miserable. And so fucking tired of all this. And there's no end in sight, either. After chemo I'll have a life of scans and drugs until my options run out. I'm 27 years old, and I keep asking myself "How can this be?"

Nothing about my life looks normal. No job. No grad school. No hair. No energy. No vitality. Everything that was once true about me and who I thought I was is gone. Just fucking gone. Like it was never there to begin with.

I feel completely and utterly broken. I'm typing this in tears.

To my true supports—the people that have come to my house for visits, have called (not texted) to see how I'm doing, have dropped by to try to cheer me up on terribly hard days like today, who have made me feel like I am still important in their lives (and not already dead)—thank you for being here for me. I'm working on finding the strength to carry on for YOU. Because I'm having a hard time doing it for myself.

I am trying to breathe. Just one breath at a time. Cuz that's all I can handle anymore.

Please pray for me, that I might be able to find some peace in this nightmare. I always appreciate prayers.

*January 9, 2017*

## READING MATERIAL
JANUARY 22, 2017

I had my palliative care appointment this morning. The doctor was very kind and I really enjoyed talking to him, but it was a really emotionally heavy and intense day. He certified me for medical marijuana, and he was filling out all the bureaucratic bullshit for the state—they really make people jump through hoops for this stuff... but anyway. He was walking me through the paperwork while he did his portion on the computer and he clicked "no" under "terminal cancer" and explained that "the guidelines for terminal diagnosis are expectation to die within 6 months"... and I'm happy that I'm not terminal by that definition... but I am still so in shock that this is even my life. (And the fact that that's a box to be "checked" as if it's nothing...).

It all hit me in a new way in those moments in his office. I've been crying on and off since this morning. My inclination sitting across from him as he "clicked" away was to get excited that I'm not dying in 6 months, and then I realized that *I'm getting excited over not dying in 6 months* and I just broke down in the middle of Strong.

I have more to say but I don't have enough energy to write right now. Instead, I'm sharing an article on metastatic breast cancer, aka Stage 4. Well-meaning people say things like "This is just a blip in the radar" or ask "When are you done with treatment?"… This article does a nice job of explaining how metastatic breast cancer (breast cancer that has invaded other organs) is different from early stage breast cancer: "Living with Stage 4: The breast cancer no one understands." (Hutch News Stories October 13, 2016)

## CT SCANS
JANUARY 24, 2017

I'm trying to get used to the fact that I will have a scan of some sort every three months for the rest of my life. With that in mind, I found the whole experience this morning to be less traumatizing than it has been in the past—and really, I've only had two other scans: the one just after I was diagnosed in April to determine the extent of disease, and the one in November (following the sudden appearance of the cancerous rash) that revealed the spots on my lungs. Maybe the third time's the charm? But really, today I do not feel the heaviness that I remember feeling in the past. I suppose a part of me is beginning to accept cancer as a part of my life. There's a part of me that is resisting that, for sure, but I do believe I am processing the implications of this disease for my life. Both good and bad. Yes, I'm acknowledging there are some beautiful things that are happening for me on an emotional level as a result of this cancer. I'm beginning to develop a tenderness for myself that I've never really known. An appreciation for my mind, a detachment from my physical body. Those are good things. And I'm putting work into myself because I'm beginning to act as if I'm worth the investment, even if I don't always believe it.

I am still frustrated by the lack of awareness around metastatic breast cancer. I do grow tired of having to explain that, no, my treatment doesn't end (until I "end"), and that, unfortunately, at this point there is no "beating it." It's something that you live with, until it eventually outsmarts whatever treatment you are on. I'm tired of having to explain that the average life expectancy for women in my position is 2-5 years because it depresses me, but I feel it needs to be said at the same time. I'm not trying to be negative, but I need people to know what I'm up against.

Metastatic breast cancer does not get enough attention or funding for research and this is a real problem since this is the version of breast cancer women actually die from. Early stage breast cancer does not kill women; breast cancer that has traveled beyond the breast is what claims the lives of 40,000 per year. What is equally discouraging is that mortality rates for this disease have gone largely unchanged in the last 40 years. This is a serious problem. We are losing our wives, mothers, daughters, sisters, and friends to this horrible disease, and the treatment available is not without immense suffering. This needs to change. I can't help but think if men's dicks were suddenly developing cancer, there would be more of a sense of urgency for answers.

I want people to be informed about the monster that I'm dealing with, **_and also_** have faith in me. I don't appreciate blind, uninformed optimism, honestly. I need my supports to try to understand what I'm going through, at least cognitively—I know people cannot empathize unless they are in the same position.

Thank you to everyone for your prayers. I can feel the heaviness beginning to lift. Please pray that the scan reveals significant improvement. I don't have room for bad news.

## GOOD NEWS!
JANUARY 27, 2017

Yesterday I woke up feeling protected by a warm glow of light and grace. I knew everything I had on deck for the day: Port draw pre-chemo at Pluta, appointment with my oncologist to discuss the results of my CT scan, and then, a new chemo that is known to cause severe allergic reactions in 5% of patients (and you don't know if you're one of them until they start the drip—how comforting)… and yet, I didn't feel heavy. I felt light.

I took a relaxing bath, went for a run on the treadmill (yes, that should be in reverse order, but I want the running to be the last thing I do before I leave the house before chemo so my lungs receive the most benefit from the cardio-induced blood flow), and ate my "twig soup"—a Chinese soup that is supposed to support red blood counts. (And it did! my counts went up last time after consuming the soup for just three days prior to treatment… I'm still anemic, but I don't need a blood transfusion; I just need to get up slowly so that I don't faint…) My mom and I headed to Pluta. As far as chemo-days go, it was a relatively uneventful morning: No closet doors slammed so hard they fall off the track (me), no picture frames thrown (me), no tears (Mom or me). **I had this knowing in my gut that it was going to be a good day.**

And thank God I can begin to trust my gut again, after the crazy shit-storm it's been for the last year. My whole world has been rocked, I've lost the ground underneath me multiple times. So when I woke up yesterday, I knew it was a different kind of day, and surprisingly I didn't really doubt it too much. I knew I could rest easy, and I was right.

My oncologist walked into my appointment with a smile on her face. "Today is a good day. We have good news!" and I blurted out, "So tell me already!!!!"

The abridged version of my CT Scan:

*IMPRESSION:*

*Redemonstration of multiple innumerable pulmonary nodules with **interval decrease in size** in some of them when compared to prior, along with decreased mediastinal, axillary, and hilar lymphadenopathy, and **interval resolution** of the previous mammary chain soft tissue densities. **These findings are consistent with treatment response.***

First of all, the spots on my lungs aren't large enough to be considered "masses" (3 cm or bigger), they are "nodules" (1 cm or less), and I'm thankful for that. Some of them have gotten noticeably smaller, which is significant because the smaller they are in the dimension, the more difficult it is to see a change in size. All of the lymph nodes that were enlarged with disease have shrunken, and the internal mammary densities have completely disappeared. I am so thankful that this chemo hell is worth it, and that, according to my oncologist, the worst (Adriamycin and Cytoxan) is behind me—Taxol (if you're not allergic to it) is much better tolerated. No more nausea!!!! CAN I GET AN AMEN FOR NO MORE PUKING!

I also won't have to take steroids after treatment, I just get them the day of treatment through the iv, so hopefully the bloating that I feel constantly will begin to subside. I still get compliments on my cheekbones which makes me feel like I'm the only one that sees the puffiness in my face. Or that people are just trying to be nice. Either way, it's nice to hear every once in a while.

Yesterday's Taxol treatment went fine. I was pretty nervous when my nurse wheeled out the oxygen tank... My eyes bugged out of my head, and my nurse said, "Relax, baby, this is just protocol. You're gunna be fine," and she was right. I was. They give everyone 50 g of Benadryl through the iv beforehand, and holy crap. I was in the middle of a conversation with the social worker at Pluta when all of a sudden the Benadryl hit me and I sincerely felt drunk. I kept asking her if I was making any sense. Apparently I was, but I don't really remember the conversation. Who knew Benadryl could make me feel like that?

I sincerely want to sing again sometimes. That's HUGE. After a year of being almost completely silent, I might be ready to start singing. I want to delve into the beauty of Schubert, Schumann, Verdi, Wolf, Massenet, Mozart, Handel, and most of all... my beloved Debussy. If not singing, then at least listening. Music heals. Music gives life. I need healing. I need all things life-giving.

When I am back in shape vocally (hopefully soon), I would like to set up a benefit recital in which some of the proceeds go to metastatic breast cancer research. I will keep you posted as this idea manifests.

Thank you for all of your love and support. It is appreciated more than you know.

## TAXOL
JANUARY 30, 2017

My first Taxol treatment was last Thursday. I was told that Taxol is generally better tolerated than Adriamycin/Cytoxan, which is what I was on for the last eight weeks. While it's nice to not be nauseous all the time, I'm certainly not a huge fan of the constant fatigue and aches and pains in my bones and muscles. I've never experienced anything like it before. It's mostly in my legs and abdomen/rib area. On Friday I came home from the day's appointments and tried to sleep. Took two Ativan, Motrin, and Benadryl… and that STILL wasn't enough to compete with the steroids they gave me through the iv before my infusion. I was up every two hours in pain. Saturday, I was in bed pretty much all day. Yesterday I power-walked on the treadmill for 15 minutes and had to stop because I got light-headed. And to think I was running five miles a day in October. I get depressed just thinking about how rapidly my physical fitness has declined. I know it will come back because I'm young and otherwise healthy. But it still depresses me.

I am grateful that the treatment appears to be working. But it is really difficult to stay hopeful and optimistic when your physical body is taking such an assault. Chemotherapy weakens the body, and I knew that going in, but I had no idea what it would do to my spirit. Not only do you feel like shit, but you're bald, and most likely gaining weight rapidly because of the steroids. You don't recognize yourself in the mirror. It's not enough to have to fight for your life, you have to confront every insecurity you've ever had around your physical appearance too. You can't be incognito. Everywhere you go, you're a cancer patient. To call this experience traumatizing would be a gigantic understatement.

I hope sometime in the very near future, we can do away with this treatment and replace it with something less harmful and toxic. Something that doesn't alter one's sense of self in such crappy ways. Something that doesn't create more suffering than the actual disease itself.

I'm struggling today. Because even though the treatment is eliciting a positive response right now, who knows what the future will bring. I guess I just have to try to think that it will make a difference in the long run...

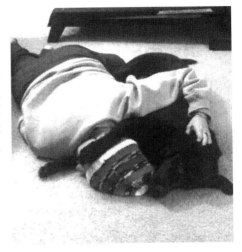

### NEED TO EXPLAIN, I GUESS
FEBRUARY 4, 2017

This is an excerpt of a message I received from someone from my past. I'm sharing this because I need people to know how absolutely painful messages like this are to receive.

*"everyday for the last 2.5 weeks since I found out, I wake up and hope to hear from you becuz i know there will be a day that i don't...that i can't, and it truly makes me feel awful. I feel awful for you, i feel awful for your mom, your dog...anyone that's ever been able to be around you and have a conversation"*

My general response to statements of this nature: I feel uncomfortable with people speaking like they've accepted my death already while I'm still here. If you were the one with cancer would it be comforting for you to hear that people are accepting your death while you're still here, or would it be upsetting? Nobody knows what's going to happen to them. People die unexpectedly and defy the odds **every *single* day**. I'm not a ticking time bomb, and I don't want to be treated as such. I don't like people talking like I'm a ghost. I don't want to hear things like this, it does nothing for my spirit. It implies that people have very little faith in me/my situation. And since my level of hope waivers on a moment to moment basis, I don't need other people's fears being projected onto me; I've got plenty of my own that require my daily attention (and Ativan). Just try to imagine what it would feel like in my position to hear people talking about your death like it's inevitable in the near future. It's hurtful. We all die. People can accept my death when it happens, not a moment before. You can't prepare for loss. And I'm still here, ***living*** and **breathing** and **thinking** and **feeling**. As my friend Holly has so eloquently stated, this is about how I forge ahead ***NOW***, not how others forge ahead LATER.

Please, everyone, just consider how your words may be received by the person who is "sick." I'm living with breast cancer. I'm not dying of it. Not now.

## SURPRISE: YOU'RE ALLERGIC! AND OTHER NEW THINGS
FEBRUARY 14, 2017

Apparently I like to keep things exciting and interesting. I mentioned after my first Taxol treatment that I did not have an allergic reaction during the infusion (though that night, I told my mom my throat felt itchy, so I took a Benadryl). Treatment number 2 was this past Thursday, and the infusion itself went fine. But Friday afternoon while driving myself to an appointment, I noticed

155

that I wanted to claw my face off due to the sudden onset of intense itchiness. I looked quickly in the rear view mirror. My face was bright red, puffy, and hot, with little spots all over it. I looked down at my neck, which was also starting to itch. That, too, was bright red. I immediately took Benadryl, 1 adult and 1 child, because I still needed to be able to drive myself home (thank goodness I had a glove compartment stash of drugs). I called Pluta and told them, and they said they wanted to see me. So I went from one appointment directly to another, which is unfortunately a normal occurrence in my world right now. My nurse practitioner told me it was a delayed reaction to the Taxol, which is extremely rare (go figure), and that I'll need to be seen by the immunologist for further testing (yay!). They prescribed a tapered dose pack of Prednisone, and I will have to take it for the six days following chemo for the remaining two treatments. So I have to take pills for a week after each treatment. Doesn't sound like a big deal, right? Except that on steroids, I am ravenous, wiry, anxious, bitchy, and unable to sleep (and the insomnia just gives the anxiety and bitchiness more fuel).

Not to mention the bloating and weight gain. ***Enough is enough.*** I am trying so hard to be compassionate and gentle toward myself at this time of healing but ***Jesus***. It seems as though I'm failing because I'm constantly frustrated in my skin, I'm not used to having a stomach, I'm not used to being so wide. I've gotten so that I won't even turn the lights on in the bathroom when I use it, or even when I bathe because I don't want to catch myself in the mirror right now. Being unintentionally bald and fat and knowing that you're just going to get fatter from these drugs you're being forced to take to prevent an allergic reaction from an ***already-toxic treatment…*** this all just feels like too much sometimes.

I'm making an effort to put nothing but nutrients in my body because I am so uncomfortable in my own skin. For example, I made a "dessert smoothie" with broccoli sprouts, kale, spinach, banana, raspberries, cacao powder, almond milk and flax seeds. It wasn't bad… it wasn't good either. Certainly not dessert. But I can tolerate just about anything if I think it's going to be good for me. That's the survivor in me, I suppose.

What's frustrating is that there's another drug in the same class of drugs (Taxol belongs to the class of drugs known as taxanes) that does not cause an allergic response in people. Abraxane, like Taxol, targets the microtubules in the cell division process, but it is packed with a different preservative—one that people are not allergic to. The problem is, you have to have a reaction to Taxol that sends you to the brink of death for insurance to cover Abraxane. Some hives on my face, chest, and neck aren't going to cut it. So I have to suffer more than I already am with prolonged steroid use because my body didn't react "enough," as in, my respiratory system wasn't affected. What a world we live in...

I've been feeling a bit better at least generally, on an emotional level, thanks in large part to cannabis, and the consequent introspective thinking and feeling I'm able to tap into when I'm high. I'm stoned most of the day on most days. And right now, that's working for me. It's making this all more tolerable. Pot helps me see things with a bit more clarity. Even my own mind—it helps me to detach from my thoughts so that I can observe my patterns, the traps I fall into, and the beliefs I seem to hold about myself and this world, some of which require some attention. Thank god for pot and meditation in helping me to recognize this!

My acupuncturist says that people who are innate healers often have an initiatory illness or some kind of trauma that propels them down the path of spirituality, and therefore, the practice of healing in some capacity. He was suggesting that he believes that I'm a healer of sorts. It is comforting to me to think that my pain might be transformed in a way that could be useful in helping others. This idea is what keeps me honest about all that I'm going through. It's healing for me to express my truth and I hope someday it might be helpful for other people to read what I'm writing or hear what I have to say. I know that I have felt comforted by the words of Augusten Burroughs, Marya Hornbacher, Pema Chödrön, to name just a few, because their words are so incredibly honest, raw, and relatable in their humanity. They make me feel less alone. (And being alone, or *feeling* alone, I've recently discovered, is one of my biggest fears...)

These days, I find myself thinking about what it means to be human, which is essentially a question the whole field of sociology is devoted to answering. Asking what it means to be human also requires us to consider what it means to be dehumanized. I think about this a lot lately. Cancer treatment definitely feels dehumanizing to me on a number of levels. And pinpointing why/what about it feels dehumanizing is helping me to understand my values as a human, and how I define being a human being.

On a somewhat unrelated note, sometimes I'm amazed with how little words do to express and connect us to each other. For example, we all know the word "sad," but we could experience the actual emotion completely differently. My concept of sadness and devastation and trauma and how those things manifest in my physical body is completely different from your concept and physical embodiment of those things, and these differences are informed by both life experiences and DNA. And yet, we all strive to feel connected. I sometimes wonder if true connection and understanding is possible, because language can only do so much.

I believe that to love is to know, and I think we have gotten so far away from empathizing with our fellow man because we are disconnected from ourselves. Meditation is helping me to confront myself in ways that aren't always comfortable. But I find that if I can sit with the discomfort for just a second longer, it usually shifts into something else. That's the thing about pain and suffering: our ideas about pain and suffering and what that pain is inextricably linked or caught up in are often worse than the actual pain itself. Our minds make things more painful, in other words. I'm trying to tame my wild beast of a brain so that I can get through the trauma of constant appointments and chemotherapy and overall cancer-centered life (right now) a bit easier.

I wish we humans could tap into each other's pain more readily instead of keeping it at arm's length. I'm sure I will talk more about this at some point but my brain is going wild with texts to consult and quotes to share and statistics to recite on this matter, and I'm just a little overwhelmed right now…

On the subject of anxiety: Two nights ago, I got **way** too high and started having panicked thoughts about death and dying. I was lying in my bed trying to listen to a guided meditation by Jon Kabat-Zinn, whose voice and words are usually soothing to me. Not that night. I was literally shaking. I had to get out of bed. I found it incredibly triggering. Probably because on some level, I equate embracing meditation and all of these more spiritual aspects of living with an acceptance of my death, which my soul seems to be resisting at this time. It's as if I see acceptance of the reality of death in general as a form of "giving up." I think it would be healthy for me to get to a place of acceptance of the impermanence of life, while simultaneously still investing in living—somehow in my brain, these two concepts seem contradictory, so that's something for me to deconstruct…

During my panicked state, my mind was racing, and this haunting image kept reappearing, assaulting me. It was literally being thrown into the center of my mind; just me, thin and pale, lying on my bed in a room covered in darkness. Alone. I would try to think about something else, but the image would just thrust itself into center stage again. Over and over and over. I had no control over it. And the more I tried to think about something else, the more intense and vivid the image became. What you resist, persists, right?

My panic that evening made me realize that I'm actually more afraid of going insane than I am of dying. Watching my brain do endless, seemingly crack-inspired backflips was absolutely terrifying. Horrifying, even. I was questioning my very relationship with "reality." Cancer itself makes me feel groundless, but this experience was like floating in the blackness of the abyss trying unsuccessfully to grab onto something—anything—to make me feel connected to something. Nothing settling about it. The thoughts and images were coming at me like lead bullets, each one penetrating my whole being sharply and violently—my physical body was actually shaking. I had no control over these thoughts and I couldn't escape them. I tried to write them down to force the gunshot-firing to slow down, but to no avail. I couldn't keep up, it was just flashes of horrible images, images of death, images from both my past and my present and my fears around the future, some things that made sense, some things that made no sense, and then I began to wonder if the things that didn't make sense to me would make sense to everyone else and vice versa.

**There is something about the isolation associated with insanity that seems unbearable to me.** Because I already feel isolated in my current situation. And I've always felt a bit isolated and ungrounded with "reality"—I suppose being an "artistic person" inclined to abstract and "colorful" thinking can explain some of that, along with my long list of disorders—take "body dysmorphic disorder," for example, a disorder that quite literally means you do not see aspects of your physical self the same way others see you. I've always felt like I've been teetering on the edge of sanity, but never fully crossing over to the "dark side." And two nights ago I was convinced that I was on *the literal edge* of sanity, heading toward a nervous breakdown, as if that sort of thing were as simple as a flick of the switch inside the brain, and my pot smoking happened to flick it, sending me reeling right into crazy land. I kept picturing—rather my MIND, not me, kept picturing myself lying in bed surrounded by darkness as my final breaths were escaping my lungs. And I was *alone*. The fact that I pictured myself dying in complete isolation really deeply upset me.

It is clear to me now that there is a lot caught up in how I define "being alone," and that is something for me to deconstruct as well. I will continue to ask myself, "What constitutes 'aloneness'? What would it take to not be/feel alone when confronting death?" My fear seems to be more rooted in a fear of isolation and aloneness (and how I'm *defining* these concepts) than of the permanence of death. Something for me to examine, for sure.

If my thoughts seem jumbled in this entry, it's because they are. I'm processing a lot emotionally which is sucking up most of the energy I would normally have to devote to making any ordinary sense…

Wish me luck for my remaining two treatments. Fingers crossed that I don't go into anaphylaxis… it's *shocking* (pun intended) that there is a larger immediate risk of death from my current cancer

160

treatment than from the actual cancer at this point. This world makes no sense sometimes. Or maybe that's just my insanity talking…

## HOLY COW NATIONAL NEWS AND STUFF
MARCH 3, 2017

I haven't written in a while because things have been so busy—not just with the usual appointments, though that's certainly part of it. The chemo fog is beginning to lift and I can see the light at the end of the tunnel, and as a result, I'm out living my life (with usual bouts of depression in between). The weather has also been a bit nicer (except for today, wtf!!!), so I've been outdoors running and walking and trying to get my vitamin D (although on my last lab, my vitamin D level was 98!). My last treatment is March 9th—less than a week away! I'm very excited to be done with this. I've got about four lashes left on each eye. But thankfully I had six for my national television debut….*

I was not involved in the study, but was recommended by the social worker at Pluta who knew I was exercising all through chemo. There were definitely days where getting out of bed was a struggle, and though I said that in the interview, they didn't quite include *all* of what I said about it (though they did keep the part where I talked about the body feeling heavy and weak).

I saw some comments on the story on NBC nightly news Facebook page that were pretty angry and negative. Some people (including some cancer patients, both past and present) were saying it was unrealistic and unhealthy to tell suffering cancer patients on chemo to run. People seemed offended by the story in general. The study/NBC was **not** trying to imply that every cancer patient needs to be out running marathons or doing anything strenuous. Any activity counts in terms of helping with the chronic fatigue syndrome cancer patients on chemo / in treatment experience. The

---

*Link available here:  myterminallife.org*

message is just "Do what you can." I think it would have been helpful if it had been stated that I was a very active person prior to starting chemo, which is why I am still able to run. But let me also make this clear: my speed has diminished completely. An 8-minute mile pace has gone to a 12-minute mile pace. And instead of doing five miles, I can do about two on a good day. **And there were definitely days where I did nothing**. Chemo has affected my physical fitness level.

Many of the comments on the Facebook page seemed really angry, particularly about the running part, to which I have to say: Running is not necessary in order to combat the fatigue (like I said). But also, **I'm 27 years old—of course I'm going to be in relatively good shape** compared to many (certainly not all) older cancer patients... Many of the angry comments were coming from "chemo veterans" so to speak, to whom I want to say: This wasn't made to shame anyone for their ability or inability to jog. Every person is different, every body is different, the biology of everyone's cancer is different. Maybe the chemo agents you were on were harsher, or maybe the anti-emetic drugs that I've been on through this whole process (which I've heard are drastically better and more effective than what people were taking even five years ago) were not available when you were going through chemo.

To reiterate, **everybody is different**. I really did not mean to offend anyone going through cancer treatment with my jogging through treatment. And to reinforce, the study simply showed *any* physical activity is beneficial. I feel badly that some people were so angered by the story :/.

NBC news also posted a separate article* on the web page.

I was also interviewed this morning by Beth Adams from WXXI.*

---

*Links available here: myterminallife.org*

So all in all, I've been very busy... I need sleep more than anything right now. Goodnight moon.

## IT'S DONE!
MARCH 10, 2017

Yesterday, I had my final infusion of Taxol, marking the end of my chemotherapy. Thank you to everyone who has supported me through this process, both near and far.

I wrote a poem* for the bell-ringing ceremony at the end of chemo, because the poem on the original plaque did not feel relevant to me as a metastatic breast cancer patient. Metastatic breast cancer patients will be in some form of treatment for life. I wrote something because I wanted people who will never fully be done with treatment to have something to commemorate the completion of an aspect of treatment.**

"My Last Scheduled Chemo
Though my treatments are far from done.
I toll the bell today,
To celebrate a milestone
And my courage along the way.

I celebrate my strength and hope
And victories large and small.
I am a METAvivor
And that's why I stand tall."

Amy Schnitzler
March 9, 2017

---

*Link available here: myterminallife.org*

**Editor's note: The Pluta Foundation will be displaying a plaque with Amy's poem adjacent to the original one, in order to give patients a choice of which poem to read aloud when ringing the bell, based on their situation.*

## **PICKING UP THE PIECES**
MARCH 14, 2017

I thought I'd be happy.

I thought I'd be ecstatic.

I thought I'd be filled with joie de vivre.

I'm not.

March 9th marked the end of my chemotherapy and simultaneously, the beginning of my acknowledgment that for the rest of my life, I will be a metastatic breast cancer patient. The last four months have been completely treatment-centered; my life has revolved around appointments related to treatment: port draws, oncology appointments, the chemo itself, palliative care appointments (to help manage side effects from the poison being pumped into me, through which I get my pot), and things like acupuncture to help me feel more human… In other words, I've been quite busy with appointments pertaining directly to my treatment, and now that a chapter of my treatment has come to an end, what I'm left with is a boatload of time. Time to relive the trauma of the past year beginning with my grandma's death, my diagnosis just 10 days later, to the scans and rediagnosis of stage 4 disease in early November, and the terror I felt all through chemotherapy. Time to ponder the implications of this disease on my future.

My life as a "normal" person is over completely. And I'm grieving that. I'm grieving the fact that I may not grow old—the longest a person with metastatic breast cancer has lived is 20 years; the majority live 3-5 years. I'm grieving the fact that I have no desire to sing anymore (because when I do sing, I don't sound like me, I sound terrible, probably due to the early menopause brought about by chemotherapy). While friends are establishing and nurturing loving relationships with partners, I'm bald and feeling hideous, and also feeling fairly confident that "I have Stage 4 cancer" is not something that typically sparks a mood of romance. (Not that I'm looking right now. But the idea of having a loving relationship with someone is something I think most people desire.)

When you're on chemo, it's your whole world. And now that I'm done with it, I feel like I've been dropped off on the edge of a cliff. I should be happy, right? The physical suffering of chemo is done. But the psychological suffering is setting in, in a way that it couldn't during chemo because I was too busy, honestly. As I said, part of the problem is  the excess time  (I would try to engage in things  I enjoy outside of my house, except that it's basically a white-out here in upstate New York.) It's not like I have a job to go back to; I quit my serving job a year ago to begin traveling for grad school auditions. I was supposed to start grad school for voice in a different state, and then I got diagnosed… and I'm not sure I'm even ready to work. (The thought of bar tending and serving to make some much needed money literally makes me want to throw up). I feel like I need to start this new treatment chapter and get a good scan or two under my belt, as well as address my mental and emotional health before I can think seriously about what I'd like to do with my life.

I am devastated. Nothing about my life is the same as it was pre cancer and I feel terrible. It's just been loss after loss after loss. I feel ready to throw in the towel on everything right now.

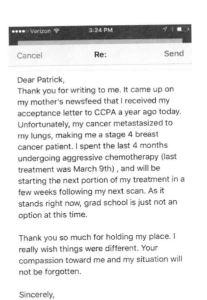

Cancer fucking sucks. As of right now, we do not know how many women (and men) are living with metastatic breast cancer, which is a problem because that type of information often drives funding for research and treatment development. This is the type of breast cancer that kills. 30% of all people diagnosed with early stage breast cancer will go on to develop metastatic disease, which actually says a lot about the inefficacy of first-line treatment. ***Until there is a cure for metastatic disease, breast cancer has no cure.***

This is an article from Huffpost (10/5/2016) explaining why this information is important: "Where is the data? The epidemiology of Metastatic Breast Cancer."

## A LETTER TO MY METASTATIC BREAST CANCER
MARCH 15, 2017

Dear Lung Spots,

First, I must start off by expressing my hatred for you and the countless ways you've impacted my life. You are dreaded, you are awful, you are terrifying, you are insidious. You came upon me completely unexpectedly. Just as I was beginning to feel like I could handle this "whole cancer thing" and everything that the last seven months had brought me (death of my grandmother on March 30th, diagnosis of cancer just ten days later, bilateral mastectomy, tissue expander "fills," beginning hormone therapy, implant placement and tissue expander exchange surgery, beginning Lupron, ending up in the psych unit…), I was toppled by your disgusting presence. I was completely blindsided. I had been running five miles a day all the way up to your re-diagnosis in November, totally unaware of your presence until the diagnostic CT scan, after my mastectomy scar presented a mysterious rash; I felt nothing in the way of respiration. In fact, I felt nothing in the way of anything— physically, I felt the healthiest I had ever felt in my entire life. Today, on March 14th, everything is different because of you.

Let's start with the basics. Because of you, I had to begin aggressive and terrible chemotherapy right away; there was no time to harvest my eggs (nor would the process have been safe for me, since you

167

are estrogen receptor positive, and the process requires shots of estrogen to plump up the eggs). Because of you, child-bearing is no longer possible for me. Because of you, at age 27, I get to experience the glories of menopause—the hot flashes that wake me up in the middle of the night, multiple times each night, the mood swings (on top of what I was already working with mood-wise). Because of you, I am in fear for my life, at the mercy of doctors and specialists and researchers and insurance companies. Because of you, I must contemplate my mortality. Because of you, I have no hair, my nails are ridged and bumpy, my energy is a quarter of what it was. My voice, the thing that has always been a part of my identity, is something I do not recognize, thanks to the last four months of poisoning, and the consequent lack of estrogen. My clear and focused bell-like top register is non existent—I try to sing and I cough; my voice is weathered and tired. I had to tell the graduate program that I was accepted into that I will not be able to attend at this time. Because of you.

You are a fuck-face son of a bitch and I want nothing more than to see you die and squeal in agony. Not only are you a sneaky, disgusting, rotten and vile piece of shit, you are also not understood by oncologists; otherwise, you would be curable, and I wouldn't have the frequent panic attacks about dying before my parents, before my dog, before ever having a truly healthy loving relationship. I hate you.

And yet, this feels somewhat wrong to me. You are part of me. My own cells. You are not an invader. I cannot simply fractionate myself from you because as far as DNA goes, we are the same. I want to know what happened to you; what your story is. I want to know the beginning of you, when your first rogue cell replicated, what triggered it, and how. I would like to tell you to calm the hell down; that your anxious dividing is tearing me apart both physically (though I don't have symptoms directly from you, but rather, the treatment you require) and psychologically. What do you need to be calm and quiet, so that I can live a long, healthy, meaningful life, you gigantic asshole?

168

I will say this: if it hadn't been for you, I would not have connected with young women like Mackenzie, Lauren, Jen, and other incredible women dealing with their own versions of you. I would not have met the wonderful nurses who took care of me through my chemo treatments—some of whom took care of my grandmother when she was going through her treatment for advanced small cell lung cancer. I would not be invested in the process of learning that I might be a worthwhile person. And sometimes, I do believe that the opportunity to ponder one's death is something we should all do, with or without your presence. If it hadn't been for you, I would have continued to float on the surface in shallow friendships that did not honor the truth about who I really am. You definitely helped me to weed out the people who were absolutely incapable and clueless in how to be a real friend to someone in tough times. The ones who have remained and the new ones who have appeared are the best people in the whole world and I am so lucky to have them.

It's this confusing dynamic of both hatred and appreciation that I have for you, and I will continue to try to hold a space for both of those things.

You are very much an unwelcome guest, and I wish you would leave quickly and painlessly.

I am trying to navigate my new life and pick up the pieces of myself that have completely shattered from the last year. I am not the same person I was a year ago, in any way. Because of you, I have to rebuild myself. Or, because of you, I have the opportunity to rebuild myself. I'm not sure which one is more true, maybe they are equally true.

You are getting your picture taken on March 29th, and it is my most sincere hope and prayer that you are nowhere to be found. I will continue to picture a radiant and healthy emptiness in my lungs in my meditations. No matter what the images reveal, I will continue to make myself healthy and well in all respects. You are a part of my story right now, but you're not all of it. Don't get cocky.

I hope this letter is returned to sender. But in the event that it isn't, know that I am working to starve you by strengthening my whole self.

Sincerely,
Amy


## EXPLOSIONS, EROSIONS, AND THE QUEST FOR INNER PEACE
APRIL 3, 2017

The end of March and the beginning of April 2017 mark several anniversaries for my family and me—all of which are laden with sadness. I truthfully am still trying to wrap my head around everything this last year has been. March 30th was my grandmother's death, and little did I know that the dawning of April would be the dawning of a very long and painful year. I've been contemplative and a little withdrawn lately because I'm trying to take this all in. The cancer-thing. The Stage-4-cancer-thing. The loss-of-self-thing. The gaining-of-a-million-pounds-thing. You know, *light* stuff. (The last one kinda *is* light, but my newfound heaviness is weighing on my heart.) (I'm cracking myself up.) (I'm high.)

I don't know where I'd be without pot. I really can't say it enough. It helps me to not take myself so seriously. It also helps me eat popcorn by the mixing-bowl-ful. And I enjoy not taking myself seriously and I also enjoy eating popcorn by the mixing-bowl-ful. So the way I see it, it's is a win-win.

More importantly, it also helps me observe my thoughts. When I'm uninhibited by pot's wonderfully delicious vapor (I have a vape pen), I'm able to get off my wheel of thinking; I can establish greater distance between myself and the wheel of thoughts and constant chatter in my mind. I think I remember reading in one of Pema Chödrön's books that Buddhists sometimes refer to the mind's

170

constant chatter as "monkey mind," and I remember picturing a bunch of red "Barrel of Monkeys" monkeys "*ooo!-ooo!-ooo!*"-ing and "*ah!-ah!-ah!*"-ing through the vines of my neurons—it really was an effective phrase with an even more effective image for me, but anyway... I've gotten much better at observing my thoughts, actually. I can recognize things a lot quicker than I remember being able to in the past. And in that recognition, I can **choose** whether or not I want to indulge in the thought.

Except around death. When I have thoughts about mortality (mine, loved ones'), they are typically all-consuming. There is no separation between myself and the thought. I was thinking about this earlier (while stoned): My struggle in redirecting away from these types of thoughts once the first thought occurs, shows me how fearful I am of death.

I acknowledge that I am actually scared *shitless*.

I have never accepted death in the ways it's presented itself in my life—that's become really clear to me as I've been navigating this new life. I have all of these intense (and unresolved) fears around my own death and I wonder if my aunt Carol and my grandma and Janet and people who have gone before me felt these fears too, at one point or another. I wonder if these fears are a natural part of aging and if cancer has just taken me from 27 to 77 in a matter of months (physically, mentally, emotionally). I wonder how much of my experience is universal among those of us with illness and how much of it is unique to me. Just things I find myself pondering...

This entry may seem somewhat of a downer, especially considering that I just received pretty great results from my scans—*bone scan was clean, abdomen and pelvic CT both clean (drumroll please), chest CT greatly improved (no more lymph nodes, just spots of a couple millimeters or smaller left here, folks)*—but I also have noticed that my mind does not trust happiness, or calmness, or peacefulness, probably due to the conditioning I've had in the last year of repeated crisis and trauma. When I experience a victory, I armor myself with negative thoughts because it functions as protection from disappointment and further hurt. The higher you climb, the farther (further? I don't know, chemo destroyed my brain) you fall, or something like that. Except that in this scenario, I'm missing out on moments of inner peace that I could be experiencing, so in that way, I'm letting the cancer run the show. To which I say: fuck *that*.

So tonight I'm getting good and high and laughing my ass off (possibly at myself and my own mental Tom-foolery, because I seem to consistently believe I'm hilarious when I'm high). Because I'm alive and all things considered, I'm doin' pretty well. I've got a little less energy (*and hair*) than I'd like to have, but I otherwise feel generally well.

My goal is to have more moments of peace and calm every day. My goal is to sit with the discomfort I have around death a little longer every day. My goal is to make peace with death: not my death or anyone else's, just the concept itself. Sit with the concept of permanence. Of what it means to be alive. Of what it means to be human. Of what it means to *live*.

I hope y'all are tokin' up with me…

## BREAK THE SILENCE
JUNE 6, 2017

I have thought about blogging nearly a hundred times since my last post, and for one reason or another, it just wouldn't actually happen. Until now.

Truthfully, I felt intensely overwhelmed by the *idea* of updating this thing because so much has happened in a relatively short period of time—the question of *where do I start?* would send me reeling so much that start, I would not…

Since my last post, I have gone from *not*-adjusted to this life as a person with metastatic cancer, to fairly *well*-adjusted (with some intense moods in between—I mean, I'm still **me**). What's been instrumental in facilitating this shift, you ask? (Maybe you're not asking, maybe you don't care at all!). So far, it's been:

## 1. Support

My mom is incredible. As sturdy and dependable as the ground beneath us, as giving as Shel Silverstein's tree. We might not always like each other, but I hope she knows how strong my love for her is. I'm lucky to have such a ferocious advocate as my mom and friend.

My dad always can divert my attention with a lengthy Scrabble game or a good pun. He is resourceful and inquisitive and loving.

My aunts, uncles, and cousins have supported me in different ways throughout this experience, whether it's sharing meals, crafting, going for walks, having meaningful conversation. Each relative has shown me they care in their own special way. I am thankful for each of them.

*(I believe earlier on in my experience with cancer, I projected a lot of anger onto those around me who truly weren't responsible for it. That's the hard part about a cancer diagnosis: there's no real place to put the anger—no person, no external source, no one to blame... )*

The nurses at Pluta Cancer Center are earth-angels. Boundless compassion and wisdom unmatched. I don't have enough words so that's all I'm saying.

Old faithful friends. Friends that have stuck around and accepted me where I'm at, regardless of how much they'd probably like to slap me when I'm in those particularly *crappy* locations. I do not have a million friends. But the ones who have shown me their character and their love for me by sticking around are as precious as the stars.

New friends. I have met some RIDICULOUS people in the last year. Good ridiculous. The best kind of ridiculous. I am so thankful. My dog. Riley is my most adored being on earth. *Sorry, turtle doves. It's just fact.* She's always there for a cuddle or a run.

## 2. Integration of mental health and spirituality

I believe I am getting well in all regards, and I think this has to do with incorporating spirituality into my mental health recovery, as opposed to my compartmentalized approaches of the past. I am integrating what I am learning and experiencing with acupuncture, reiki, meditation, reciting the rosary (and other prayers) and other spiritual teachings and practices with concepts like mindfulness, radical acceptance, and other skills from CBT and DBT—and suddenly, the world makes more sense to me. The two worlds of mental health and spirituality seem inextricably linked to me now. Healing is spiritual…. (Almost like ***how the hell did I never see this before?***)

By addressing my mental health, I am also addressing my spirituality, and vice-versa. I am doing a lot of painting lately as a mindfulness practice which makes me feel connected to source and altogether more centered. I want to share my latest thoughts on all of this but it's 10:20 p.m. and I'm pooped, so I'll save it for another time…

## 3. Being off chemotherapy

Pretty self explanatory… chemo is a soul-suck. And a body-suck. It just *suck*-sucks. I have so much more to say, but this was as good a start as any.

# "MEDITATION" ON THE CLOUDS
JUNE 24, 2017

I stormed in the door hot and dripping with sweat from my slower-than-normal 3-mile run with my unruly dog, and my unrulier thoughts, and announced in an icy tone to my mother that I was in a terrible mood. She asked what she could do, and I shot back hastily, my voice fraught with angst, "*Nothing*, I need my water and I'm going to sit outside."

I unleashed the dog, grabbed my bottle off the counter and the door slammed behind me. (Was that the *wind*, or did *I* just slam it?) I made my way to the back of the house and sat on an area of flatness I found amidst the slopes and slumps of my backyard. The sky was foreboding: a dark and heavy shade of grey tinged with dark blue, and the air had a sudden sharp coolness suggesting rain was in my immediate future. I didn't care. The cloud straight above me was the darkest cloud in my view. *How appropriate,* I thought. I looked to either side of me; the right had lighter shades of grey, like someone smeared grey-blue dyed whipped-cream across that part of sky. I looked to my left and saw a similar picture, though the left looked slightly more defined and less hazy than the right side. I took a deep breath and decided to focus my attention on my breath, and on the clouds.

As I breathed and took in the picture to my left, I was surprised to find several patches of cerulean blue amidst the light grey whipped-cream clouds. (Were these patches there all along?)

It began to rain. Pour, actually. I was chilled, but a smile made its way to my lips. I stayed present for a few more breaths before getting up from my place in the grass, thanking the sky for its mercy, and made my way back inside.

## DAYTRIP TO MY PLACE OF WORSHIP
JUNE 26, 2017

Some days, you just gotta get away....

## MY EYES ARE WATERING
JULY 17, 2017

I was chopping onions for a nice spicy lentil daal for my friend Stephen and me, listening to some reporter and interviewee on tv discussing the importance of health care proxy, advance directive, financial planning, "because we just don't *know* when a health event will occur." My impulse was to march over and change the channel because like, not today, please... I've been feeling so *happy*. But I didn't. I stayed with it. I cried. (And not just from the onions.)

I have been resisting the health care proxy thing since the inception of my terminal diagnosis. Fuck "terminal"—that isn't how I feel. But how *do* I feel? For now, we'll go with confused, sad, angry, happy, pissed, joyful, grateful, devastated, angsty, scared, vibrant, dull, and like I could eat tater tots for days.

I think about death often. As a person who spent much of her 20s feeling passively suicidal, my thoughts about death are a bit different now (I will post about this next; there's a draft I'm working on now). Will I fill out my health care proxy this week? Probably not. I've got some emotional roadblocks that must be worked around/through in order to do that.

What I will say is this: when I'm on my way out, I know where I want to be, and who I want to be there.

I want shamanism to be a part of my transition (Dr. Londorf and Dr. Graber). I want acupuncture to help with pain and discomfort (along with allopathic medicine). I want to die at home in my own bed in my own room with my own sounds and smells and familiar sights. I want the overture of Traviata played frequently, along with Berlioz's "Les Nuits d'Été," and Debussy's "En Sourdine," "Claire de Lune" (vocal), and "Nuit d'Étoiles," preferably all sung by Elly Ameling. I want good counselors in place for my closest loved ones.

All of this from chopping onions.

Two tears fell into the simmering pan.

This will be one authentic meal.

## FAT TEARS
JULY 19, 2017

I have not had a good ugly cry in a while. And I have a feeling it will be happening soon. Possibly tonight.

I am exhausted. Since my diagnosis (2016), I have yet to sleep through a single night (minus nights in the hospital after surgery). I wake up multiple times each night, sometimes from hot flashes, sometimes from terrifying dreams where I am literally startled awake, sometimes just to pee. Most nights upon waking, I make my way to the fridge. I eat blueberries (sometimes a whole pint. I'm not kidding), sometimes some almonds, occasionally dark chocolate (last night. Oops). And then I go back to bed thinking how terrible it was that I ate at 2 in the morning, and what that must be doing to my IGF-1 levels, and how disgusting I am, and how I'll always be "fat" because I have no "self control," and on and on. And at 2 or 3 in the morning, I don't have the clarity of mind to talk myself down from that place. So then I somehow fall back asleep (though not necessarily quickly), and wake up the following hour. Sometimes I stay in bed after the initial awakening. Sometimes I get up and go to the living room and try to read. But I hear the cupboards taunting me from the room next door. Some nights I feel so terrible about it all that I just cry.

The real issue here is... well, there are several. Let's start with number 1: I need to sleep. Sleep is very important. We hear it all the time. It's the body's chance to repair and restore. If you're not sleeping, you're not repairing or restoring.

When I wake up during the night, I'm often pissed, shaken, sad (and sometimes actually hungry, but most of the time, not really). So I go to the fridge. Because rather than sit with the feelings, I am looking for a distraction, a diversion. So the impulse to consult the refrigerator makes a lot of sense, but the problem is it leads to regret, self loathing, and SHAME (this is problem number 2).

Typing this out has been difficult for me because I feel a tremendous amount of shame around my night-eating. I feel shame for the "you have cancer and you're fucking up your hormone levels so if you die soon it will be all your fault" reason (that's issue number 3). And shame for the "normal" American female reasons. (They might be common/nearly universal, but they're not healthy.)

The stuff with food and weight still plagues me. In some ways, it's comforting to have some things carry over from my previous life.

In other ways, I'd rather not deal with the food stuff at all and just eat like a normal human being.

Since I have not had adequate sleep in a year, and since I am on drugs that shut down my ovaries and stop my body from making estrogen, and since I can never have children, and since I statistically may not make it to 30, it is really no wonder that I am a fucking moody wench.

I forget all of this, probably because I'm adjusting to this new life... (But fuck statistics, seriously.)

I need to cry. I can feel heaviness resting on my chest, and that needs to be released. Sometimes, I think it's okay to throw yourself the pity party, as long as you don't stay in the party hat too long. (Or eat the cake at 3 a.m.) (Whatever that means.)

Edit: Or, you could puke in a neighbor's driveway (not your own, of course) after a run in 85-degree weather. That's a release, too.


## SCAN DAY / HAPPY BIRTHDAY, GRANDMA JOELLEN MANCARI
AUGUST 1, 2017

I had a scan this morning at Strong's new Imaging building, which is really more like a hotel than a medical building. I first walked into a comfortable lobby with high ceilings, an electric fireplace, large tv screens, a set up for assorted coffees and teas. Very quiet, and almost peaceful. Well, as peaceful as a medical facility can be...

I arrived feeling very calm, and very very loved and supported. (Thank you to everyone who sent me some love last night/today!) Interestingly, I am still feeling peaceful, though the waiting ('til Thursday) SUCKS.

The man at the front desk looked familiar to me. After a couple of "what's-your-date-of-birth?" type-questions, he told me that I looked very familiar. We laughed when we realized that it was from the hospital, as he used to check me in over there. He handed me the usual paperwork that has me answer questions like Why are you here? *(why not?)* What type of scan are you here for? *(CT of chest, abdomen, and pelvis)* Why? *(Because I have ductal breast cells in my lungs)* When was your last menstrual period? *(10/25/16, enjoyed at the psych unit at RGH)*, any chance of pregnancy? *(HA!)* etc., etc.

A tech came out moments after I began my paperwork and brought me into a room in the back, decked out with a fancy large screen tv mounted on the wall. ***This** is where my port gets accessed?* I wondered. Looked more like a room at the Woodcliff. (K not really, but you get what I'm sayin', the place was spiffy).

After the 20-minute ordeal that is known as power-port accessing, I was free to watch a bit of a cooking show. About 8 minutes into it (they were making savory pastries; holy butter, Batman, though), I was called in for my scan. I got on the table, and was told that my shorts needed to get a little lower (dumb metal buttons). First, they took pictures without the iv contrast to get a baseline, and then several images with the iv contrast (the kind that causes the warm, flushed feeling all over; I always feel as if I've just peed myself), which highlights any potential problems. I'm lying in the machine with my arms over head (flashy CT pose), when all of a sudden, I get hit with the sneezes. One after the other, as the machine whirs around me, telling me to breathe and hold my breath… I sneezed about 10 times. When the tech came back in, I was convinced he was going to say we needed to get more images, because my sneezing messed it all up. Not the case. He came in to tell me I could pull up my pants, and that I was all set!

Pulling out of the parking lot and onto East River road, a yellow butterfly circled around my mom's car. Hello to you, too, Aunt Mary. And hi, Janet! And happy birthday, Grandma Jo. Three angels who are rooting for me on the other side.

## UPDATE
AUGUST 4, 2017

On Wednesday, while in the ED for chest pain (more on that later), I received a phone call from my oncologist. Literally, I just got unhooked from my EKG. I told her I was in the Emergency Department at Strong, and she was sorry to hear that, but then asked, "Do you want to talk about your scan now? I mean, will that upset you?" And I said, "I don't know, you tell *me!*"

It did not upset me. It's by far the best lookin' scan I've had since November, when this whole mess began. Prior CT reports have consistently read "innumerable pulmonary nodules ranging from 5 mm to 2 cm"; Tuesday's scan actually had a number, and they are all "itty bitty" according to Dr. Shayne. Like pin-prick small. Like wouldn't-show-up-on-a-PET-scan small.

I don't have words to describe how this feels, really. So I'm just trying to soak it up.

Thank you to everyone who has walked behind me and beside me through this journey. Every text, every phone call, every happy surprise visit… your support really means the world to me.


## THE BRIGHTEST LIGHT
SEPTEMBER 6, 2017

On August 30th, 2017, the world lost a gorgeous glowing force that was known as Lauren Morelle. She was an amazing woman, and her presence was an absolute gift to me, and to all whose lives she touched.

Lauren was my hero. I was diagnosed with metastatic breast cancer just shortly after her. The day we met at Pluta, we were sitting in chairs next to one another in the infusion center. I had actually recognized her from the news story she was in about a year before. She looked over at me with her elbow resting on the arm of her chair, her head resting on her hand, her eyelids fluttering, and with a slight smile on her face, asking "Sooo, whatchya in for??" "Metastatic breast cancer," I replied. She got up from her chair, walked over to me saying, "HEY ME TOO!!" and proceeded to high-five me. In that moment, I knew we would be friends.

She had an infectiously radiant, beautiful, and bubbly spirit. In times when I was struggling to stay afloat, I would text Lauren, and she would call me to remind me of my own strength. Once, after a particularly painful experience at a friend's bridal shower (where I was forced to acknowledge, yet again, just how abnormal my life is), I sent her a message saying that I was having a hard day, and she called me right away. She listened to my kvetching with such compassion and understanding. After about 10 minutes of that, the two of us were laughing together about any and everything, and then we planned our next lunch date. She stayed on the phone with me 'til after I got home to make sure I was in a good place.

The last time we saw each other, we had a lunch date at Panera, and she gave me a shirt. I am so lucky to have something of hers. I feel genuinely blessed to have known her. Her light will shine on in the lives of the many people she touched.

Until our "epic lunch" and Mickey Mouse waffle breakfast on the other side, you will be so treasured and so missed, sweet girl.

## HI!
OCTOBER 22, 2017

Things have been absolutely crazy for me lately (in mostly good ways!). Unfortunately time for blogging has been scarce. I'd like to make a once-weekly (at least) commitment to this thing again. A lot has been happening; I don't really have the mental energy to write about it now. So in the meantime, I'll just share my most recent online interview with Maimah Karmo from the Huffington Post.*

---

*Link available here: myterminallife.org*

NOVEMBER 3, 2017

Things have been an exciting brand of crazy lately, so I haven't been able to write, tho' I've wanted to! Today I have a scan—normal, routine, but the scheduling of it was a bit abrupt. I was expecting it to be scheduled in the upcoming weeks, but after my appointment yesterday, I received a phone call that they couldn't get me in then, but could get me in TOMORROW (today) for CT and bone scans. So, here we are, en route to the River Road building (luxury hotel). Prayers for a good outcome are welcome. Happy reading!–sorry, it's long!

*Who is Amy Schnitzler?*

I am a daughter, a sister, a dog-mom, a girlfriend, a friend. I am a singer, a painter, a writer, a world traveler, a runner, an amateur yogi, a Community Relations Coordinator, an advocate, a teacher, a lifelong student.

*How old were you when you were diagnosed? What Stage?*

I was diagnosed with breast cancer at 26-years-old. Prior to my mastectomy I was tentatively diagnosed Stage 2 invasive ductal carcinoma, ER/PR+, HER2- (that's jargon for "my cancer likes hormones"). I was officially diagnosed with Stage 3 disease post-mastectomy, as there were more lymph nodes involved than originally thought. There was a note on my diagnostic CT scan referring to a 2mm speck on my left lung, which was "too small to characterize." This was in April of 2016. By November, following the sudden appearance of a mysterious rash along the incision on my right side, I was re-diagnosed with Metastatic disease (Stage 4), with metastases to both lungs.

*What was your mindset at diagnosis?*

I don't think I had a mindset; I think I was terrified and confused, looking for concrete, black-and-white absolution in a world of grey uncertainty. My grandmother had died just ten days before I was diagnosed. I was processing tremendously heavy grief, and then was diagnosed with cancer. My feelings were all over the map. I was numb, shocked, despondent, and full of terror and rage all at once. I also sensed a bit of pressure to be "brave" and "strong," to "fight" and "win" very early on, and I think that pressure was coming from both outside of me (cultural conceptions of the disease/"Pinkness") as well as within me. As a result, I felt very isolated. There was also great pressure from my oncologist to move forward with treatment quickly, which added to the sense of overwhelm. Making life-or-death decisions is not easy, especially around something as complex as cancer. I think in the beginning, I tried to say, "I got this, don't worry, I'll be fine, I'm tough!" when in reality I was a scared-sh**less little girl, longing for someone to scoop me up and transport me back to a world where life made sense. I vacillated between feeling powerful and powerless every 10 seconds, which was exhausting. Powerlessness is not a comfortable state for me (or any human). I think when we humans experience loss of a loved one, of a relationship, or of health and vitality, we feel out of control. If it weren't for the support of those closest to me (and mental health rehabilitation services!), I honestly don't think I'd be here today.

*How did your breast cancer diagnosis change your life?*

How did it not? To start, I was diagnosed the same week I received acceptance to Graduate Programs at Peabody Institute, Chicago College of Performing Arts, and Rider University for Classical Vocal Performance/Opera. I had to let them know that I was diagnosed with cancer and would need a decision extension as I was waiting for more information regarding what treatment would look like. Chicago College of Performing Arts responded with such compassion and told me they would allow me to defer for a year, should I need to. At that point, I was still trying to comprehend this diagnosis and processing all the feelings around it, so I decided it was not the time for me to move to a new city, try to find a new oncologist there, etc. Writing to them that I would not be able to attend that Fall was heart-breaking. Music is no longer my career-path. I recently began working with a new company called Harmonigenic as a Community Relations Coordinator. Harmonigenic is a diagnostic assay that uses photonics to analyze the collagen of breast tumors to predict the risk of metastasis, giving patients more information to inform their treatment decisions.

Socially, this disease terminated a lot of friendships that probably would have ended anyway, and it also led me to some incredible people I most likely wouldn't have otherwise met. I appreciate the people in my world more (Mom, you're the best). My values are also a bit different. In my life before cancer, my identity was very much wrapped up in my physical appearance—my weight, my body, my face, my hair. Nothin' like some good ole' chemotherapy to zap your hair off, give you 20 extra pounds (thanks, steroids!), and force you to challenge your ideas about yourself. I've had to find my worth outside of my physical identity, and truthfully, that's been a pretty healthy thing.

*What do you wish you'd known before being diagnosed with breast cancer?*
I wish I was aware that breast cancer can and does happen to young women. Maybe I would have gone to the doctor the moment I discovered the lumps under my arm instead of putting it off for several months. I wish I had known about the impact of everything we consume and put onto our bodies, the harmful things we are exposed to on a daily basis. Diet is so important! We live in a culture of processed food, and we are also the sickest we've ever been. There's a link there.

*How has this experience awakened you to yourself and your purpose?*
Cancer has been the ultimate perspective-shifter for me. I think I was always an empathetic person, but receiving this diagnosis has opened me up further to the pain and suffering of others—I don't think that I was exceptionally selfish before cancer, I think I was just young and naïve. This diagnosis has illuminated the role of human connection in the facilitation of healing on all levels. I

advocate for women with metastatic disease because it is an isolating and terrifying diagnosis and we need each other's support.

*Tell me about your advocacy work.*

Most of my work is centered around conversation with people about the reality of this disease. When I was first diagnosed, I began a blog to chronicle my journey with breast cancer. I was most recently featured in a Facebook live interview on Metastatic breast cancer at Pluta Cancer Center, where I receive treatment. Last February, I was featured in a NBC Nightly News story on a study about the benefits of exercise for chemotherapy/cancer treatment induced fatigue. In October of 2016, I was in a local news story discussing breast cancer in young women and the power of self-awareness. I am currently co-facilitating a grief group at a local mental health rehabilitation center, where I openly share my experiences with the disease. My new job at Harmonigenic is all about patient relations.

*What word do you wish you could take out of the breast cancer vocabulary?*

Mortality. We need a cure. This is a disease that kills 41,000 women (and men) per year—113 women per day. It angers me that people believe breast cancer is "curable" in the early stages, when 1/3 of all women diagnosed with early stage disease will become metastatic at some point after completing treatment—whether it's months or years down the road.

*If there was one thing you could change about breast cancer and how people view it, what would that be?*

It is not a pretty pink disease. Not everyone who gets diagnosed gets to walk away. Metastatic breast cancer is the only version of the disease that kills, and yet it receives the least amount of attention (people don't even know what it is!) and the least amount of funding for research. Less than 7% of all the money received for breast cancer research goes to metastatic research. This needs to change, and it needs to change NOW.

*Why is it so important to you to support other women with breast cancer?*
Receiving this diagnosis and needing to make decisions regarding barbaric, though possibly life-preserving treatment is pure unadulterated Hell. The isolation I felt is something I can't explain well with words. I can only speak of the constant clenching in my chest, the empty gnawing feeling in the pit of my stomach, those delicious weary moments between sleep and wake where all of it felt like a terrifying nightmare, where if I put my two feet on the ground, I'd walk into the world I remembered from the life before breast cancer... and then the crashing back to reality... No woman should have to experience that (or any variation of it) alone. This diagnosis has led me to some extraordinary women who are also dealing with this disease—I've lost some dear friends, too. Connecting with other women who are facing the same unique challenges, navigating their journeys in their own way, has been full of opportunity for learning, growth, and healing. I also believe that systemic change is only possible when we come together, inspire one another, and educate our communities on the ugly reality of this disease, and point people to the organizations that actually support us with research, such as METAvivor, and METup.

*What would you tell a newly diagnosed young woman?*
Breathe. Focus on surviving in these early days. Balanced, healthy eating, hydrating, and sleeping will help, as will laughter. Reach out when you are feeling vulnerable, which will probably be often. Don't suffer in silence; you are not alone. Harvest your eggs even if you aren't sure about children. It's better to have the option than not. And most of all, be gentle with yourself—you just stepped into a whirlwind. Allow yourself time to process and grieve. And as far as treatment decisions go, do your research, ask lots of questions, tune out the noise around you, and do what feels right to you—it's your life.

*Has cancer changed how you see adversity?*
I certainly do not get upset over "little" things as often as I used to. I've always been an anxious, easily flustered person, but these days I reserve my panic attacks for doctors' offices, scans, port draws,

etc. I think getting diagnosed with cancer forces a person to face adversity head on.

*What one word defines you?*

Determined. I am determined to live an awesome life, a life not dictated by my treatments or side effects, or cancer in general. I am determined to love the beautiful people in my life. I am determined to contribute to this world in a meaningful way.

---------------------------------------------------------

Dear expensive hair, stay out of my eyes please. Also, this is what the end of Ibrance look like (note the eye-bags).

Peace and love to you all!

## CANCER ANNIVERSARY (THE METASTATIC ONE—SORT OF)
### NOVEMBER 6, 2017

This is a week of cancer-related anniversaries, and I'll be receiving scan results, too. My head and heart

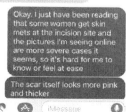

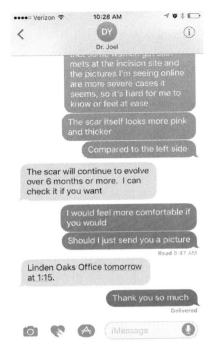

feel full, but I have great people in my life to lean on, should the results be less than good.

On this day last year, I was on my way to an appointment with the amazing Dr. Joel Yellin following the sudden appearance of an angry-looking pink rash on my mastectomy scar.

A year ago today, my mother carted a skinny, shaking-and-shivering (despite a full head of hair!) little girl to her surgeon's office. I was carefully examined, and since my surgeon is amazing, a biopsy was scheduled for the following day.

I don't identify with the little girl lying back in the chair listening to the *scritch-scritch* of her own flesh being scraped away from her. I remember the voices of my surgeon and PA sounding muffled, like they were under water. I remember a slight ringing in my ear. I remember looking down at my chest and seeing blood and iodine through the strategically cut hole-y sterile napkin gently draped over me. I remember thinking that I was dissociating. Today, I do not identify with this skinny, terrified, little girl. Today, I am sure as shit not skinny, I am still terrified, and at times, still very much a little girl. But receiving this terminal diagnosis crushed a part of me—maybe even killed it, I'm not sure. Or maybe that's just the emotional space I'm exploring lately. Lately this little girl has her outstretched hand behind her, painfully reaching to the past (possibly a glorified version of it) and looking ahead upon the fanged monster, shrieking loud as a freight train. This monster wants to swallow her whole. This, I believe, is terror. It is my terror.

It is a willful tantrum, a lack of acceptance of my reality that I'm experiencing pretty intensely right now. This first cancer-versary feels heavy.

I am, however, so glad I followed my heart and my gut and spoke up when I felt something was not right. I'm glad I pushed for a biopsy which revealed that we were not in the clear. It was this sudden and mysterious rash and biopsy of this rash that prompted the whole battery of tests. The chest CT showed the spots on both lungs, which changed my diagnosis to Stage 4 Metastatic Breast Cancer and changed my life forever.

Sometimes I think about what might have happened had I not noticed the rash, or had the rash not been present at all. I feel grateful to have had a loud flashing neon warning sign on the outside showing that something was very wrong on the inside. The rash went away after my first chemo treatment, and hasn't made a peep since. I believe that my angels were looking out for me then, and I believe they are continuing to do so.

I am ending abruptly because I just realized I'm running late. Keep me in your thoughts and prayers this week. I do not have room for bad news.

## LYMPHEDEMA
NOVEMBER 12, 2017

Dear Lymphedema,

Oh no you *didn't*. You picked the wrong girl to eff with. (Trying to clean up my language, we'll see how long this lasts…)

So, last Monday, the crease of my right arm (above my elbow) felt sore and achy. Didn't think much of it since I'm a busy (and clumsy) girl. Tuesday, it was achy, slightly swollen, and also red and hot to touch. My thoughts were: blood clot, cellulitis, lymphedema. I decided to call Pluta. They did not seem very concerned. I had an upcoming appointment on Thursday and "worst case scenario, it's a blood clot, so we can order an ultrasound on Thursday if it's still swollen then." Fine. I asked if I should wear my lymphedema sleeve just in case; they said that wasn't a bad idea. So I did. And I slept in it. (Apparently you are not supposed to do that. Oops). Wednesday morning, I woke up, looked at my arm, and then noticed that my hand looked a little bit puffy. And this began the longest-feeling state of panic in my whole life. Okay, maybe not my whole life, but in recent days.

Long story short, I called Pluta four times, waited around for them to call me back, called my primary, finally said, "Screw this waiting shit!" and went to the ED, waited for five hours with my mom, made friends with the triage nurse, got a room (my three best friends brought me food and love), had an ultrasound (unanticipated PTSD kicked in—brought me back to diagnostic ultrasound), had bloodwork, and at 10 p.m. I was discharged with no answer other than "edema."

I have lymphedema, a permanent, incurable, disfiguring, and not-at-all-understood condition.

Stay tuned. If I do actually have it, you can expect my potty mouth to kick back in full swing.

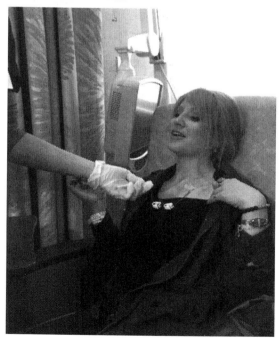

## QUESTIONS AND BLABBING
FEBRUARY 3, 2018

*"It's that knife-edge of uncertainty where we come alive to our truest power."*
—lady from a documentary I watched a year ago (I saved the quote). (Sorry, don't know who she is…)

Do I agree with this? If I'm being honest, it really depends on the day. Things have felt turbulent lately, and I have been more anxious, more sensitive, and certainly more tearful than usual. I have my scan this month, following this last month and a half of dose reductions and scheduling adjustments of Ibrance due to neutropenia. I have discontinued the Chinese herbs I was getting from a Doctor in California due to the inconvenience, terrible taste, and cost. I have been a little lax on certain things (like a decrease in the overall number of salads per week), and a little more diligent in other respects (like personal training 2 times a week, gym 5-6). I am quite nervous about this scan because of all of these shifts. And because I'm on so many supplements and drugs, it's hard to pinpoint which of those things aid in keeping me alive, which are inconsequential and therefore not worth sticking to (and of course, which might be harmful—though fingers crossed that none of them are—with the exception of the pharmaceuticals and the laundry lists of side effects).

This constant fear and uncertainty around my treatment, around my life, and around my death weighs heavy on my mind and on my heart. And yet I'm here. I'm living and I'm loving and I'm tremendously aware of the fragility of it all. Sometimes that awareness makes me anxious and sharp-tongued and angry and explosive and sad. And sometimes it makes me completely grateful for the entirety of it. The uncertainty is a gnawing ache in the center of my chest, the clenching in my abdomen, the tears in my eyes. But this is my life now, and I'd take grappling with uncertainty and fear with the support of loved ones any day over the alternative (not being here and therefore having nothing to be uncertain about).

If someone had told me that I would be diagnosed with a cancer typically seen in 60-year-old women at the age of 26, become terminal at 27, go through the hell of chemotherapy and come out alive with a thirst for meaning and life greater than ever before, I would have said, "No way! I would have killed myself at diagnosis. No way I would have let that shit drag out." But "that shit" has been some of the most beautiful, tender, moving, powerful, soul-opening moments of my entire life.

Sometimes cancer is background noise. Sometimes it's center stage. I am grateful for both positions and spaces it occupies. Because I am here. With breath in my lungs—the same lungs, peppered with cancer. I am here.

"Don't be afraid of your heart breaking open. The heart that breaks open can hold the whole universe."

## SCAN DAY
FEBRUARY 18, 2018

Hello everyone. I've got scans (bone and CT) tomorrow (the ones I mentioned in my last post that I'm feeling pretty scared about) and would really appreciate any good thoughts, prayers, juju, and vibes sent my way. I appreciate you all more than you know. I will be sure to update once I receive the results on Thursday. We are hoping for stable or better! These 2-6 mm spots have taken up residence in the wrong lady...

Xoxo
Amy

## "SLIGHT PROGRESSION"
FEBRUARY 25, 2018

Progress usually implies good things. But cancer has a way of tossing all aspects of life on its head. My latest scan showed two areas of millimeter growth. The rest of my "spots" were stable. I sort of had a feeling about this. Like I mentioned in my last post, I've been off my game. I haven't been as great with diet, I've discontinued some herbs and supplements, and adjusting to medication dose-adjustments and various other life changes… but even if I was on my game, progression is always a possibility. And that really sucks. This lack of control is sickening and terrifying. I'm trying to keep calm and keep my head above water, and that is one hell of a challenge. I met with the NP on Thursday and she did not seem worried. We are continuing on the same treatment (Ibrance and Letrozole). Please keep me in your thoughts and prayers, I am so grateful for all of your support.

## TIRED OF BEING "SICK"
APRIL 14, 2018

I still can't wrap my head around everything that I've adjusted to over the last two years. I went from being a normal 26-year-old with a plan for a life to being a terminally ill cancer patient in the blink of an eye. I've kissed my breasts goodbye, my hair (goodbye and hello again), my ability to have children, I've watched my weight go up and down and up again, and experienced the highs and lows of my roller coaster life. And the whole time I've thought, "Things will level off. They have to."

What does that mean? Seems foolish to have ever had that thought as I sit trying to absorb and process the fact that my cancer is progressing today... my 6.7 mm guy shot up to 9.9 mm in two months. Leveling off is not a possibility in my experience of the disease (today). There is always something to adjust to, to process, to cope with, to accept. And frankly, I'm fucking TIRED of it. I'm tired of the hot flashes. I'm tired of the weight gain. I'm tired of the tearfulness.

I am working with an incredible integrative oncologist in Oregon (she came from Sloan Kettering) and she recommended I get off the wheel of failing 1st-2nd-3rd- (etc.) line treatments and pursue something that has potential curative benefit. She connected me to an immunotherapy trial at the NIH/NCI in Bethesda, Maryland. This trial appears to have "cured" a young woman like me in 2016. Unfortunately, it was determined last week that my cancer is too small for their trial at this time. That's kind of a mind fuck. So you want your cancer to *grow*?! Kinda.

I am going off of my treatment next month. To help grow my tumor for this trial, and to give myself a Fucking break. I am done playing cancer whack-a-mole. I want out. This immunotherapy trial gives me a shot at that. There are no guarantees. The only guarantee is that if I continue on toxic treatments that work for a little bit and then stop, I'll be doing that until I'm dead, and statistics say I'm about halfway there. We know that this is what tends to happen with metastatic breast cancer, as this is standard of care practice. Getting a cancer that is most commonly diagnosed in 65-year-old women in your 20s is hardly standard. I require a different approach. And if it doesn't work, it doesn't work, and we will figure that out. But I know I can't stay on these hormonal drugs much longer. If it's about quality, not quantity, then I need to do what's going to make me feel okay in the time I have left, however long that is.

This is a cranky and poorly written post because I have slept about three hours due to hot flashes and anxiety. Which is why I need a break... Thank you for thoughts and prayers as always.

# WRITING MY STORY
MAY 14, 2018

I know my pursuit of immunotherapy has made some people uncomfortable and I know some would feel more comfortable with my complying with the standard of care. I want people to know where I am with things, and also express my gratitude to you.

I appreciate your care and concern for my well-being, first and foremost. Cancer is a terrifying thing for all who are caught in its clutches—this includes those diagnosed, as well as their supports and loved ones.

What we know about metastatic breast cancer today: Women (and men) diagnosed with the disease have treatment options, not cures. These treatment options are highly toxic, and are generally only effective for short periods. When one drug stops working, the next-line treatment is implemented; from the Susan G. Komen site: *"With each line of treatment, it becomes less likely the cancer will shrink. And, if the cancer does shrink, it's often for a shorter period of time with each new drug."* It is also worth mentioning that each new drug is more toxic and more difficult for the body to handle than the last, largely due to accumulation. Your liver has to process a lot of garbage, in other words.

To give you a picture of my experience: my Ibrance and Letrozole combination is considered first-line treatment for hormone receptor positive patients like me. It worked for about 9 months, and was generally well-tolerated, minus the neutropenia and fatigue. So 9 months, feelin' okay! and then we saw progression. Yikes! Based on what we know, the next-line treatment, Exemastane, for example, will likely only work for about 7 months, and that's being generous. (I do realize, however, that every drug works differently for every person, but I'm being general here.) The next treatment maybe 4 months, and so on… for a couple more treatments (because that's all we have left). So 7 months + 4 months + 3 months + 1 month…. so, about a year and 2 months of life left if I follow this track, making me a walking statistic. Most women (and men) live between 2-5 years, and younger women tend to do worse.

I find this unacceptable. I love this life too much.

This is why I am doing everything in my power—constant research, corresponding with some of the best doctors in the country—to write a different story for myself, and for my loved ones. I know how much my supports and loved ones love me. I am so grateful for that, and I want to share this life with you.

The National Institutes of Health (NIH) are home to the most cutting edge research—particularly for cancer. I was fortunate to have been connected to Dr. Dawn Lemanne, oncologist originally from Sloan Kettering, who now practices integrative oncology in Oregon. She connected me to the folks running two immunotherapy trials under Dr. Steven Rosenberg at the NIH. He was the leader of all of the interleukin 2 discoveries (look it up), and was also featured in the documentary "Cancer: The Emperor of All Maladies" (the book, too). I have been told that if there is going to be a cure in our lifetime, it will come from him and his incredible team. And I believe it. I believe in immunotherapy. (Also, look up Judy Anderson/ TIL trial).

So I stopped my medication for 1.5 months. I will be rescanned in June, and hopefully the 9.9 mm nodule has increased a little bit (or those dust specks have disappeared completely—there's documentation of people in my position stopping hormonal treatment and having their disease disappear at their next scan... that would obviously be ideal:). In addition, stopping treatment is also a therapeutic measure for people who have had two hormonal therapies: (me)

Antihormonal therapy withdrawal could be considered a therapeutic measure, at least in some selected patients, such as patients treated with two or more hormone therapies with a good clinical response before disease progression and without life-threatening metastases. A short duration of aromatase inhibitor or tamoxifen withdrawal may be considered before starting additional anticancer treatment.

## disclosure

The authors declare no conflict of interest.

## References

1. Small EJ, Vogelzang NJ. Second-line hormonal therapy for advanced prostate cancer: a shifting paradigm. J Clin

Are there guarantees? This is cancer. Further, this is life. There are no guarantees in anything. But I am not going to be a statistic. As I said in my article and probably in other blog posts, I am done playing cancer-whack-a-mole. My case is so unusual, so my approach needs to be different. The standard of care is not for me.

Thank you all for your support and concern for my well-being, and most importantly, thank you for your love.

*Editor's note:*

The essays and poems framed in the following pages were written
and shared while Amy took part in the spring 2018 session
of the Bristol Bookends memoir writing class
at the Bristol Library, Bristol, NY

# The Wisdom of the Willow

When I was a young girl—maybe four or five—to escape the shrieks and screeches of my younger (autistic) brother's tantrums, I would slip outside to sit beneath the willow tree in the backyard of my childhood home. Countless strands of leaves like long hair on a woman—I would often stand beneath the enormous tree and try to reach the thin branches to practice weaving *over, under,* and then later, braiding. These leaves always looked and felt very much alive to me, dancing, giddy with laughter and excitement in the wind, gently swaying and shimmering in lighter breezes, with a faint sound of whispers. Sometimes I would grab clusters of branches in my hands and try to swing across the yard like Tarzan; sometimes I would get a couple of feet under me before falling to the ground, other times the branches would snap instantly, and I would fall onto my knees. And when Disney's Pocahontas came out, I was telling all my secrets to "Grandmother Willow" of Partridgeberry Way, singing to her, and asking for her guidance. We had a hammock nestled beneath it and another tree in that yard. I always felt cradled by the willow directly when swinging in the hammock, somehow.

Years later, I tried to climb the tree, but always needed a boost from an older cousin or neighbor. I could only get to the first "converging point"; I was not tall enough or strong enough to hoist myself up to the next one. On our eighth birthday celebration, my cousin Michael (whose birthday is two days before mine) fell out of the tree and broke his arm. There would be no more tree-climbing after that, at least not in front of grown-ups.

When I was 19, my mother moved out of that home. I was living in the dorms of Nazareth College then. Her new house was being built about two miles away, in a new housing development.

Today, when I visit her, I go for runs to visit my childhood neighborhood. Much has changed, but Willow remains. I wonder if the new residents retreat to the back yard for moments of escape, or peace. Do they have a little one who braids her hair, and whispers secrets to her? ♦

# Once a Singer, Forever a Singer

The buzzing, ringing sound of a choir perfectly in tune is one that instantly triggers the "yawn-space" in the back of my throat to lift and expand, my eyebrows to rise as if I'm about to start singing, and my eyes to well (slightly). I close my eyes and a surge of warm light from the ceiling rushes in, I see tall risers in an auditorium of velvet-green seats surrounded by brick walls, a sea of long, black dresses and tuxedos in various concert halls, ornate cathedrals in Italy and churches throughout NY. In place of whoever is conducting in the present moment, I see the long arms of Mrs. Sargent, my fittingly-named choir teacher, passionately waving, the distinctive furrow in her brow. I feel the almost-pleasant "pre-nausea" bubbling in my stomach I used to feel so often before making an entrance in a solo with the R-H Singers, my high school select choir.

*****

The R-H Singers (otherwise known as "Singers" in our district) developed in the 1970's and were known throughout the community for their talent, academic achievement, acts of service, as well as their gigantic fundraising undertakings for trips overseas (ask any current or former Singer about the can and bottle drive and you are guaranteed to get a shudder…). From the first time I heard them perform the National Anthem in 5th grade, I knew I needed to be a part of it.

I was part of a group of select elementary school students asked to sing at the start-of-the-year superintendent's conference. Elementary, middle, and high school (regular mixed choir, and R-H Singers) each had their own song, as well as one final piece all together. The ceremony began with the Singers' National Anthem, and the moment Mrs. Sargent raised her baton and breathed in an audible downbeat, I knew I was going to hear something moving. It was an acapella arrangement, in perfect tune-shimmering, buzzing, and completely enchanting. And then, the final phrase:

*"O'er the la-and of the free-**Eeeeeee!**...."*

A glorious leap to a High C (though I didn't know what note it was at the time), sung by a curly-haired girl in the front row on the right side of the risers. *I'm going to be that high singing girl.* Maybe it was more a gut feeling than a thought.

*"And the home of the braaaaave!"*

I remember bouncing around at my grandmother's house after school with all of my cousins, annoying them all to no end with my relentless singing. I sang the ending of the anthem over and over and over that year... playing with what I now understand as "resonance", intuitively adjusting the shape and aperture of my lips, trying to find what offered the greatest sense of buzzing in my face. I recall trying to see if it was possible to reach the high note without raising my eyebrows. (It wasn't). How blissfully curious I was then! This whole magical world was beginning to unfold for me. It was my world, alone. And it was safe. I did not need to share it with Ryan (my brother), or my parents, or my cousins, or my friends, unless I wanted to, of course. It was mine.

*****

It almost didn't happen... When I was in middle school, my mother announced we would be looking into private schooling (Allendale Columbia, Harley), as Rush Henrietta was becoming a bit "worrisome". The high school was having some issues with fights, and my mother did not want me in that kind of environment. She was a high school teacher at the time, and her school district had many problems of this nature, so she felt it was in my best interests to pursue an education free of that kind of trouble.

At first, I was excited because there would be *placement exams!* I was the type of student who found the opportunity to prove my knowledge of subject material completely thrilling- unless that subject was math, in which case I would have rather hid in a cave somewhere. Then, I was sad. I would miss my friends, of course. But my real sadness was that I would miss the opportunity to become an R-H Singer. I begged and pleaded with her to let me stay in Rush-Henrietta if I was accepted into the group. She finally agreed.

*****

I auditioned for the group in 9th grade, before entering the high school (we had a Ninth Grade Academy). We were required to learn a snippet from a large patriotic work the Singers had performed at the Kennedy Center the year before. Standing face-to-face with "The Sarge" felt how I imagine being suspended in air would feel. There were no smiles, no nods of approval, no anecdotal conversation. I remember shaking, I remember a slight quiver in my voice that matched the one in my knees, neither of which I was used to. But I also remember walking out of that room with the knowledge that my little world was opening before my eyes.

*****

I was 16 when I had my first overseas adventure. I was singing with the R-H Singers. We traveled throughout Italy in just 11 days. My brain does not recall order. I relive the trip in colorful bursts and smells and feelings. I remember covering my shoulders with a shawl as all 67 of us stood in line to enter St. Peter's Basilica. Walking inside, gazing up to the ceiling, I felt like we were all ants milling about, overwhelmed by delicious beauty in every direction. It was covered in gold on the inside. My friend Holly and I sang the "Laudamus te" from Vivaldi's Gloria Mass for a Sunday Mass there. Hearing the ring of our sound fill the air, expand, and continue long after we were cut off was dizzying. We gave several impromptu performances on the Spanish Steps, sang spirituals on the gondolas in Venice while the boatmen rolled their eyes and likely insulted us in their beautifully buoyant and musical language. (Our guide joked that they hadn't yet had their espresso, so we figured they weren't saying anything nice.) I remember arguing with my mother about one petty thing after another throughout that trip (because I was 16 and she was my mother), and both of us agreeing that she would never chaperone a school trip ever again.

Sneaking wine in our un-chaperoned time. Getting completely separated from the group and lost in Venice (but figured while I was lost, I might as well shop, and I bought myself some beautiful glass pieces…). Getting lost in Milan trying to find the Duomo, where we were to rehearse next after lunch, asking a group of cute Italian boys (in poor Italian), *"M-m- mi scuzi, dove il Duomo?"* They looked at one another and laughed as they pointed directly ahead. Getting lost in Florence and ending up in a leather shop (there's a theme here…). I remember countless acapella performances of Beatles tunes on the streets of Rome, Florence, Sienna, Milan, Treviso because it seemed that's all the Italians wanted to hear… I remember a rainy day in Florence, huddling together singing Edward Elgar's gentle, lilting "As torrents in summer…," making eye contact with an older man peering out his window and smoking a cigarette up above us (why I decided to look up, I have no idea, perhaps looking for validation that a raindrop did indeed fall on my head and not pigeon poo).

After our last concert at a small church in Treviso, we were served fresh cantaloupe and prosciutto, along with plenty of wine—alcohol was strictly forbidden throughout the trip until that night. I was a vegetarian then, but I dove right into that prosciutto-melon combo like a seasoned carnivore. A choir of 53 students… all of us in a choir of tears on that last night. We got drunk off wine and the balmy magic of moonlight in one of the most beautiful places on the planet on that electric evening in July. The choir of chirping crickets in the church courtyard even seemed to be for us. ♦

# Awaken, My "Sole"

Every morning now, the sweet (but persistent) chirping of the birds outside my window is the first sound to greet my ears. Their waking cries a beckon for me to do the same.

I stretch out my arms horizontally, picturing the distance between my shoulder blades gently widening as I sit up slowly on the edge of my bed.

I lengthen my spine, roll my shoulders back and down, and remember just for a moment what it felt like to dance for all those years (though I hardly considered myself a dancer). Port de bras forward, then the other way, tiny clicks like the snapping of buttons up and down my back.

Drearily I make my way to the sizzling coffee pot, which has just awoken as well, and I am grateful for the person who created the automatic setting on the coffee machine. Resting against the counter as I pour, I take some belly breaths, and then some sips. The red curtains give a pink and orange cast to the sunlight coming through the living room window. I wonder if it's going to be a hot one today...

I put on my gym capris, a long-sleeved t-shirt—a safe choice for any early spring morning—followed by my headband to keep my now-brown and curly hair out of my face. I feel enormous gratitude for this hair, however different it may be, for there was a time not long ago when I had no hair at all. I lace up my cobalt blue Nikes, head to the door and open.

A surge of air rushes to me, brushing my face, sending my chestnut curls fluttering. I drink it in. Birds, bugs, buses, cars, thumping music, the lulling voices of talk-radio, splashes of color in every direction, and the golden glow from above tickling my nose—I can almost feel my freckles coming to the surface. Every morning, this life greets me.

I crack my head from side to side, and then I'm off. Sweat dangles from the hair that has come loose from my pony tail, and I feel the cool beads trickling down my neck. This, too, is a gift. I fill my lungs, release, and repeat to the steady ostinato within my footsteps. I am home. ♦

*Sailing with my friend Mackenzie, Canandaigua Lake, June 30, 2018*

## BURNOUT
JULY 12, 2018

WOW! It's been such a long time... I think my last entry was in May, and now we are in JULY?!?! So much has happened in the last few months. Things have certainly been a bit more adventurous than I'm comfortable with, but I don't really have much of a choice in these matters. Sometimes I feel like I'm just along for the ride; the cancer is what's running the show here.

I was invited to the NIH at the end of June to begin the screening for the clinical trial I was pursuing. Holy crap, is that place huge. I will update at some point on the specifics of my experience there, but I wanted to paste in a sort of journal entry that I wrote in the days leading up to my travel to Bethesda, Maryland (NIH). This was something I was planning on editing and submitting to TheUnderBelly.org. Today when I read it, I feel such deep sadness. These little erosions along the way—blood count trouble, stopping treatment, progression, new sites of disease—all of it makes me wonder if this is where it all begins, if THIS right HERE is the

208

beginning of the end, the declining, the turning for the worse, crossing the Rubicon. I remember thinking that I was beginning to decline when I had to stop taking Ibrance due to neutropenia. And today, the bulk of my anxiety exists around these thoughts and fears.

I don't believe I see this disease entirely "accurately"… I think what I mean is that my experience is just that, my own. Statistics haven't really helped me to understand or process my disease because I'm not actually represented in them, being young, and metastatic is not incredibly common (though I wouldn't say it's particularly rare, either, given that I interact with several young Stage 4 women through support groups and online communities every day). I don't believe I'm always as mindful of the amount and degree of suffering inherent in this disease as I should be; I tend to get caught up in fear of the future, and I don't think I practice gratitude for my present circumstances because I often get stuck in a place of anger or victimhood. In truth, I know I've had it so much easier than other women I know who are currently suffering physically as well as psychologically, or they are no longer with us at all. So yes, I feel pretty blessed—two years in and living a fairly comfortable life; I'm still able to exercise and do what I love. No, it hasn't been a walk in the park, but as far as metastatic breast cancer is concerned, I am often referred to as one of my doctors' healthiest patients. I don't know if that's comforting or downright terrifying.

Anyway, this is my journal entry in the week leading up to my NIH trip:

*In this moment, I am encountering heavy resistance to writing. This entire week, I've welcomed the excuses, the distractions (food, Netflix), even the chores! Seriously, my kitchen is unusually clean. Avoidance is something I am familiar with. A cousin of denial, avoidance (for me presently) is undergirded by undeniable fear.*

*I was accepted into the NIH immunotherapy trial last week. I am absolutely thrilled and absolutely 110% terrified.*

*After about two months off my medication, all of my tiny 2-4 mm pulmonary nodules remained exactly the same. The only spot that grew was the nodule that was right on the cusp, measuring in at 9.9 back in April. This most recent scan shows that it now measures 1.5 cm; the trial requires a lesion that is between 1 and 2 cm, so my body certainly delivered right smack dab in the middle! That feels awfully serendipitous. In addition, no new growths were present. When deciding to go off my anti-neoplastic, hormone-depleting, side-effect-filled medication, I was aware of the potential risks. I was counseled by my long-distance Integrative Oncologist, and she laid out two reasonable paths to entering the trial. One was to go off my medication for a month or two and hope that growth occurred only where it needed to (9.9 mm spot on my left lung increase to a 1-2 cm spot). The other was to stay on the current meds until we see the progression we need over a longer (more miserable) stretch of time. Initially, I went ahead with Lupron (ovarian suppression received once a month) as usual, in April, with the plan to continue Ibrance and Letrezole for the rest of the month. After three days of the Ibrance and Letrezole, it dawned on me: It really made no sense for me to accumulate more toxicity and misery if I was having break-through progression anyway. If I wanted to get into the trial quickly and efficiently, stopping my treatment was the best way. So I stopped my Ibrance/Letrezole combo, and felt some safety in the fact that I still had some protection from the Lupron I had received that month. My transition to "No Meds Land" would be a gradual one. In May, I did not receive the Lupron. I felt a sense of relief with that decision (because menopause sucks, and I have never been more uncomfortable inside my skin with the constant sweating and weight gain if I even LOOK in the general direction of, say, a cookie, despite my running 10-20 miles per week). I also felt worry, I suppose, because worry is a natural response to terrifying things, and the growth of metastatic cancer, whether it's intended or not, is certainly terrifying. Would the progression get out of hand now that I was truly off everything?*

*Many nights in May in particular, I was startled awake by visions of maggots swimming around inside my organs. When my breath would come to me, it was shallow and short. I've learned that emotional safety is something I need to actively cultivate now, in this life with cancer, otherwise known as, my life. There are triggers everywhere. Hospital waiting rooms, someone else's shitty scan results, your own shitty scan results, the death of someone in the MBC community, health insurance coverage under threat... I am dancing this dance to the best of my ability. Some days it looks like an adagio movement in a ballet, graceful and refined; other days, it looks like a seizure. I found myself taking inventory of how I was feeling. Checking with a capital "C" as I've done since the beginning of this ride. Tightness in my chest? No. Wheezing? No. Shortness of breath? None. Was I feeling well? Yes. So I tried my best to carry on, revisiting my checklist as often as I needed to.*

*I cannot express how much better I started to feel just three weeks after I discontinued the dynamic duo. I thought I felt pretty great on Ibrance. I was exercising regularly; my energy seemed good, no real physical symptoms aside from hot flashes and the ridiculous weight gain associated with menopause (and believe me, I am NOT downplaying the wretchedness of menopause). In general though, I thought I was feelin' good. Just three weeks after calling it quits, I was no longer anemic. My neutrophils, hemoglobin, hematocrit, iron, MCV and basically all of my CBC looked astonishingly healthy. I had no idea how worn out I was until I started to feel better.*

*I leave in two days for the NIH. This first visit is really just a meet-and-greet, with some brain scans and pulmonary function tests tossed in. Even though I have a schedule of where to be and when, I have no idea what to expect. What does this place look like? What does it smell like? Is it cold and sterile in energy and vibe? (I'm sure it is sterile in the literal sense…) Are the nurses and doctors scary? I'm experiencing some fear around this brain MRI business. I've never had one, and I'm pretty scared of the possibility of brain metastasis, which could disqualify me from the trial. I don't believe this is very likely at this point in my disease. My metastases are quite small and not widespread, contained in the lungs. I am hormone receptor positive, HER2 negative. Triple negative and HER2 positive breast cancers have the highest occurrence of brain metastasis. Still, anything is possible. I'm not really allowing myself to think too far ahead in this respect; I know that whatever the case may be, it will be dealt with.*

*And that's really all one can do, right? Take things as they come, and deal with them. And if you need medical marijuana or the occasional Ativan in order to do that, so be it…*

One of the toughest aspects of this disease (for me) is the constant evolution of fear. It seems the fear has a way of becoming more defined, more specific as time goes on with this disease. A new circumstance arises, and then your brain wonders, "Oh, so maybe *this* will be the thing that kills me." Maybe the re-focusing of fear is just reflective of the initial shock wearing off and fading into a gradual acceptance.

When I was first diagnosed, I was just terrified of death, period. Nothing in particular about it other than the ceasing-to-be-here because my mind wouldn't really allow me to unpack it any farther. Death had a vagueness about it to me then. Since then, death has become a focus in my world. Living with this disease for the past two years has steered me toward relationships with many women who have also faced it, and are sadly no longer with us. I've seen the horrible ways in which people with cancer die. The decline that starts off slow, and then takes off at lightning speed. With each of my new cancer "events," I always wonder, is this my decline? The slippery slope? I suppose generally, the diagnosis of cancer was the start of my decline, but since I've felt physically well (aside from drug side effects) from the beginning, it's hard to imagine that I began declining at 26. In all actuality, if a diagnosis of cancer occurs around 10 years after the initial cell went rogue, then I've been steadily declining since I was 16 years old. What an odd thing to think about.

Why all this talk of declining, you might be thinking? Well. At the NIH screening, four lesions were discovered on my brain. Having no neurological symptoms, having HER2 NEGATIVE disease, and having very little tumor burden in general (contained in lungs, or so we thought) this was not on my, or my oncologists' radar. Can anyone explain to me why we are not giving brain MRIs at the point of diagnosis of metastatic disease? And I do not accept the "We scan when people develop symptoms" answer, because by that point, the treatment options are less successful, and more invasive, impacting cognition and quality of life in general. This is a systemic thing that really requires attention. More on this in a future post.

No one knows how long these lesions have been there, and that's pretty scary to me. The good news is they were discovered very small (hence no symptoms), and I'm able to have Stereotactic Radiosurgery, which is a type of radiation. It allows for very precise treatment to small areas with about 95% effectiveness, and very few side effects. Right on!

So tomorrow is my birthday, and I get to have fun at a radiation mapping appointment at the hospital, along with a brain MRI at 7:30 p.m. (like wtf?!). I'm complaining, but only slightly, because they are squeezing me in quickly so that I can complete the treatment, have another scan that demonstrates stability (as far as cancer goes HA!) in the brain, and then head right back to Bethesda, Maryland, for round #2 at the NIH... I've also been completely off *all* medication for two months now. I have to remain off medication until the NIH removes the lesion from my lung, and then I can resume any treatment my oncologist and I decide upon. I'm feeling pretty fantastic off the meds, but of course, that's a bit scary, especially because I've felt fantastic all while things have been growing inside of me...

## MY VEINS ARE SLIPPERY, ROLLY BASTARDS, AND MY PORT IS MIS-BEHAVING, TOO. WHAT TO DO?

JULY 15, 2018

Friday was my birthday, and it was also a full day of appointments. In the morning I went to the hospital for the radiation simulation.

They molded a warm mesh mask to the contours of my face and let it sit for 30 minutes or so. Not super pleasant or comfortable as you are breathing out of tiny holes…

I went to my MRI at 7:30 p.m. I had to leave my own family birthday party—part 2 of the celebration is today, though, which should be more relaxed…!

So the MRI: Too bad I have no veins and no one bothered to tell me they wouldn't be using my port for this brain study. So after nurses examined my arm, they agreed I had no veins to offer them, and got the doctor to change the order for the contrast administration.

Only too bad my port has decided to stop working… accessed just fine but with no blood return… This has never happened to me before. Blame it on Friday the 13th?

So these images from the MRI are necessary for mapping out my treatment for stereotactic radiosurgery. No MRI = no radiation. Hoping this issue can be resolved tomorrow so I am able to resume my scheduled radiation this week. Time is of the essence as I am still trying to enter this clinical trial, and that requires me staying off meds until after surgery… and staying off meds for many months in a row (while it feels physically great!) is also a bit terrifying.

I will try to keep things up to date here, but I'm not able to make any promises as things feel quite hectic…

## NOTE TO SELF
JULY 17, 2018

Amy,

When you enter your brain scan today, this is what I want you to think about: The day before you turned 29, you got to hold a baby deer!*

Onward!

Amy

---

*Link available here: myterminallife.org*

# I'M FUMING. I'M BREATHING.
AUGUST 3, 2018

In the last two days, I have lost TWO separate blog posts. I have no idea where in cyberspace they are, but I am so angry and frustrated, and sincerely hoping this one doesn't disappear into the abyss as well...

The first post that was lost was a reflection on my experience with Stereotactic Radiosurgery. I also discussed my latest research focus: the systemic issues around diagnostics and screening for the brain in the metastatic breast cancer setting. Perhaps when I am not riled up as I am in this moment, I will try again.

The second post was about returning to my regular yoga practice. When I discovered my posts were gone, I took myself right to yoga. I needed to breathe.

I don't have the motivation to try to recall what I said right now. I'm too annoyed with the whole thing.

Today has been an odd day, with energy that seems to keep shifting and evolving. I am trying to become more flexible. Not just physically, but with my whole being. Yoga helps facilitate this in me, and it's good to be back.

I'm pushing through this brick-wall-resistance to write.

Yesterday I received a very overwhelming report (18 pages!) on my RGCC test. This is a circulating tumor cell test which looks at several different aspects of the cancer, including tumor-related genes (over-expression or down-regulation), resistance, as well as sensitivity to pharmaceuticals and other treatment methods. These results are super complex and overwhelming to look at, and did I mention it's an EIGHTEEN-PAGE REPORT??

I am not a patient person. And I feel like I am sitting on a gold mine of information, and because I don't have a medical degree, I do not know what most of it means in terms of the overall picture. That doesn't stop my imagination from conjuring up the worst case scenario, with every "HIGH RISK" "RAPID CELL PROLIFERATION" highlighted in red on every page, I think of myself breathing into lungs that are incessantly filling with broken versions of my DNA, and I wonder if... or when... I will actually feel it. And lately, I've felt a sensation (not pain, not discomfort, just "something") below my right rib, the location of the liver. Would that be where my long-legged cancer is adventuring to next? My liver enzymes were fine last week—how long does it take for cancer in the liver to be reflected in a lab...?

What is my path? Well, unfortunately, my path is determined by ITS path. I said in a recent post, and I'll say it again: sometimes I don't feel like this life is mine. Sometimes I am forced to respond to however the cancer is behaving at that particular moment. There's not a ton of freedom or space or ease in that aspect of my world... which is essentially my whole world. So I don't know where anything is headed, honestly. I have my hopes, but I don't know what's happening inside my body, or what's been happening since my last CT in June. I have scans at the end of this month, and if the brain looks stable, I head back to the NIH. That's about all I know right now. And this:

I sit in chair pose. I sink my heels deep into this life, this moment. I root down, I feel the subtle lift in my toes as I anchor myself lower, the burn of the lactic acid swirling in my thighs. I straighten my legs and fold myself over, reach my head and arms to the ground, a sigh for my body. I lift halfway, shining the crown of my head to the front of the room that always smells like nag champa. I peel my shoulders away from my ears in this space, I search for ease in this pose. I fold forward. I rise up, reaching my hands to the warm ceiling lights, rooting into all four corners of my feet. And I breathe. And I breathe. And I breathe.

I fold forward again, this time, ah, yes, a bit nicer on my low back, allowing my arms to hold opposite elbows, swaying in rag doll, honoring the heaviness of my head in this inversion. I feel release in my jaw, my neck, my low back as I slowly, lightly swing from side to side. I place my palms down on my mat. I step my feet back into high plank, the subtle earthquake in my abdomen reminding me of my strength. I lower slowly to the ground, untuck my toes, open across my chest while my palms ground into the mat, sending my weight forward. I press my hips to the back of the room for downward facing dog and feel a zip up my hamstrings. And I breathe. And I breathe. And I breathe.

….

I leave class. I am breathing.

## **THIS BODY**
AUGUST 14, 2018

This body went up into an assisted handstand today. This body played in crow pose. This body is capable of so much more than I give it credit for. So much of my life is centered around the various ways this body of mine is failing me. But there is so much this body does right.

This body, 27 lbs heavier than it has ever been, "sicker" than it has ever been, still serves me well. I'd like to try to remember this when I am feeling down. I am healthy. I am strong. And I am determined to live well.

And in reality, I already am.

Namaste.

## ANXIETY
AUGUST 21, 2018

Racing thoughts, clenching jaw, shoulders creeping up to my ear lobes, a tightening in my stomach, heart beating wildly, can't sit still, and can't move forward.

Perseverating. Replaying. Constant worry.

I am trying to make sense of my past, my 20-something years of life. I think this type of reflection is probably normal in the wake of trauma. I'm trying to understand where I have come from. Who I am. Placing pieces of my puzzle together. Replaying events, conversations, asking myself questions, trying to be compassionate with what arises because self-hatred gets nobody anywhere except further entrenched in darkness.

I have feelings of gratitude, and also sadness and remorse and perhaps even regret for things I've said and how I've behaved with people close to me. I am very lucky to have the support of family and friends, especially after my tumultuous college years (my depression and often mal-adaptive coping made my mother and others worry about me constantly). And even more, especially after my lashing out when I was first diagnosed. I really can't believe how awful I was in the beginning of all of this. I find myself ruminating on that time constantly, and when I'm alone, I often cry.

I am also facing an uncertain future.

The future is uncertain for everyone. But I think those of us with cancer experience a more in-your-face type of uncertainty. Heaviness looming over one's shoulder, hanging like a cloud of personal oppression with the weight of a million bricks concentrated in one's thoracic region.

Lately my anxiety has been extremely... present. I'm managing okay, but I have been actively coping constantly it seems.

Next Tuesday, I have scans. Brain MRI, and CT of chest abdomen and pelvis. I have had NO cancer treatment in over four months, aside from localized brain radiation (SRS). So who knows what things will look like. But really, I'm most concerned with the stability of the brain, since that's what's required for me to re-enter the NIH.

I keep coming back to gratitude. I am so grateful for the love and support I've had from so many people. Especially those I haven't always shown my gratitude to (mostly family). I love you.

And… thank you, anxiety, for showing me I am very much alive. And that I want nothing more than to live a life of love and peace. And I think that journey starts within.

## SHARP EDGES
AUGUST 22, 2018

Sometimes cancer feels like a very complex etch-a-sketch. You begin with a single point (diagnosis), and from there, your experience grows, taking numerous turns, sharp, jagged, and angular.

I am wondering lately: how does one soften these sharp edges? How do people lean into the places they fear the most? **Do they do that? What does it look like?**

How can I soften my sharpest edges? Often in yoga, the teacher will liken the challenge of "staying" in a pose—really sinking the heels into the mat, really activating the breath, really lengthening when the impulse is to shrink—to challenges in life.

How can I find ease in this very crunchy and uncomfortable pose?

I feel like much of the time, I'm either saturating myself in the sadness and fear, or running away from it. Neither option feels right, or particularly good. What does it take to integrate the reality of the situation with hope? I have moments of both in isolation, but they very rarely synchronize. Things are either great and hopeful, or bleak. It's harder to allow these things to coexist. But I think that's what's needed here.

How? Is it through finding connection? To spirit? To people? To facts? To stories? I don't know.

Am I bringing any ease to my dis-ease? What would that look like? Is it in my constant state of active coping? My self-care routine? I would like to find the ease. I have faith that it exists.

Sometimes I feel like I live in a state of inescapable fear. This angers me. And saddens me. It scares me to think that my life will have been about how I coped with terminal illness and not about who I really am in the end. I think aspects of my identity got royally fucked, for lack of a better word, simply because of where I was in my life when I was diagnosed. 26 years old. On the verge of huge transition, moving to a new city to start graduate school, ready to start something new and examine my life through fresh eyes and the perspective new life experience often brings.

Well, I certainly have had shifts in perspective (I guess that part would have been true regardless). The world as I knew it, or anticipated it, was within my reach. And then, in a two-minute phone call, it vanished.

On April 11th, 2016, my inescapable fear was born. And it has not left my side or subsided, but has since settled deeply into my being. It has changed shape, color, and size many times, but it is always there. It is inescapable.

I am trying to see if that inescapable-ness can be transmuted into comfort somehow. When you can feel the breath of death on your neck no matter how fast or far you're running, maybe the answer is to stop running. Maybe the answer is to turn around for just a few moments and look and see and feel. Maybe death is not jagged and harsh as it feels to the living. Maybe it is soft and round. After all, death should have roundness to fit inside life's circle. Or maybe that's just my desire for resolution, my hope for ease to exist for all when life no longer does.

Where can we find that softness? Where can I find it? Is it in living well despite cancer? Or living well because of it? How are those things the same? How are they different?

I'm searching. In the days leading up to these pretty significant scans, I am searching for ease. I guess that's all I know now.

## INDOLENCE
### SEPTEMBER 3, 2018

This week was a huge week for me. I had all my scans on Tuesday, and played the waiting game 'til Wednesday afternoon. I received an email from my coordinating nurse at the NIH saying that she had my scans, but was missing the scan reports, so as soon as she receives them, they would be getting in touch with me; I was "on their radar," and I should hear from them by Tuesday, since Monday is a holiday. I called Pluta to request the reports be faxed over to the NIH ASAP. I spoke to Erin, my NP, who was able to tell me the preliminary reports for the CT's (they hadn't been finalized yet), the MRI-Head hadn't yet been reviewed.

So: in almost five months off ALL treatment, there is no evidence of disease in my abdomen or pelvis. The innumerable 2-4 mm pulmonary nodules in both lungs have stayed inactive, with the exception of the nodule of interest to the NIH—previously measured 1.5 cm, currently 2.2 cm. Seven mm. In five months off treatment, my disease has grown 7 mm. A US dime is 17.9 mm. Seven mm is not very significant growth. My disease is approximately the size of a peanut. What sweet relief! This was not what I had expected. I truthfully expected there to be disease in my liver, and more lesions in my lungs. My lung mets actually grew just as much on the Ibrance… makes me wonder if it did anything for me aside from causing side effects.

Erin told me she would try to nudge Radiology to read my scans quickly, and that she would call me if she heard anything. Five o'clock on Wednesday came and still no word, so I figured I would be finding out at my appointment Thursday afternoon.

In just one month following stereotactic radiosurgery, my brain metastases have nearly vanished. And radiation continues to have effect months following treatment, so we aren't seeing the full impact of the radiation yet. Considering that all I needed to hear was "stable" for the clinical trial eligibility requirement, this is amazing news.

My NP referred to my disease as "indolent" and "slow-growing." Can you imagine? My cancer has never been described to me in that way; in fact, it has always been very much the opposite— "aggressive" "fast-growing" "high proliferation rate" "nuclear grade 3." Those are words I'm used to. Slow and lazy cancer is definitely a new and welcome concept to me.

Good scan results have always been a bit confusing to me. There's an added layer of complexity when good scan results = growth. Back in April I was HOPING my disease would grow in order to enter the clinical trial—what a mental shift that was!

I want so badly to stay in the present and relish the joy and happiness and relief. But I find this difficult. I think I've grown accustomed to waiting for the other shoe to drop, I think that's just life with cancer. If not now, when? After my phone call with Erin,

226

I started to question if these were actually my results, if perhaps they confused me with someone else.

Cancer is so jerky. I feel like I'm always on the edge of my seat, even when things are "calm." I don't fully trust the calm. I think the last two years have cued a constant low-grade anxiety like a background hum that can turn up without warning.

I am so grateful, and truthfully, so scared for what lies ahead. I think that's okay. Tomorrow I should hear back from the NIH. I'll write a more thoughtful response to all of this once I know exactly what is happening, but I definitely wanted to write an update on the facts and where things stand now.

Thank you for all the love, kindness, and support.

## AWAKE AGAIN
SEPTEMBER 10, 2018

I started writing this on Saturday around 3 a.m.:

Every so often I wake up around 3 a.m., the "witching hour." It just so happens that I saw "The Nun" tonight (horror movie), so my trips to the bathroom / to the kitchen for water have been extra harrowing.

I can't sleep. I've suffered bouts of insomnia before. I actually slept terribly when I was on Lupron, Ibrance, and Letrezole, as well as my twice-daily thyroid medication. I am no longer on hormonal treatment, and my endocrinologist changed my thyroid meds at my very first appointment, as well as the dosing schedule. He told me to stop taking it at night as thyroid hormones are stimulants and were likely a huge piece of my insomnia puzzle. Since that appointment in July, my sleep has become more regular. But every once in a while, I encounter nights like this one.

I'm woken up by a nightmare, sometimes thrashing about, heart beating fiercely, usually damp with sweat. My first move is typically to the bathroom, then the kitchen for water, then back to bed. And then the thinking.

After I've contemplated my death from cancer, life's meaning, and my purpose within it for a while, the water I consumed begs for its exit.

Some nights I check my phone, some nights I research (that's been a thing more recently) and sometimes I put on The Office. I'm usually awake from 1 to 3 hours. Only to wake up and repeat the restlessness again, perhaps for an hour or so.

Tonight's anxiety and restlessness are due to recent events.

The NIH rejected me from the trial, based on the existence of brain metastases. Are you as shocked as I am?

I was led to believe (both in person and on the clinical trial website) that brain lesions just needed to be stable "for a bit and I'd be back in no time!" to enter the trial. (#3)

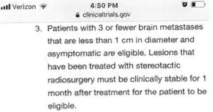

3. Patients with 3 or fewer brain metastases that are less than 1 cm in diameter and asymptomatic are eligible. Lesions that have been treated with stereotactic radiosurgery must be clinically stable for 1 month after treatment for the patient to be eligible.

4. Clinical performance status of ECOG 0 or 1.

5. Greater than or equal to 18 years of age and less than or equal to 70 years of age.

6. Willing to practice birth control during treatment and for four months after receiving the treatment.

7. Willing to sign a durable power of attorney.

8. Able to understand and sign the Informed Consent Document.

9. Hematology:
   - Absolute neutrophil count greater than 1000/mm(3) without support of filgrastim.
   - Normal WBC (> 3000/mm(3)).
   - Hemoglobin greater than 8.0 g/dl.

I am so disgusted with the NIH for this egregious "error"—I went off treatment for five months in order to be eligible for this trial, only to be told over the phone on Thursday, by some resident, "I'm not sure why you were under the impression that one month of stability is long enough, as patients are waiting years and years.."

Oh really? Years and years? First of all, this trial has not been around for "years and years." Second of all, most of us applying for this trial do not have "years and years" to wait.

I wrote to the head of the trial as well as the nurse coordinator and the doctor I saw back in June. I also reached out via text to Judy Perkins, the woman who was cured by this trial. She promptly called me; she was disgusted. She wrote to them as well. She got a response; I did not.

Judy shared their response. They do not know why I was told something different from their policy. They will change the wording on the website to "avoid ambiguity" and have a discussion with the team so that this never happens to anyone in the future.

Avoid "ambiguity"?! I was told something completely different from the reality; that's not "ambiguous," that's fucking **WRONG**, as in INACCURATE.

It sounds like I'm the only one this has ever happened to and I am sincerely thankful for that, no one should ever have to experience anything like this, especially in the case of terminal cancer. But I'm appalled that I was not part of the conversation considering that it's *my* CLINICAL CARE that was impacted, as in, my whole plan for a shot at long-term health completely shot to Hell. And when I asked the resident on the phone what she recommended I do next, her response was that she wasn't sure because she only knows the happenings in the immunotherapy branch.

So in one 4-minute phone call, my path is blown up, with no suggestion of where to put my focus next.

I've been off treatment now for five whole months. I stayed off treatment even after the brain involvement was discovered, to protect the lesion the NIH was interested in harvesting for the trial. Thank GOD that during this time, we were able to see how my cancer behaves organically, without any kind of pharmaceutical intervention. Thank GOD my cancer seems slow growing at the moment. Thank GOD it didn't spread to other organs. Lots to be thankful for, this I know. Lots to be pissed about, too.

Right now, I am trying to find the ground. Yet again. This life with cancer demands such flexibility and openness to change at the drop of a hat. It's sickening. You can't get into a promising clinical trial unless you are "sick." You can't just be "sick," you need to be the right amount of sick; you might not be sick enough—so get sicker? Good luck to you if you are deemed "too sick." This dehumanizing health care system does not care about people.

I cannot tell if it is bile creeping up my throat to the back of my tongue, or the taste of disgust.

Perhaps a bit of both.

***Editor's note:***
The essays and poems framed in the following pages were written
and shared while Amy took part in the fall 2018 session
of the Bristol Bookends memoir writing class
at the Bristol Library, Bristol, NY

*Reading
"Three Octobers"
at the Poetry and
Prose Sharefest,
Bristol Library
Fall 2018*

# Living in the In Between*

I walk down the hill to the pond alone. The lush green grass tickles my bare feet, a pine needle or two poke through to the middle of my arches, the sting reminiscent of the time I stepped on a yellow jacket. I was five then. I'm twenty-nine now; I still remember.

I sit cross-legged on the slightly damp and fringy blanket of grass to find a moment or two of peace and inner quiet, my perpetual pursuit as of late. I turn my head from side to side hoping to find release in the form of a "pop" in my neck, a terrible habit I have no interest in breaking. Behind me, my path is still visible in vague imprints from my feet, grass lying low in submission. I wonder if the grass is as bothered by my current weight as I am.

Golden rod, bronzy cattail and purple flowers blend like stippling in a painting. *If this were a painting, what would it be about,* I wonder.

I tilt my head down to my right to see if I can coax just a click or two more out of my neck. The glint of something small catches my eye, and I squint in the sunlight to focus in on it. A tiny pearl? I quickly touch my ears to see which earrings I am wearing (aquamarine, phew!). No, not a pearl, but a perfectly round drop of dew, nestled gently inside the palm of a clover leaf. Not two inches away, several brilliant shimmering beads line a single blade of grass. The desire to touch one, to hold one in my hand is present, despite knowing that I would wreck it all. I behold. I think about other things we humans destroy with our grubby hands, how we always want more, more, more; how I am always wanting more. More dessert, more wine, but mostly more time, as if it has already been stolen from me. (According to statistics, thirty would be just short of a miracle.)

I am learning to live in this state of in-betweens, of squeezing all I can out of moments, like the juice of a lemon, both sweet and bitterly stinging. I am learning to die, too.

The honk of a single pissed-off-sounding goose interrupts my melancholy musings, and I realize my eyes had

*Published in "Self Care," April/May 2019 issue of Wildfire Magazine

been fixed on the water in a daze—my body so completely still, apart from my breath; my mind, a violent hurricane. I am grateful to this angry goose alarm for saving me from the wreckage.

I breathe in through my nose and exhale through my nose, sounds of the ocean created by the constriction of my throat, a close-mouthed, drawn-out "huff," like the sounds I used to get scolded for making as a kid when asked to do anything I didn't want to. Today I still feel like a petulant child; a scared little girl longing for someone to take the wheel of this ship and steer across these murky and turbulent waters to safety, to the other side.

Is there another side to metastatic cancer that is not death?

Like an electric blue string attached to the heavens, a dragonfly zips past my face. I follow it with my eyes as it zig-zags, hovers, and bounces in a syncopated sort of rhythm. Its sharp movements are like a visual hemiola, reminding me that no path is linear. Not the dragonfly's, not the one I made to the pond, nor my path to healing, which has simply become, "my path."

How strange, this dichotomous separation between "then" and "now" in my mind, like the Wizard of Oz movie, from black-and-white to color… or would my life story be more like color to black-and-white?

Has cancer taken beauty from my life? Beauty. My mind drifts to my physical self, what I used to look like. That former self cannot be found in the mirror today. Today I am just shy of 30 pounds heavier than my former life's heaviest weight. I am scarred, my hair is a different color, my breasts have been replaced by foreign objects that feel like the Haribo gummy bears I used to love. My eyes droop now, probably from stress, or aging, or both. My eyebrows are patchy and uneven since my oncologist became my hair dresser. "Damaged goods" comes to mind in moments when I'm feeling particularly sorry for myself.

I do miss the ignorance of my former life. I also miss simply pulling out my debit card and praying there's enough money for gas—this still happens today as I've never been great with money—but it's often coupled with the sobering acknowledgment, as my hands graze over the raised bumps on the plastic, that I may expire before 4/21, the expiration date on the card. I miss the petty concerns that weren't really petty because they were real to me then. I miss it all.

And yet, I don't. I had no idea what life was then. I still don't know, but I'm aware of my uncertainty today; I was not before. I had great expectations from myself, from this life. Today, expectation comes with trepidation and weariness, with the knowledge that the ground could disappear from beneath me at any moment...

A deer fly bites me on my left arm, and I swat, reflexively, too late. There is nothing like the sharp sting of pain in this life to nail you to the present moment. ♦

## I know a girl

I know a girl
who was given a year or less
to live

unless They removed her tongue
(where all the cancer is)
along with her ability to speak
and eat
and sing,
unless They gave her poison
intravenously
and scorched and burned
her neck and throat.

She told Them, "No thank you,
I'll live out my days
*MY* way. I'll drink
my organic juices
bright and tart,
sweet, alive…
I'll sit in an oxygen chamber
and breathe the air through a Darth Vader mask
and bow my head in prayer.
You will not take my Voice
for as long as I'm here."

I'd like to think
I'd choose the same.
For what is life
without chocolate
smooth and velvety.
Or the buoyant and bubbly dance
of champagne on the tongue.

What is this life
without hearing
and feeling the buzz
of your own vocal folds
oscillating
in your throat.

Today she speaks
in an obstructed sort of way
air leaking out
in places it isn't supposed to.
She winces in pain sometimes.
I wonder if it feels raw
and hot
and if she always tastes the salty
metallic taste of blood
like when you bite your lip
by mistake.

I wonder if she's grateful for that, too.

◆

# Awake

Awake in the black of night
again. Mind searching,
hungry,
and yearning
to step out
of the dark
abyss
into the light,
onto the flesh
of ground.

Awake in the black
of night again. Hands
trembling
shaking,
reaching,
grasping.
Gasping for air through a stir-stick straw.
Thirsty capillaries winding like tributaries
forgotten
or frozen over in the dead
of winter.

Awake in the black of night
again.
Will water not squelch these rising flames
in the chest
spreading wildly through blood
to tired organs?

There is no rest for the dying.

◆

## Three Octobers

*October 2016*
Trapped in the merciless undertow of grief,
shock, and horror.
I am sinking fast, barely swimming.
Images of a pale, gaunt version of myself lying
in my childhood bedroom, dressed in all white,
surrounded by candles,
my grieving mother kneeling in prayer for me—
images like this one violently thrash about my mind each time I dare
to close my eyes.
Do not call. Do not write. I am not home.
Most likely at therapy, perhaps at the hospital,
trying to find the parts of myself that were shattered and
scattered like broken glass
just 6 months before.

Every day, a fight. Every day, I succumb
to the skeletal bitch hissing in my ear,
"You can't do it, this life isn't worth it,
just give up, your life is over, why do you bother?"
Her voice has replaced my own.
I am not here.
I am bleeding out.
I am hardly alive.

*October 2017*
Hair growing in, sharp as porcupine needles
Trapped underneath the oppression
of a very-expensive, very-believable "cranial prosthesis"
and therefore, passing as "normal."
"Normal" with a side of hot flashes and night terrors,

"Normal" with tentative sips of wine, eating "with abandon"
once again, after months of rabbit food.
The self-consciousness of new love (don't look at me without
my wig!), onboard its unstoppable train,
moving with magnetic force and a wild momentum.
A new home that has feelings of forever
like I've been here before,
like we've been here before, somehow...
The big bad wolf makes itself known only at workouts and
blood draws.
Huffing and puffing with each furtive step, MCV, MCH both
elevated ("not to worry, just 'anemia of chronic disease'" or,
"it's just the chemo")
Stable scans.
Turning my cheek away
from the sea of pink emerging in the name of "Awareness."
Waiting,
tirelessly waiting,
for the other shoe to drop,
for the slippery downhill slope to my grave
to begin.

*October 2018*
The shoe has dropped, 5 times over.
I put that shoe back on, lace it up tightly and
run.
I pass as healthy without any help;
full head of hair that can be wrangled into a pony tail,
rosy cheeks, bright eyes
legs that run miles,
arms that bear my full weight—no small feat these days.
I feel the familiar resonance of my own voice
This voice, once quivering
barely a whisper, not long ago

This voice, today,
it sings.
Perhaps not the Mozart or Puccini of a surreal lifetime before
but a song of its own
in haunting harmony with a select choir of 155,000 Americans
Dying for a cure.
I am singing my own song.
The melody writes itself.
Unrehearsed.
Not for some grand performance,
not for some display
that fits into the triumphant pink narrative
relentlessly shoved down our throats.
This song is gritty and dissonant.
It is edgy and sad
It is filled with longing
It is beautiful

It has only begun.

◆

# GRANDMA JO
NOVEMBER 24, 2018

It's been almost three years since my Grandma Jo died. And three years since I was first diagnosed with cancer... hard to believe. She died ten days before that horrible day, and someone once said she's no longer with us on this realm, but she's still holding my hand through all this. I'd like to believe this is true even though I don't often feel her around me.

Last night she visited me in my dreams; she hasn't done this in a long time. I woke up in tears. It all felt so real. Her wrinkles and laugh lines, watching her put on her dangly earrings. I even heard her voice. The plot of the dream wasn't memorable in itself, but her face and her eyes and her voice were exactly as they existed when she was alive. I believe it was her. I woke up crying because I think my brain knew I was leaving the dream, which meant I wouldn't see her anymore.

My grieving process (of her sudden death) was completely interrupted and overshadowed by my cancer diagnosis, and I feel like I am beginning the process all over again these days, almost three years later.

This woman took care of me every single day after school, helped me get ready in the morning so my mom could focus on Ryan (my brother), made me countless meals and drove me CRAZY with her obsession for neatness—she would often have me run the vacuum and point out when I missed a spot. She loved to help people organize and purge, and as an adult, clutter makes me anxious. When she came to my mom's house on the weekends to help out with Ryan (who has autism), she would always bring a stash of candy with her. We would cuddle and giggle and call ourselves "the chow hounds." I think I inherited my love of food from her.

Homework time after school at Gram's was actually a lot of fun (most of the time). My cousins and I would sit at the kitchen table, giggling and nibbling on homemade cookies and milk, comparing handwriting and cursive, asking Gram to judge whose was the neatest. (I never won that contest.) She tolerated me in my terrible (moody, mouthy) teens, and even stood up for me when she felt my mother was being too tough. I never went without anything because Grandma Jo wouldn't allow it. She always found a way to get Ryan and me whatever the other kids had.

I wish I had some of the perspective I have today when she was still alive. She used to talk about her childhood and early adult life; I would give anything to hear those stories again. I wish I had listened better. I wish I had been more interested then. It's sad to think that they've died with her.

I remember when she was going through chemotherapy for advanced non-small-cell lung cancer. They gave her an 18-month prognosis. (She lived for another 17 years; prognostication is stupid and pointless.) I was in middle school at the time. I would hear her retch endlessly in the morning before waving us on the bus for school (sometimes she would just tell us she'd see us later as her head was in the toilet bowl), and again in the afternoon after we got off the bus. I knew nothing about cancer then. I saw her devastation when her hair fell out. I think I probably told her, "It's just hair, don't worry, it'll grow back," or something slightly dismissive, and this saddens me today. I wish I could have been more present to her then. I wish I could have said, "I'm sorry, Gram, it does suck. You're still beautiful because you're still you, but I understand this aspect of the situation is really hard," or some 12-year-old's version of that. I wish I had held more of a space for her then. But I guess most 12-year-olds are wrapped up in their own middle school drama and unable to wrap their heads around the psychological challenges of cancer.

She supported me financially during my graduate school auditions, paying for plane tickets and school application fees. She said she was leaning toward Peabody Institute for me (probably because I'd be close to family). When I told Peabody about my cancer diagnosis, they basically said, "So sorry to hear; unfortunately we won't be able to hold your spot for the next year while you go through treatment, so you'll have to reapply and re-audition." I think that would have changed her mind.

Gram, you deserved everything. I wish I had listened more, talked less, and savored each moment with you. I had no idea about the fragility of life when you were still here. I wish I had. Thank you for everything you've given me.

# THOUGHTS ON THE FIRST SNOW
## NOVEMBER 27, 2018

fingertips pink with the sting of cold
from brushing off snow—
heavy, in its semi-melted state
a wet sloshy thud as it hits pavement
from atop my car.
this snow, somewhere between water and ice
comforts me in my own state
of in-betweens.
I suppose I am more
water than ice
in this moment
moving with life
like water droplets down,
down,
down a windshield.
the heaviness of this life has a gravity of its
own,
a momentum pointing to an end.
and nevertheless, we rise.
day in and day out
to kiss the smoothness of our loved ones'
heads,
to breathe in sweet cedar-y smoke from a
fire,
to choke and cry from laughter so deep it
hurts.
I know one day I will freeze as we all do
"someday"
fluidity and motion through this life as we know it will cease to exist.
The thing about ice, though:
it melts
becoming water
again.

# SCANS TOMORROW
DECEMBER 2, 2018

When I was first diagnosed with Stage 4 breast cancer, two years ago, I had no idea of the wild ride I was beginning.

I remember when I was first diagnosed with early-stage disease, I thought I'd "just be able to take a daily pill or two" if the cancer ever came back. Because Stage 4 breast cancer is the elephant in the room. We don't talk about it. It's not something that is discussed upfront in most oncology settings until the official Stage 4 diagnosis is made. And this is probably because it generally lacks the happy triumphant narrative that our society expects when it comes to breast cancer. You know, the one where people survive—albeit scarred and bruised, they can walk away with their lives.

I had no idea that the metastatic breast cancer experience was so incredibly different from the early Stage 1, back in 2016. I had no idea that 30% of all early stagers become metastatic, and that mortality from breast cancer hasn't changed in over 40 years despite all our "awareness." There was so much I didn't know in 2016. But I was about to find out…

Tomorrow I have scans of my entire body. Bones, chest, abdomen, pelvis, and brain. And I am particularly worried about the brain. For a couple different reasons.

I've been off treatment for nine months now, but even if I had been on systemic treatment, the drugs available to me do not protect the brain because science hasn't figured out how to negotiate the blood-brain-barrier, and unfortunately for me, my cancer cells have. So this is where we are in 2018. The average life expectancy for this disease is 2-5 years. I'm coming up on year 3 of living with this disease, and while I'm happy for every day that I'm here on this earth, I am also terrified for what's to come. It's sad to me that despite feeling so great physically for the past nine months, with two prior scans showing minimal disease activity, I haven't really been able to settle in any of it. I'm always on the lookout for signs of "the beginning of the end."

Two weeks ago, I had my first ocular migraine experience, and of course, my first thought was, "It's the cancer." I called my Cancer Center right away and they said that one isolated incident isn't necessarily something to worry about, but to keep them posted over the weekend (this happened on a Friday) and if it happened again, I should let them know. It didn't happen again… until last night. Same exact experience. Aura, flashing ring, followed by a headache an hour later.

It's pretty hard to find peace or feel grounded in this situation. I am doing my very best these last few days, and that has included serious snippiness with pretty much everyone I'm close to. I have such good loving people in my life.

Someone asked me this week if I am used to the scans by now. It was a perfectly fine question, but for some reason, I wanted to scream. The answer is a loud HELL NO. Perhaps I'm used to the rhythm, every three months, the anxiety in the week leading up to them, the anxiety in the period of waiting for results, and then the adjustment based on whatever the scans demonstrate. But no. None of this is "routine" or "normal"—it's just a huge part of my "new normal." By the way, I hate that phrase. It implies a sort of "settling in." And I suppose we settle in as best we can, be it cancer or other life challenges. But I'll be clear: Nothing feels normal about this, not the uncertainty nor the flexibility required to adjust your understanding of your outlook every three months.

I'll find out the brain results on Tuesday, and I'm thankful that I don't have to wait terribly long. I'll get the rest on Thursday, unless I can persuade my brain radiation oncologist to give a quick read on the others…

Anyway. I'm no peach right now, but thank goodness for cbd oil. Hoping to get through this week. And I know I will, no matter what. I have a great team.

246

# LAST CHRISTMAS?
DECEMBER 5, 2018

Will this be my last Christmas? I've had this thought before, but with nine new tumors in my brain and growing cancer in my lungs, this feels more like a possibility than before.

My scans results were not good. Time to get back on a systemic treatment of sorts to address the lung mass and circulating tumor cells, and zap the shit out of my brain. Quite honestly, I had a feeling that these scans weren't going to be good. Stress has been crazy high, and despite feeling well physically, I've been feeling really "off."

Brain metastases are a huge threat to survival, and they are also becoming more common as people live longer with this disease today... which is why we need more research and development of drugs that can penetrate the blood-brain barrier. Life expectancy drops significantly with a diagnosis of brain metastases. And what's crazy is that there are probably more of them in my brain already that just can't be seen yet. My radiation oncologist said these tumors were probably already there at the last scan, just too small to see. Scans don't see individual cells, they see masses.

Thankfully mine are all very small, so I'm able to have SRS again as opposed to whole brain radiation.

A lot of unknowns, but my integrative oncologist is helping us navigate systemic treatment options right now.

Not the way I had hoped to start the Christmas season, but I'm eternally grateful for all the love and support I have in my life.

## NEW
DECEMBER 13, 2018

I'm in victim mode right now and I'm aware of it. This is a place I visit and I don't intend to stay here, but this is where I'm at right now.

The biggest trauma of metastatic cancer (for me) lies in the repetition of wounds ripping wide open— wounds that are doing their damndest to try to heal—and tirelessly bleeding out from these places, emotionally speaking. I guess that's sort of how I see PTSD with regard to cancer. But "post" doesn't really apply here; the trauma is not only in the past, it's in the present reality as well, and most likely in the future—unless a cure is found. So I guess it's more like "present and post traumatic stress disorder."

IV Chemotherapy was my oncologist's first recommendation for me. The moment the word left her lips, I stopped listening—not intentionally, of course, but from shock. My four-and-a-half months of chemotherapy in 2017 were probably some of the darkest days of my entire life. Physically, it was uncomfortable, but psychologically it was almost unbearable. Because for me, this aggressive treatment was just the start of a life filled with treatment. I heard the words "you have Stage 4 cancer," and was rushed into chemo just two weeks later. My ringing of the bell at the end of chemo didn't signify my "survivorship," nor the end of treatment, but the start of a daunting road ahead. The start of a life revolving around treatment.

So last week, when that dreaded word left my oncologist's lips and lingered in the air, I felt sick. I actually tasted metal, like I did so often on chemo. Are we really here in this place again? I guess so. Though I hesitate to say "again" because where I am at present is much more threatening than where I was at my original Stage 4 diagnosis. Instead of one site of metastasis, I now have two, and this second place is the brain, which is an immediate threat to my life. Kind of a "pinch-me" moment, in a horrible sort of way.

Her second recommendation was an option she's brought up in the past. Another hormonal therapy pairing. She favored the chemo slightly over this approach because chemo tends to work faster; hormone therapy needs a few months to kick in.

After a full day of digesting shit news (aka "eating shit"), my family and I had a phone call with my integrative oncologist, who had already reached out to three clinical trials on my behalf. It's really a shame that she isn't covered by insurance, but she is worth every penny.

In an hour I fly to NYC for a consultation, MRI, and neurology and oncology appointments with Weill Cornell for a trial that combines SRS for metastatic brain lesions with an already established immunotherapy drug, Pembrolizumab. I am eligible for the trial, so really I just need to decide based on these appointments if I think it's right for me.

If this isn't a good fit, my plan is to come home, get SRS for the brain lesions here, and then head to MD Anderson in Texas for a trial of a new checkpoint inhibitor in combination with radiation.

A decision needs to be made quickly, as these brain lesions are a threat to my survival and they will keep growing, eventually causing symptoms, which would disqualify me from most clinical trials. My integrative oncologist advised me to begin treatment of some kind to address the brain in one to two weeks. It's been one week since I received the shitty news. So. We are pushing ahead. Onward!

Thank you for all the love and support. I will keep you posted as best I can.

# CLINICAL TRIAL LAND
## DECEMBER 20, 2018

Hello from New York City!*

Since my last entry a week ago, I have enrolled in (and started) the immunotherapy clinical trial for brain metastasis at Weill Cornell / New York Presbyterian. It has been a CRAZY week, and I am so grateful for how quickly all of this has been able to happen.

I found out about this trial on December 6th, and on December 13th at 4:30 a.m. we were on a flight to NYC for a consult, followed by a late flight home on the same day. December 14th was a day of back and forth phone calls with Weill Cornell, my oncology office in Rochester for complete medical records/pathology slides, and various hotels to look into discounted rates for people coming into town for treatment. And this past Monday, we were back in New York to meet with the team and start treatment the next day.

I really have been blessed with the presence of earth angels in my life… in the form of family, friends, and complete strangers. I am so overwhelmed with gratitude for all of the support we've received to get us to the city to start treatment.

---

*Link available here: myterminallife.org*

As far as these clinical trials go, we had really been dealing with roadblock after roadblock up to this point. But this all came together so smoothly, miraculously even. Out of such devastation, we have found new hope.

My first infusion was Tuesday, and I didn't feel anything other than tired, and maybe slightly queasy. The infusion nurses were wonderful. I got a lymphatic massage on my lymphedema arm, and a foot rub! Truly felt like a VIP.

Yesterday I had my first SRS treatment (targeted radiation to select brain mets), today was my second, and tomorrow will be my last. Today immediately following treatment, I developed an ocular migraine—I've only had two before, both were recent, just weeks/days (respectively) before my shitty scans. My radiation oncologist in Rochester didn't think they were cancer related, but of course I'm slightly paranoid (which I think is normal when you have cancer). Today I texted my trial nurse and she arranged a quick meeting with my radiation oncologist within five minutes. He told me that these are just run-of-the-mill ocular migraines, nothing to do with cancer. I don't have any tumors near the optic nerve, which was a relief to hear. It's also a relief that both radiation oncologists were in agreement.

I will return to NYC once every three weeks for infusions of the drug, Pembrolizumab, and every two months for scans. Unfortunately those trips don't often line up, so we will be doing a lot of back and forth.

This is not a particularly well written entry, but I wanted to give a quick update while I'm still awake (I won't be for long). I am so grateful to everyone who made this possible. Susan Rahn, Linda Carey, Dr. Dawn Lemanne, PALS and Tracy Milgram from BRCAStrong, and to those who donated to and/or shared my gofundme. Thank you. NONE of this would be possible without you.

I am patient number ONE for this phase 2 trial. I'm actually really excited about that. I'm praying this approach revolutionizes the treatment of brain metastasis for all cancers, not just breast.

I will write a more thoughtful entry when I'm not so exhausted!

Thank you all again, from the bottom of my heart.

Amy

# *2019*

## DEATH
JANUARY 2, 2019

My relationship with death has taken different shapes over the last (nearly) three years of living with cancer. Generally, it follows a pattern: something devastating and derailing occurs (i.e., diagnosis, cancer rash, Stage 4 diagnosis, progression, discovery of brain mets, more progression, more brain mets, etc.). The thing from left field (whatever it is) ushers death into center stage. And then over time, we (my team—medical and otherwise) adjust and find some normalcy in the new paradigm shift. Until the next shoe drops.

Right now, I'm in the throes of grief and pain over it all. It's a raw depression I haven't known before, and for me, with my history, that's saying something. And yet, this depression feels somehow different from the dark places I have been before. There's a lightness to it. I don't know if that makes sense. Perhaps the lightness comes from my ability to validate my own feelings about a really difficult thing, instead of looking for others to interpret and reflect what I "should" be feeling back to me. Today I know that what I'm grieving is valid. And I'm going through the process of acknowledging my grief in all its forms.

Perhaps it is that I feel nestled, protected, and surrounded by a community of wonderful people. (And guess what! People who feel supported tend to have more intact immune systems!)

Today I feel like the depression I'm experiencing is completely understandable (and I wish it weren't). For the first time in my life, I haven't tried to tell myself that I SHOULD feel better, and that has allowed me to begin to move through some of this oppressive heaviness.

I will be doing some speaking and co-facilitating in an under-graduate religious studies course this spring semester. The course is entitled "Meaning of Death"—you know, nice and light.

I discovered the flyer for the class on my way out of the gym back in November (I'm an alumna and I use the rec center at the school). It immediately grabbed my attention and I decided to reach out to the professor to see if I could possibly sit in on the class. I explained a bit about my situation, and he responded enthusiastically, asking if I'd be interested in collaborating for parts of the curriculum. I said yes, I think because I'm trying to make peace with death while I'm still alive.

Does accepting death mean accepting defeat? This is something I've thought about lately. And I've come up with an answer, but I think that deserves its own post, so I'll hold off, for now.

This is sort of an incomplete entry, but it's reflective of the space I'm in. I don't have answers, just lots of questions.

Happy new year. May 2019 be a year of learning and growth and understanding.

And more reading and coffee-sipping... (Am reading *The Healing Code* by Alexander Lloyd.)

Runs in gloom and sunshine alike...

And listening to my body for cues to slow down...

And many walks in the woods with people I love.

I hope it's a peaceful, loving, and inspiring year for you, too.

# ACCEPTANCE AND CANCER: ANY ADVICE?
JANUARY 6, 2019

A considerable amount of my hair came out in the shower yesterday morning. I don't think I can adequately describe the shock and horror I felt as I peeled the innumerable wet strands from my hand, and watched them swirl their way to the drain. It may have been a little bit easier if I were at home, but I was in the shower at the gym, in public, crying silent tears.

I had labs drawn on Friday showing that my hypothyroidism was being a bit over-treated, pushing me once again into the hyperthyroid zone. This happened once this summer, interestingly around the same time I received stereotactic radiosurgery (SRS) for the first set of brain lesions. Both thyroid issues and SRS can cause hair loss, and both times I've had the SRS treatments I've also had (unrelated) concurrent thyroid upsets from synthroid doses being too high. Pembrolizumab (the drug that I'm on as part of the clinical trial I'm in) can also cause hair loss, but it's generally not full hair loss like seen with chemo. So it seems there are many forces at play possibly contributing to my current state. I've got two dime-size (maybe slightly bigger) patches in the back of my head. Between yesterday and today, I couldn't even guess how many strands I've lost, and I'm terrified that this is just the beginning. Luckily they are not visible at this point because they are underneath a lot of hair, so unless you move hair out of the way, you're not going to see them.

Even so, I am so devastated. Yeah, it's just hair, and also, regrowing this hair that I have today has been such a long and difficult process. Losing my hair the first time was so traumatic, and yesterday's shower brought me right back to that place. Once again, confronted with feelings of powerlessness that are so connected to mortality for me. It isn't really about the hair, though that part really sucks. It's about feeling this life slip through my fingers, it's about watching the remnants of my vitality make its way down a shower drain. Again.

Accepting all of this feels really difficult. I feel so ungrounded lately, and I don't know how to manage my energy or where my focus should be. The anxiety is constant—whether it's about my death and how that will crush the people closest to me and the tremendous aching guilt for all the suffering they are enduring with me... or more seemingly petty things like my weight or my hair, or the fact that I'm nearly 30 and my life looks nothing like my 30-year-old-peers' lives... (Yes, I still feel tremendous pressure to have a "normal life"—intact health, meaningful career, family etc.). Or should my energy be used to cultivate positivity, to shut off the negative stuff, or drown it? Or should I focus on seeking spiritual guidance?

I have reached a breaking point, I think. I'm not a "sitter," I don't like naps; they make me anxious. Doing "nothing" is uncomfortable stuff for me. Today all I did was cry in bed.

And you know what? That's okay. Because some days are like that. Out with the yuck to invite in something else.

Something new.

We leave this coming Thursday for my next round of treatment.

Happy to report that I haven't had an ocular migraine in some time. Immediately after my SRS and infusion in NYC, I was having them pretty much every day for about a week. And all of a sudden... they've vanished.

I know that the radiation oncologist didn't think they were related to the presence of brain metastases because I didn't have any lesions near the optic nerve, but I find their timing pretty suspicious. They were worse and more frequent right after treatment (which I think could POSSIBLY be related to normal and expected swelling from the SRS). And the fact that the migraines disappeared shortly after my first round... well, I'm choosing to view it as a sign that my treatment is doing what it's supposed to do.

I'm in an odd space of trying to accept all of this while trying to be as positive as possible. And I'm struggling to find a balance in it all.

I guess the only way to find the positive is to let the "shit" have its stage time. Maybe that's what today was about. Hopeful that tomorrow will be a day full of movement, in contrast to today's sucky (and inescapable) stagnation.

Okay 2019, I'm ready for something good.

*Always we hope*
*someone else has the answer.*
*Some other place will be better,*
*some other time*
*it will all turn out.*
*This is it.*
*No one else has the answer.*
*No other place will be better,*
*and it has already turned out.*
*At the center of your being you have the answer;*
*you know who you are and you know what you want.*
*There is no need*
*to run outside*
*for better seeing.*
*Nor to peer from a window.*
*Rather abide at*
*the center of your being;*
*for the more you leave it*
*the less you learn.*
*Search your heart*
*And see*
*The way to do*
*Is to be.*

                             –Lao Tzu      (Thank you, Rebecca!)

## LET GO.
JANUARY 18, 2019

For the last three (diagnosed) years, parts of me have been growing and going where they shouldn't. I'm growing too. I had a lesson in letting go this week. It's too long to get into completely so I'll try to summarize.

My December 3$^{rd}$ scans were what prompted all of this movement and change. I hesitate to call them "bad" because they motivated a change that I am beginning to trust in, wholeheartedly. The scans on the 3rd made us look into other options beyond standard of care, and that is what led me to my current clinical trial.

As part of treatment planning with the trial, I had another brain MRI in NYC ten days later. I didn't really think too much of it because in just ten days, it's not really likely that anything will change. I wasn't terribly interested in the report for that reason. So you can imagine that when I happened to peer through my patient portal and find the MRI report with an overall impression of slight "progression" from my last scan ten days before, with mention of "superficial lesions, possibly leptomeningeal or dural in origin"… I lost my shit.

Leptomeningeal carcinomatosis is pretty much a death sentence. Typically people survive 2-4 months. It often leads to invasion of cerebral spinal fluid, which is deadly.

The fact that that word was written in my report (leptomeningeal, not leptomeningeal carcinomatosis, and there is a big difference, as I would later hear) and that this was the first time I was hearing about it—reading a report in my pajamas, alone in bed, one month after the scan was performed—was absolutely devastating. *This is it,* I thought. And also, *why didn't anyone tell me how sick I was/am?*

It turns out that not all diagnostic equipment is the same. The trial in NYC has better, more precise diagnostics than Rochester. After a long and emotional day of attempting to calm my nerves and writing to pretty much everyone involved in my care, I received a phone call from my radiation oncologist in the trial at 6:30 p.m. explaining that NO ONE believes I have leptomeningeal carcinomatosis (and he even brought my case to a neuro-oncology conference, in addition to the normal scrutinizing involved in routine radiology). I just happen to have some lesions within the leptomeningeal margin of the brain. This is not the same as leptomeningeal carcinomatosis. And further, my situation did not change in ten days, but their diagnostics allowed them to see a more precise picture of what was happening in my body. The fact that I have not had any real symptoms is a good sign at this point.

Speaking of symptoms. My migraines have pretty much gone away. I had one a few days after my most recent treatment, and part of me thinks that it could be due to the expected swelling that occurs when treating brain lesions. Despite no one believing that these ocular migraines are connected to cancer, the fact that they've only occurred immediately following treatment (since treatment began) is somehow comforting to me. I'm choosing to believe this is a sign that things are working, that my immune cells are responding to the treatment and going to my needy brain to clean things up, and perhaps causing some swelling from all the cancer-killing activity.

I was also told my first scan in two weeks will likely look worse before it starts to look better. That type of response is common in immunotherapy. So I'm not hoping for worse looking scans, because that seems weird to do, but I am hoping for evidence that things are moving in the right direction.

So, the letting go part: I think I'm coming to accept that *THIS* is my path. It may change. But this is my path right *now*. And I owe it to myself to stop torturing myself, indulging in my every fear and anxiety. I owe it to myself to LIVE. I'm not dead yet.

Thank you for all your support and love through all of this craziness.

## THERE IS NO THEME—JUST READ IT
JANUARY 21, 2019

With all of the money taken in under the guise of "awareness," I find that people still don't know what "metastatic" means, and how metastatic breast cancer differs from an early stage diagnosis. I can't tell you how many times I have heard *"You'll beat this! You're strong!"* from well-meaning people. So much of the time, I just say, "Thank you for your encouragement," because I feel like sharing the truth of what I'm up against is not welcome; it would just be "Depressing" with a capital D. Sometimes it's easier just to smile and nod. I'm not proud of these moments. I feel that not sharing my truth is part of the problem. By keeping quiet, I am allowing the breast cancer narrative that people know and love, to continue to thrive. And that isn't the reality—for myself, or the 41,000 women who lose their lives to the disease every single year in the US alone. And this number is only rising. (The majority of these women were once deemed "cured"…)

This is all symptomatic of a culture that celebrates (deserving) survivors, while (perhaps) unconsciously turning away from those who are told they will not survive, that they will succumb to their disease. I think the problem lies in how we regard aging, illness, death and dying in the West. There is an unwillingness to explore these aspects of life. I spent up until my cancer diagnosis at age 26 thinking about death as an event that would occur "someday," perhaps when I am 90-something, someday far far away.

But really, because I carry life inside of me, I also carry death. All the time. This potential energy within the kinetic. It is as true as my bones. It is as blaring as the silver-dollar patches of white scalp amidst tufts of chestnut colored hair. We hide this inevitable truth from ourselves in the same way I try to conceal my patchy treatment-induced baldness—every day checking the mirror countless times, *"Is my death showing?"*

I know it's there, but I try to conceal it. For myself, maybe, maybe for others. But why? I "know" the facts of metastatic breast cancer. I "know" what I am up against. And then there is this small voice—

as airy and sweet as a child's—that whispers, *"But, **hope!!!**"* And to be honest, it sometimes feels good to hear people telling me I'll "beat it." Can I just say that? Sometimes I'm more than willing to give up my own authority on the matter and replace it with someone else's reflecting a cheerier outlook.

Is hope a form of denial? Is it foolish? Sometimes I obsess over this thought, especially on nights I've had some medical marijuana in me. Tonight is perhaps one of those nights.

I think true acceptance is about being at peace with what is. I cannot say I'm there yet. I can say I'm trying to plant the seeds for it. (Too bad they keep spilling out of my hands.)

With each passing day, I am facing my death in new ways. Headache? You're dying. Nauseous? You're dying. Hair loss? Tired? You're totally dying. (I refuse to give in to napping due to this line of thinking—I know it's a bit irrational.)

What am I so afraid of? The uncertainty? The ambiguity? *What happens when you go? Where do you go?*

Or maybe it's the certainty of it all. The permanence. *(Or is it?)*

Or maybe it's the process of dying. The suffering of the body, the withering of the mind, the devastation of loved ones left on earth.

We fear aging because it represents loss—loss of sight, loss of hearing, of mobility, of agility, of "beauty," of sensation, of vitality, of ability…

… and eventually, loss of life. Of course that's part of it, right?

Life and loss are inextricably linked. Whether I die at 90 or 30, loss will be part of it. That's guaranteed. Buddhists say, life is suffering. I say, *agreed. But it's pretty amazing too.*

You know what I did on December 4<sup>th</sup> after I found out my brain metastases tripled? I went out for breakfast. Somehow the ordinary act of ordering an omelette made sense.

And I wish I could say it was the best omelette I've ever had because I suddenly appreciated life more, savoring every bite, that I was flooded with awareness and appreciation, but that would be a big fat lie. In fact, I probably barely tasted it.

I cried some ugly tears between stringy bites of egg, mushroom and cheese.

*And isn't that beautiful?*

It is. Because grief exists proportionate to love of existence. Even when it SUCKS, this life is something to be prized.

Which brings me back to death and dying. What would it mean to have death inform one's life? What would that *look* like? What of meaning and purpose?

My "Meaning of Death" class at Nazareth College met for the first time last week. We had a lengthy discussion about various hypotheticals: *"What would you do if you knew you were going to die in **10** years? **5** years? **1**?"*

My first thought regarding these questions was, *"Well, what **quality** of life?"* It was interesting to see that I was alone in this thought. No one else brought up quality of life. No one else seemed to consider that their bodies might change or fail them. Because death exists "out *there*." We are *invincible*.

And of course no one else had this question. I'm in a room of healthy 20-year-olds. Why would they assume that they would be less healthy or able?

I miss the innocence and the illusion of it all. And also, I *don't*.

It's both. I'm in a perpetual state of in-betweens.

I want to work toward a place where I am okay with whatever happens. Living another 3 months or another 60 years.

I'm not sure what this requires. Maybe this is where spiritual guidance comes in.

I will say this: I am not unhappy with my life. But it is a struggle.

We need a cure.


## TREATMENT NUMBER 3
FEBRUARY 3, 2019

I left for NYC this past Thursday for treatment on Friday and scans all day Saturday.

I'm currently in my Uber heading to the airport to go back home. I'm dealing with some discomfort from being loaded with both oral and iv contrast for imaging. It generally makes me feel pretty sick. Doing lots of deep breathing!

This particular visit was "mostly business." Treatment day on Friday ended up taking five hours for what should have been maybe one. This is because my port mysteriously decided it didn't want to give good consistent blood return. We literally tried everything. Aerobics, yoga-esque moves, odd positions (including jutting my chest out, hunching my shoulders forward, coughing), strange arm movements, saline iv after saline iv, TPA (a treatment to break up a possible clot or fibrin sheath around the port)… and nothing worked.

They were able to give me treatment because things were going into the port fine, but my labs needed to be drawn peripherally, which is something I try to avoid because my veins are extremely superficial and roll-y. It ended up being fine, but I was concerned about my scans for the next day. My veins would likely blow if they tried to access them for the contrast required for scans; this wasn't my opinion but what my trial NP told me.

On Friday night, my grandma Jo visited me in my dreams. This has only happened one other time in the nearly three years that she's been gone. Nothing remarkable took place. We were in my childhood home and I was younger, maybe high school age. She was watching my brother (and me, I guess?). I told her I was going for a run and she said, "Not too far."

I'd like to think she was dropping by in dreamland to let me know that she's here with me, and that she never wants me far out of her sight! (Some things never change…)

By some miracle, my port issues resolved and I was able to use it for my scans. Thanks, Grandma Jo!

So now, we wait. I should find out tomorrow. My oncologist and NP are hopeful and optimistic. My neurological exams have been unchanged since December, and my ocular migraines have pretty much disappeared. I am looking and feeling mostly well, aside from the fatigue that hit me pretty hard last week. My oncologist said that she doesn't need blood work to know that I'm healthy despite this cancer; I am a picture of health! She also said that if this approach isn't working and we need to regroup, I'm healthy enough to tolerate anything any doctor recommends for me. She believes I am in a favorable position.

Because I like to be prepared for the worst, I asked her what she would recommend next if these results aren't good. She said most likely a single-agent chemotherapy, not a taxane (as I've had Taxol before), but something like Eribulin, or Capecitabine. Trying not to get too ahead of myself...

Regardless of what these images show, I am healthy. These results won't change that. And as I've learned over the last three years, health is truly an invaluable thing.

Thank you all for your continued prayers, love, and support.

# WAITING
FEBRUARY 5, 2019

I have not mastered the virtue of patience.

I am not a graceful "wait-er."

Each time has echoes of the first: Mom and I waiting by the phone in a pile of blankets watching birds outside the window on a cool but sunny day. Missing Grandma.

The second time, too: Teetering on the edge of hope and fear. Mom throws a tissue box across the living room as we learn my mastectomy scar is riddled with cancer. Onto repeat diagnostics.

The third, just weeks later, walking the tight rope again. Has it spread? Lungs look like constellations in the night sky. Stage IV. What does this mean? (I still am trying to figure this out.)

The fourth time was different: I felt hazy and calm. (Maybe the benzos and pot, or maybe my gut knew.) The sun was shining that day. I went into my appointment with a smile. I left with a bigger one.

The fifth does not stand out in memory as particularly agonizing in the waiting. Maybe because I was in the middle of aggressive chemo and already saw a response from the first four rounds. I do remember feeling slightly disappointed that the Taxol didn't debulk as much as the AC. This was my first lesson in the "healing isn't linear" concept. I still had expectations that things would automatically get better. I had no idea about the reality of this disease then. I had no idea that a response to treatment is not guaranteed. I had no idea just how groundless my world was. I'm learning this now.

Sixth, seventh, and eighth: Some highs (stable off-treatment), some lows (discovery of brain involvement). Feeling well, but unsettled and unsafe in the body that contains me. Disconnected. Threats lurking around every corner. How can I feel okay if I'm dying?

266

With each scan, the stakes are higher. With each new breath, I hear the faint whisper of my last on this earth.

I was told I would find out results on Monday; Monday came and went. I went for a run in the morning, and came home to my familiar "awaiting-results-position," nestled in blankets with some show on for background noise to try to drown out the shrieks of panic in my head. Surrounded by a pile of books, searching for peace within the pages—to no avail. Touching my phone every few seconds to check the time, to check my email, my patient portal, close my apps, etc.

Waiting is almost worse than hearing bad news. In the waiting, there is no plan or approach, only catastrophes. In the waiting, I am flailing in the dark, left to try to ignore the fear experienced in every cell of my body.

I should hear soon.

## RESULTS ARE IN
FEBRUARY 6, 2019

I received a phone call yesterday around 11 a.m. from my radiation oncologist at the trial, shortly after I wrote my last entry about Waiting. These scans are such roller-coasters, and each one is its own thing. Each one has its own flavor, and its own set of potential threats. It's crazy-making…

Okay.

There are no new lesions anywhere in my body! I haven't received this kind of news in MONTHS, since the discovery of my first scan for brain lesions back in June, to be precise. Each scan (with the exception of one) showed new brain lesions, new lung lesions, or both.

No new lesions.

I keep repeating this over and over in my head, like the little engine that could. This is REALLY fantastic news. New lesions would most definitely indicate treatment failure.

Immunotherapy is a newer treatment approach, and it is truly a unique one. So unique that it receives its own set of criteria for measuring progression and treatment response, which differs from how radiologists typically interpret scans. For example, RECIST (the tool radiology uses to evaluate images and assess treatment response) for other forms of treatments regards tumor growth of any kind as progression, which indicates treatment failure. For immunotherapy, though, there has been a well-documented phenomenon of patients' tumors increasing in size initially. This sometimes correlates with an immune response.

It's impossible to separate true progression from immune response in a scan. So oftentimes, if the patient is feeling well, the therapy continues with close monitoring.

So, for results: The brain lesions that were treated with SRS have all shrunk in HALF in just six weeks from my first treatment. The lesions that were not treated with SRS have mostly increased slightly. It's too early to tell if this is true progression versus "pseudo" (immune response causing swelling and inflammation). No new lesions in my lungs, either. Some small millimeter growth in some existing nodules. Again, could be progression, or an actual immune response. It's too early to tell.

Given that I am feeling well, we have decided to continue with the current treatment and re-scan in another four weeks. This will give us more answers. But I have a good feeling. My neurological exams have been unchanged since December. I am running and lifting weights and feeling strong and healthy. Also, my migraines have decreased significantly. Last one I had was three weeks ago!

This weekend, I will be walking the runway in New York Fashion Week (NYFW). Such a crazy amazing opportunity. I am modeling for AnaOno, a lingerie line for women who have had breast surgeries related to breast cancer. AnaOno has been in NYFW for three years, in collaboration with Project Cancerland. This year, all the models in the show are metastatic patients, and the funds taken in go to METAvivor, an organization that gives 100% of its money to METASTATIC breast cancer research. I am so thrilled to be part of this once-in-a-lifetime experience.

So for now, I'm celebrating. Because I feel good, and that matters. Putting this cancer stuff on the shelf for a bit (or at least trying to!). Thank you for all the support and prayers and love.

## NYFW 2019
FEBRUARY 17, 2019

I participated in New York Fashion Week last weekend. It was an incredible experience (and admittedly, a bit terrifying—walking the runway in my undies is not something I ever pictured myself doing, and especially not 30 lbs over my natural weight...). When Dana Donofree (owner of AnaOno Intimates) first asked me if I might be interested, I honestly cringed at the thought of taking the stage in all my overweight glory. My body and I aren't really on the best of terms these days; we haven't been for quite some time...

And then I thought, *screw that. I don't want to keep giving my critical inner-bitch power over my life.* And also, **this isn't about me.**

This year, all the models who walked the stage were metastatic breast cancer patients. We raised over $100,000 for METAvivor, funding MBC research. Pretty freaking amazing!

269

On Saturday morning, I headed over to Soho for an interview and photo shoot with Natrelle Implants (they are the creators of the implants I chose for reconstructive surgery). I had my hair and makeup done, which I normally don't really like, but the hair and makeup artists made it so fun—I had such a great team.

Following my interview and photo shoot (and a bit of singing on camera!), I went over to Soho Ink to participate in another interview on metastatic breast cancer and the importance of MBC research, and had my fitting for the show. All of the other models in the show were there, and we worked with a fabulous runway coach to learn how to strut our stuff!

I'll be honest, the runway was probably my least favorite part of the whole experience; I wasn't as comfortable as I'd hoped to be up there (and simultaneously about as comfortable as I expected to be, if that makes sense). But I loved connecting with the other amazing women in the show, and I loved all the interviews. I've learned that I'm actually a pretty good public speaker. I feel myself coming alive in those settings. I had a great time advocating for MBC on Capitol Hill this past October. It felt very comfortable and freeing to share my story with legislators and their correspondents, and I felt similarly comfortable in the interview setting last weekend.

Now I'm left with: what next? I've got some ideas for community fundraising for MBC... stay tuned.

In the meantime, here are some links and pictures from the show and interviews.[*]

---

[*] *Links available here: myterminallife.org*

"People aren't dying from a primary tumor in the breast. They die when it spreads. And so we need more allocated funds toward research to stop it from spreading. One-hundred and sixteen lives are lost every single day to this disease and that needs to change. It's unacceptable."

I think it was an important step for me in terms of self-acceptance. Instead of giving power to the voice in my head that says I'm unworthy because I'm too fat or too sensitive or lacking in some big way, I chose to say yes to owning my body (as opposed to trying to detach from it).

I wish I could say that the experience was transformative and that my body and mind are at peace with one another now, and I no longer hate my stomach or my thighs or arms, but that wouldn't be true. But I did plant the seeds for something new and different for my relationship with myself by saying, "Yes!" Last week I felt like I was almost observing myself feeling all my fears without getting stuck in them. And that's something I'm proud of.

# ALL OVER THE PLACE
FEBRUARY 26, 2019

I had no idea when I was first diagnosed that the fear of "recurrence" would completely consume me, to the point that I found myself wishing it would just happen, because I couldn't handle the anxiety, uncertainty, and fear. And then when I was re-diagnosed metastatic seven months later, I had no idea that the end of chemotherapy would be more challenging for me than the chemo itself. Cancer is not a single event or experience. It is a gaping flesh-wound, with all the appropriate coagulants rushing to its aid, simultaneously exposed to all the lemon and vinegar this life has to offer, stinging and biting. It is shock and horror. It is a diagnosis date, it is the eyes of your oncologist welled-up with tears behind the sheen of glasses. It is a series of horrendous treatments, it is the pain of needles penetrating a newly placed port, it is the steely smell of the infusion center, it is the neon red of Adriamycin, watching the nurse in protective clothing pump hazardous substances into your body. It is the thin-metallic taste on the back of the tongue. It is the shrill but subtle wheeze in your chest at night, a whispering reminder of your impending mortality.

Beyond anything, it is grief. It is saying goodbye to so much, allowing the space for so much Hell to enter in, all in the hopes that someday this will end, that life will begin again without death's icy chill breathing upon your neck.

In just a few days, I have scans to evaluate my body's response to my current clinical trial, immunotherapy combined with stereotactic radiation of select brain lesions. My last scans in early February were a bit inconclusive, as is often the case with the earliest scans for immunotherapy treatments. Most of my brain lesions looked larger, with the exception of those that were irradiated, and a few that appear to be stable, and one that possibly went away, or was possibly a blood vessel all along. Immunotherapy has its own set of criteria for radiologic evaluation. It is not entirely uncommon for lesions to initially look bigger, or "new" lesions (that aren't actually new but are now swollen and enflamed enough to be picked up on a scan) to appear as part of an actual immune response. Unfortunately, it is impossible to distinguish between "pseudo progression" (immune response) and "true progression of disease," so if the patient is feeling well and symptoms have not developed or increased, the therapy is likely continued. That has been the case for me. That is, until this past week.

It has been impossible for me to differentiate between anxiety, side effects from treatment, and potential cancer symptoms. I know anxiety often manifests itself physically, but my body is also under attack here, from both cancer and cancer treatment. Is shortness of breath related to cancer growing in my lungs, or the immunotherapy drug, or am I just on the verge of a panic attack? Is the headache I had yesterday morning a side effect of Lupron (restarted hormone therapy in January) or is this a symptom of swelling in my brain (swelling that we know exists based on my last scans on February $2^{nd}$). Numbness in my hands—neuropathy from treatment, or brain lesions pressing on nerves, or anxiety?

I recently discovered that my body can do headstands and handstands—something I've wanted to incorporate into my yoga practice for quite some time. I asked my oncologist if inversions in yoga should be avoided based on the presence of brain metastases. She had never been asked this question before, but her advice was to not spend *too* much time in those positions. I posed the same question to my integrative oncologist who advised not to do it until things in the brain have been quiet for six to eight months, as the increase in pressure to the brain can cause bleeding. I'm glad I asked, but I'm now a bit worried that I caused irreparable damage to my brain.

*Fucking cancer.*

I suppose I will have more definitive answers on Monday. Waiting is always hard, and each scan is its own thing. I don't know what to expect with this one, and I find myself searching for evidence that this treatment isn't working, not because that's what I want, but because the uncertainty of it all is unbearable. I've been conditioned to expect the worst over this last year. Hope is a hard thing to maintain for me lately.

This entry accurately reflects where I am at present: all over the place.

## HELLO NYC
FEBRUARY 28, 2019

*On my way to NYC, with the pilot of this tiny plane—*
*made possible through the PALS program*

Scans are tomorrow. I was anxious for most of the morning, until our tiny little plane broke through the clouds and into the clear blue sky. Sometimes we all need a reminder that the sun exists, even if we can't see it. I mean that literally as I live in grey Rochester, NY, but I think it also applies metaphorically...*

---

*Link available here: myterminallife.org*

Fingers, toes, and eyeballs crossed for good news to come on Monday... Even if things aren't what we are hoping for, I still have standard of care treatment options, and clinical trials to explore. I so wish I wasn't trying to calculate my life expectancy through average progression-free survival periods of the drugs still available to me, but until MBC gets the funding it deserves for research and new treatments, this is my reality, and the reality of the estimated 250,000 others living with this deadly disease.


## MY BODY IS A STRANGER
MARCH 5, 2019

I received my results yesterday. The microenvironment of the tumor plays a huge role in its ability to survive and thrive. The why's and how's of cancer metastasis still need further clinical investigation. Science does not understand why or how certain cells break off and find new homes in other organs, and in order for new treatments to emerge, this needs to be addressed. This is why funding for metastatic cancer research is critical.

The brain is a unique and complex organ. Unlike any other organ in the body, it comes with its own shield, the blood-brain barrier (BBB), designed to keep things out that don't belong (bacteria, viruses, rogue cells, etc.). Unfortunately, because cancer cells find a way to evade the immune system, certain cells are able to bypass this shield and find a comfy cozy home inside the brain. There is an understanding that cancer cells that make their way to the brain are also biologically different from the cancer cells that have taken up residence elsewhere in the body.

With all that being said, the treatment appears to be working on the brain. I am so grateful for this, as CNS metastases are the biggest threat to my survival at present.

As for the rest of the body: Pembrolizumab alone is not cutting it.

The main tumor in my lung almost doubled in size since my last scan four weeks ago. And that particular lesion is very close to my heart, which is worrisome. The scan before this one showed a very slight increase in that particular lesion from 3.1 cm to 3.4 cm. Today it is measuring at 5.5 cm. Imagine my shock upon hearing this, and seeing it on the screen, as I feel completely fine. No respiratory issues whatsoever.

I also have two very small new hypodense lesions on my liver, most likely representing disease.

My oncologist at the trial is trying to obtain special permission for me to stay on the trial, with the addition of a new hormonal therapy drug to address the disease in the rest of the body. If this is not approved, we will be applying for Compassionate Care in order to receive both treatments.

Insurance can deny this.

This is my reality and the reality of countless others living with terminal illness. Welcome to metastatic breast cancer, where your literal survival is at the mercy of people who don't know you or anything about your life, other than the fact that you have cancer and your request to have treatment outside of the standard of care would cost them money.

They can hear my oncologist's plea and still say, "No, her life isn't worth the money, her life expectancy isn't that long, it will cost too much to try to keep her alive, it's not a worthwhile investment," essentially. What a world we live in.

So now, we wait. I am trusting that things will work out as they are meant to, and that everything I need will come to me, but trust does not mean anxiety-free 100% of the time. I haven't cried since I got the results, but I've had a few bouts of crippling panic today.

If this disease is growing so quickly, how is it that I still feel well? How is it that I'm able to run and jump and lift weights and stand on my head and enjoy food and live a relatively normal life? The images the docs showed me yesterday don't seem to correlate with my experience.

I am grateful for this. I am also scared. It is a strange thing to be housed in a body that is also a home to such insidiousness.

## ORDINARY
MARCH 13, 2019

I spent the better half of Sunday night (into Monday morning) in the ED, receiving bags of fluids and anti-emetics. Non-stop vomiting courtesy of my new treatment regimen, most likely. I've been popping Compazine and Zofran like tic-tacs every day since.

Today I took my doggo for a few miles' run and made a tiny haven in my room. It took getting rid of about eight garbage bags worth of clutter in order to make my little meditation nook, but I'm grateful for the sudden burst of energy and inspiration, for the sweat in my brow, the ache in my back and legs from moving bookshelves and furniture myself.

Sometimes it's not about the monumental, but grounding in the mundane.

## THE ART OF WAITING
MARCH 23, 2019

This title might be misleading because I don't actually have "the answer." But I do know that if I can keep up a routine of some sort, generally the waiting is less excruciating. Maybe the art of waiting is not waiting, but living.

I was told that I would receive the yay or nay regarding the compassionate use of Pembrolizumab early this week. I made several phone calls both to my doc's office and to Merck Pharmaceuticals. Apparently there was a missing form that needed to be filled out before Merck could begin its "benefit investigation" for me. I was told last evening that all my documents are in and I should hear by Monday or Tuesday of next week.

It's frustrating, but I've tried to keep myself busy this week. I gave a talk at Nazareth College on Wednesday, went to yoga and the gym, got together with friends, ate lots of delicious food, went to several appointments (medical and acupuncture) and pretty much refused to wait by my phone.

I think I've discovered that this is a better approach than what I have normally done in the past (anxiously waiting in a pile of

blankets for my phone to ring, nervously checking it every three minutes…). I can't do that anymore. I can't do it to myself. My anxiety impacts the people I'm closest to, in addition to the anxiety they already have, walking this road with me. I didn't let the waiting run my life this week, and I'm glad for it. I made myself get up and out, and even dared to put my phone on silent a few times— how absolutely *ballsy*!

Moving through it. Not sitting in it. I think that's my plan from now on.

Puppy snuggles help, too.

## APPROVED
MARCH 26, 2019

PEMBRO WAS APPROVED!!!!

Thank you to Merck Pharmaceuticals for granting access to this potentially life-prolonging treatment free of cost!

Celebratory post-run BLISS!!!!

Thank you for sending all the love and good vibes! Onward!!!!

**BCCR SPEECH** *(See text in Introduction, pages 21-25)*
APRIL 8, 2019

This was my talk from the 16th annual Cindy L. Dertinger Advanced Breast Cancer seminar through the BCCR.*

## HOLES IN YOUR HEAD ARE A BITCH
APRIL 26, 2019

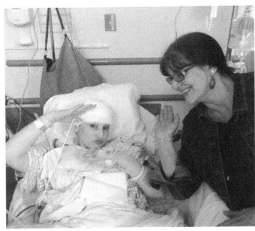

Last weekend my mom and I went down to NYC for "routine scans." I was tentatively booked for surgery on Good Friday to remove a 3.2 cm lesion from my right frontal gyrus, an area of the brain responsible for balance, movement, coordination, sensation. The doctors seemed somewhat surprised that my giant lesion was not causing any symptoms for me; they'd expect to see seizures, one-sided weakness and numbness, in addition to horrible headaches and visual disturbances which I thankfully have not experienced. Yes, in the middle of these shit storms, there is much to be grateful for. My docs brought me in for a PET/MRI combo scan (one of the few hospitals in the country offering this technology) to help clarify the nature of the brain lesions (pseudo-progression or true cancer growth), and they were somewhat surprised to find not a whole lot of PET activity in the scan (PET activity/ increased FDG Uptake correlates with more active tumor). The large tumor was 100% resected, and we are heading to NYC this weekend to do some treatment planning, remove the

---

*Link to video available here: myterminallife.org*

staples from my head, and get some radiation. Check, check, and check.

I am feeling a lot of things right now. I have never ever been a particularly patient person. I am discovering through this recovery process that in order to reduce suffering, I need to put my expectations on the shelf for a while. The body is such an amazing blessing when it works well, moving you through the world with ease and softness and light, and then becomes more of a burden when it no longer does this as you feel it should. I can't work out for a month. No heart rate elevation. Confession: I've been sneaking in calf raises and slow and controlled squats when no one is looking my way because I am a defiant little shit, and "no, you can't do that" generally doesn't work for me. For those of you who know me well, you know that physical activity is hugely important to me. It has allowed me to move through these last three years with some semblance of sanity and composure (not oodles, but some). Yesterday I went for a long walk but was so frustrated with my sudden lack of ability. I've never encountered such emotionally brutal, painful and obvious "no's" in my whole life. With every turn, this body of mine saying "nope, slow down"... how old am I, really? And yet, I have to be grateful that I went into this surgery 100%, and rehab isn't a necessary part of my recovery plan.

My pathology report from surgery introduced me to some new information regarding my disease. Apparently the lesion they removed tested positive for HER2+ gene over expression. We are waiting on the final report, but this actually appears to be good news as HER2+ targets have made huge headway in the breast cancer scene in recent years.

## QUIET TIME
MAY 15, 2019

I know I've been pretty quiet on here for a few weeks. There's lots to say, but in general my surgery/recovery has been pretty challenging. Taking away my ability to exercise (granted it's only for a few more days for a total of four weeks of inactivity) has really been messing with me psychologically. There's also the issue of moodiness brought on by steroids and no real way to diffuse it... We've had to increase my steroid dose twice because I can't seem to stop throwing up, and my headaches are constant (probably from a combination of the aftermath of surgery and SRS, both of which can cause swelling and inflammation in the brain...). I have not been a peach lately. My poor family has had to deal with so much garbage from me.

There's only so many water-color paintings* a girl can start (and not finish) in one day!

I spent yesterday throwing up; today looks a lot the same. Hoping the Ativan will help me sleep a little bit today. I feel like I live in bed lately and I hate it. I'm worried, as I always am when cancer takes center-stage, that where I am in time and space marks the beginning of my decline. I have already outlived the three-year overall survival statistic, which is something to both celebrate and fear. I have been living this life with MBC long enough to know that the story ends the same for each of us facing this diagnosis. I try to balance hope and fear, and lately that balancing act is challenging me in a way I'm

---

* For copies of original paintings shown here and in the following pages visit: myterminallife.org

not used to. Every day during this recovery period seems to have its own flavor of nauseating misery. Either my head hurts or I'm hovering over the toilet bowl, or if I'm lucky, both. I don't want to increase my steroids anymore because I'm afraid I might kill everyone I love in my life (or they might kill *me!*). Apparently the FISH test came back negative for HER2, and I was a little disappointed because negative results remove drug options, and those drug options are my literal life-lines. But luckily my pathology showed that I am still very hormone receptor positive, which is a good thing at this point, as there are many treatment options still available to me.

I'm feeling a nap coming on...

## SELF CARE IS HARD
MAY 25, 2019

I am finding that I really don't know how to care for myself in this place. On top of processing the shock and trauma of my most recent news, I am also fighting my way through a bad cold, steroid rage and depression, and all the demons that come with it. Regular exercise was just approved at the beginning of last week, which is great news. I went to the sauna to try and sweat out some of these cold germs and attempt a light workout to ease back into physical activity. I ended up bawling my eyes out at the gym. I don't think I've ever cried this much in a stretch of time, let alone in public. I tried to run and got through ten minutes of sprint intervals before I felt like I was going to throw up. So then I tried to redirect with some weight training, which I was just advised is more important for me during chemo than cardio. I had a panic attack after one set of lat pull-downs. Somehow managed another two sets, tricep kickbacks, squats, medicine ball thrusts, and abs before darting out in tears.

I don't know how to give myself what I need right now because I don't know what I need. Do I push through the shitty physical feelings and try to soothe my emotions in the ways I'm used to, or do I have to find other ways to achieve some suggestion of peace and calm? I don't know. I'm fucking tired. Of all of it.

**MAY 26, 2019**

*"What matters most is how well you walk through the fire."*
-Charles Bukowski

I'm ready to burn, release. Loosen my military grip.

Like a pissed off phoenix—set me on fire. I need a new beginning.

## CHEMO TOMORROW
MAY 27, 2019

Today I woke up feeling like garbage, which is sort of becoming normal—nauseous, sweaty, and full of mucus... I ended up going to my mom's and napping and bathing and then going for a run with Riley, in that order (which is not exactly the right order). And then I did 22 minutes of HIIT before calling it quits. I hate how out of shape I feel right now. Huffing and puffing after a single SLOW mile is not normal for me. Incomplete workouts are not normal for me, and yet, here we are.

But. I was able to get through today and take care of myself. I'm scared about tomorrow, but I'm also looking forward to it in a way. The Eribulin was tested on my circulating tumor cells when I sent my liquid biopsy to Switzerland last year. The test showed this particular chemo killed 83% of my cancer cells in the lab. Let's pray that it does that much or better in vivo.

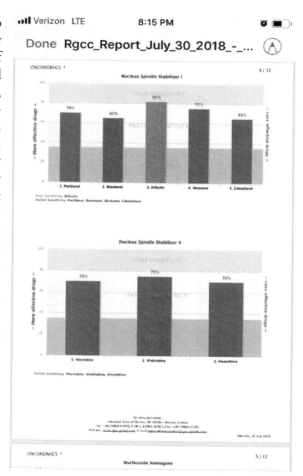

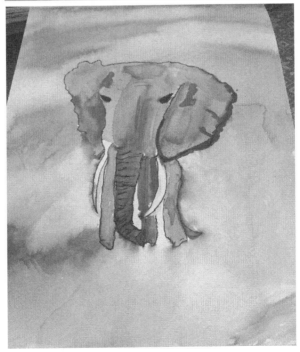

I'm finding tremendous comfort in water-color painting. The process is calming and it takes my mind off of the scariness of life.

Wish me luck for tomorrow—I'll be fasting 'til 2:30 on Wednesday to improve the efficacy of the chemo and prevent nausea and vomiting—a common side effect of this drug.

Thank you all for your continued love and support as I adjust to all of these changes.

## CHEMO 1
MAY 28, 2019

I woke up today with a migraine, which was probably brought on by lack of sleep from steroids, stress, or (my biggest fear) progressing brain mets. No one can tell me the cause of my migraines. I find them at best, unsettling; at worst, pretty terrifying.

I felt sick to my stomach and had all kinds of fun visual experiences, auras, flashing lights. Every day seems to bring on its own unique flare of discomfort. But chemo was relatively uneventful; I had an appointment with my oncologist, labs, and then treatment. The treatment itself took about ten minutes. My labs somehow looked better from the labs that were drawn in NYC on the 23rd. My liver function looked normal again! Praise be!

Pluta Cancer Center is such a blessing to me. I was greeted with hugs and kisses and the "I'm-sorry-you're-back-here-in-this-chair-again-but-let's-turn-this-ship-around-and-kill-some-cancer" pep-talks, and it was just what I needed. So grateful to Kitty and Gail (nurses) for all the love today.

I went into chemo feeling not great (migraine), and left feeling a little queasy, but not terrible. All in all, today was a good day. I am hopeful in this moment. I took Riley for a couple miles' walk today too, and that was nice. Fresh air is a blessing.

Thank you to everyone who has reached out to me. I am grateful for all of you.

## PAINTING MY WAY THROUGH
MAY 29, 2019

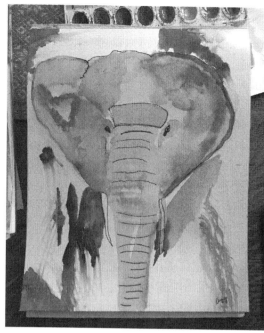

Not sure what the obsession with elephants is all about lately, but I'm just going with it.

Hmm...

Especially as yesterday was the start of a new beginning. "Although he is known by many attributes, Ganesha's elephant head makes him easy to identify.[8] Ganesha is widely revered as the remover of obstacles,[9] the patron of arts and sciences and the deva of intellect and wisdom.[10] As the god of beginnings, he is honoured at the start of rites and ceremonies."

wow how fitting!

Yup!

# I THINK I'M HUMAN AGAIN
MAY 30, 2019

Today I officially re-entered the land of the living. I woke up feeling a little queasy but went to acupuncture and left with a smile on my face, which happened when I was going through AC/T in 2017 pretty much every time. I don't know how acupuncture works, but the fact that it does is wonderful and something I'm truly grateful for.

I went to the sauna and gym at Nazareth and was able to get through a good, compassionate workout, followed by a meeting with my professor friend for a smoothie at Breathe. My nausea started up again, unfortunately, and I've had to take a few anti-nausea meds today. But overall it was a very good day.

I was able to go for a nice long walk with my friend Mackenzie. We had talked about getting coffee beforehand, but with my stomach situation, I didn't want to add anything to it that might complicate things.

I came home and made a "savory oatmeal dish," which sounds weird, but it's essentially oatmeal with tons of veggies and seasonings and some farm fresh eggs (thanks Mrs. Bayer!!). I was finally a little bit hungry and craving something both earthy and bland, and I figured eggs would agree with me.

So far I'm okay, but I really can't taste anything and I'm wondering if this new chemo is altering my tastebuds. Nothing actually tastes right. Even my smoothie at breakfast tasted wrong and chalky. Hoping that if it's a side effect, it will go away. What's life for if not enjoying good food?!

## PAINTINGS
JUNE 2, 2019

I've been painting up a storm lately and I'm finding it really helpful. Just sharing a few of my new pieces. Steroids don't allow me to sleep, which means I'm awake most mornings between 4 and 6 (I am NOT a morning person). And I'm not just sort of awake. I'm wide awake with energy to clean and read and write and, lately, paint.

I think creative outlets are so necessary for my spirit and help to facilitate mental and emotional shifts. I feel like I am shifting lately, and it feels good.

This inability to taste food is really messing with me, though, because food, although always complicated for me, does bring a lot of joy into my life. Not being able to taste or smell is so strange. For example, I know that I normally love Indian food. When I tried to enjoy some spicy Indian veggies the other night, my mouth was watering like crazy, but there was no taste. That's been the case with pretty much everything I've eaten this week. I will say fruit tastes pretty "okay". I enjoyed a really delicious peach yesterday, but what made it delicious was not really the taste as much as the texture— really juicy and ripe. I know that nothing tastes right right now, but I'm not a quitter. I'll keep trying 'til I find my food love again—it's part of who I am, and I am missing that part right now. A lot.

Happy to say the queasiness has dulled, and my energy seems to be returning a bit. I'm still taking it pretty easy, and finding peace with that. It's hard sometimes to be patient but I can feel some of my strength returning and it's encouraging me to just keep on this path and give myself what I need, knowing that my needs are likely to change day to day, moment to moment.

## ODE TO SPRING (POEM)
JUNE 4, 2019

I wrote this poem yesterday in sleepless hours of the early morning. Thanks, steroids, for inspiring some early-morning creativity. (Photo by me as well.)

Ode to spring

The wind and the wisteria dance together
to a song of hushed intensity,
a whisper,
a secret.
It shimmers golden yellow, or silvery blue.
It is the call of the red winged black bird, or the spring peepers at night,
persistent, insistent, as if shouting:
"I bring you perfectly round pearls of dew in the morning in grass and leaves and petals alike.
Pay attention, I come bearing gifts;
The promise of balmy sunsets reflecting on a pond, pink as rosé, seamlessly merging into orange, grey, cerulean, an almost-imperceptible blending, as if God had a watercolor brush in hand and felt compelled to create a series of perfect moments for all eyes to devour and feast upon.

I bring all this to you, and soft kisses from gentle breezes. I bring you hazy heat, and steamy May-showers whose breathy vapors tickle and caress your feet as they evaporate to the heavens once again.

I bring you the budding beauty of bright new flowers beaming yellow and royal purple and fiery unashamed, assertive red.

I bring you the buzzing, electric pulse of insect and wild life in the palpable hunger of the nighttime."

Renewal itself fills the air,
Sweet, fragrant,
clean petrichor sipped through the nose,
a delicious subtlety.
New life abounds.
An abundance of hope, too.
*Sigh.*
Thank you, Spring.

*-Original poem, 6/3/19*

## HOME SWEET HOME
JUNE 9, 2019

I had a brain MRI on Friday, and it was not a bad scan! I have two "punctate" lesions that we will monitor, but even if they are cancer, they are too small to treat at this time. They could be "vascular in etiology," aka blood vessels. So the plan is to re-image in six weeks and see what's what! This is the first not horrendous scan I've had in a while!

I feel myself shifting right now. Releasing and letting go of a lot of emotional stuff. I'm reading a book by David Hawkins currently and it's helping me to process and release a lot of my dense and heavy feelings. I'm grateful for it. Now more than ever, I want to live a life embodying love and connection. I want the people in my life to know just how much they matter to me. I want to be grateful... and I think I'm finding gratitude more easily these days... (Exercise makes me a better person. I swear.) Most of all, I want to be kind. I want to help others. I feel myself healing from the inside out.

I just got home and the first thing I did was hit the water colors. I'm calling this piece: "Home."

## <u>MORE PAINTINGS</u>
JUNE 11, 2019

I am officially an insomniac. Thank goodness for writing and reading and watercolor. I feel so productive lately, though I'm

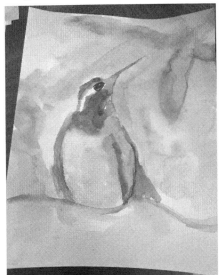

completely exhausted… I'm up early (between 3:30 and 5) every day, to exercise, read, write, paint, make breakfast and coffee, grocery shop, etc… I don't know what's gotten into me over the last few weeks but I'm not entirely mad about it. I could use some more sleep though. Stupid steroids…

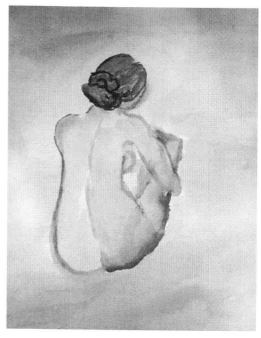

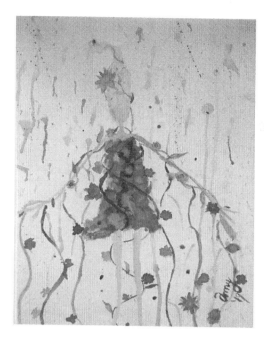

I'm feeling like I have all the "good" aspects of a hypo-manic episode or something.

Dexamethasone can induce mania in some patients, and with my propensity toward moodiness, it's not out of the question, so who knows. Hopefully only a few more weeks on this stuff, and then we will see if this surge of creative energy was all due to the 'roids.

## NEW WIG WHO DIS
JUNE 12, 2019

I picked up my new wig today! Prior to chemotherapy I always had gold-medium-brown hair, and I always got highlights. My hair grew back super dark after chemo, and I got used to being a brunette. In fact, my blonde wig felt sort of wrong... I feel like myself again with this brown hair. (Thank you, Mom!)

*Editor's note:*

The following essay was published by SHARE, a national nonprofit organization that supports, educates, and empowers women affected by breast, ovarian, or metastatic breast cancer.*

---

_* Link available here: myterminallife.org_

# Moving Through Grief: Tips for Living with Metastatic Breast Cancer

I received my metastatic breast cancer diagnosis at 26 years old, on April 11th, 2016. I had just been accepted to my top 3 graduate school programs for Opera Performance and Classical voice the week before and was in the middle of trying to decide between them—all while attempting to process my beloved grand-mother's sudden death on March 30th, 2016. To say this time in my life was "full" is a monstrous understatement. I went from excitedly planning my future to mourning the devastating loss of my grandmother, and of the illusion of the control I had over my life, in a matter of seconds.

The cancer diagnosis felt like a cruel joke. I was not overweight, I was not a smoker, I exercised, I valued health and wellness, and I lacked any of the associated high-risk factors for developing this disease, which is thought to typically impact women in their 60's. I remember expecting to wake up from a terrible dream in the Spring of 2016 and have everything suddenly return to "normal."

My life course has been forever altered by the insidiousness of cancer. Today I live with Metastatic Breast Cancer, with the disease in my lungs, liver, and brain. This also means I live with anxiety, depression, PTSD, and tremendous grief—grief for the countless losses I've already experienced, and the anticipation of how my terminal illness will play out and impact my loved ones. I believe that the experience of living with cancer is inextricably linked to grief. Cancer has a way of stretching and sinking its ugly claws into nearly every aspect of existence. It is a larger-than-life-diagnosis, and it changes so much. In my over three years of living with MBC, I have discovered some tools that allow me to not only cope with all the heaviness associated with the diagnosis, but to lead a life shaped by meaning and purpose.

**1. There is no shame in seeking out therapy and/or medication for management of depression, anxiety, PTSD, grief associated with cancer.**

In my experience, the state of my mental health is equally important to that of my physical health. Cancer is as much psychological as it is physical, and oftentimes the two intersect. My cancer is considered hormone receptor positive (HR+), meaning that the female sex hormones fuel its growth. Because of this, my treatment to this point has been largely based on starving my body of estrogen and progesterone to slow down disease progression. As a 26-year-old, being thrust into the "joys" of chemical menopause through drugs like lupron and aromatase inhibitors had devastating effects on not only my body, but my psyche. I gained weight, I developed severe hot flashes, my bones hurt, and my mood became unmanageable. I honestly wanted to die, and I believe some of the despondence I was encountering was due to the rapid physiological transition from "young maiden" to "old crone," biologically speaking, in addition to processing the sadness and pain around a life interrupted— a life that no longer felt like my own. I ended up in the hospital. I was given mood stabilizers to help me better tolerate menopause and all of its emotional effects, and began Dialectical Behavioral Therapy to help cultivate some much-needed mindfulness in my life. The combination of medication (temporary) and new skills has proven helpful for me, and the techniques I learned in DBT are ones I still use regularly today. I am much more calm and centered today, even in the face of the constant unpredictability and upheaval of life with cancer.

**2. Exercise is good for the soul.**

Exercise helps facilitate emotional shifts and transitions for me, and I don't think that's just the endorphins (though the mood boost doesn't hurt anything!). For one, it increases self-efficacy and encourages a ripple effect in making other healthy and balanced choices in my life (nutrition, sleep). The feelings I encounter in association with MBC are weighty, dense, and often overwhelming.

There is something to be said for physically moving through the feelings—whether it's yoga, dance, kick-boxing, weight-lifting, running, or walking. Movement of any kind helps my feelings move, soften and shift as well. When my oncologist first told me that my diagnostic CT scan showed innumerable pulmonary nodules (lung mets), I immediately took myself for a run, and I realized in the course of my 5 miles that despite the news I had just received, my ontological reality had not really changed. My lungs felt the same as they had before I received this new information. I wasn't suffering physically in any way. Despite my new diagnosis, I was healthy—healthy enough to run 5 miles, to enjoy food, to feel connected to the ebb and flow of my breath, and free of physical pain. That was an invaluable realization for me, and one that I reflect upon often. And luckily, this all remains true today. On days when I'm not feeling my best physically, I often find that some light yoga, stretching, or a walk in the fresh air helps me to reset.

In this article from NBC News *[see p.162]* I spoke with journalist Maggie Fox about how exercise can help fight the fatigue of MBC.

### 3. Get your creativity on!

I have always been drawn to the arts (classical music, drawing, painting, photography). Much like exercise, the arts boost my spirits and give me great pleasure. I believe that positivity attracts positivity, and like exercise, my creative tasks help me feel immersed in a joyful process. At the end of April, I underwent a craniotomy to remove a large metastatic tumor from my brain. During my month-long recovery, I was restricted from engaging in any physical exercise, which challenged my sanity and sense of self. I was forced to get creative with how to pass the time and cope with the emotional stagnation that was rapidly accumulating from my inability to do very much. I found tremendous comfort in watercolor painting, writing poetry, and blogging. Some of my creations are centered on cancer, and some of them are whimsical, light-hearted, and have absolutely nothing to do with "the big C".

## 4. It's okay (and sometimes necessary) to take space from cancer.

One of the trickiest aspects of this disease is how it sneaks into nearly all corners of your life without your permission. It has a way of impacting virtually everything. For the first year of my diagnosis, I struggled with my identity in a significant way. My life trajectory was permanently altered, and suddenly I had taken on the role in my family and friendships as a "sick person," a person who suddenly required more care and attention, and even special-handling. My life felt swallowed up by this new identity— an identity I certainly did not sign up for. I think it is fairly easy for a person with an illness to fall into the role of a helpless victim. That certainly happened for me, somewhat sub-consciously—I was terrified and looking to be led in any way that I could. I was craving safety and security. It took about two years for me to realize that living my life from a place of "why me?" and victimhood was not good for anyone—not my supports, and certainly not myself. At that point, it was time to get empowered. What could I control in this life of mine?

I am generally a very articulate person when it comes to how I'm feeling. I'm pretty open with my experiences around cancer. BUT: sometimes I tell the people in my life that I need a couple of hours or days off from cancer. In reality, we (my loved ones and I) are never fully "off" from it, but this is my attempt to center conversation and focus around things that have absolutely nothing to do with my health. By creating that space for myself and my supporters, I am able to reinforce that cancer doesn't have to touch every corner of my life. In the "no-cancer-zone," I don't want to talk about treatment or clinical trials or research or latest scans and labs, or even how I'm feeling physically. I want to talk about THEM! I want to genuinely share and connect over things that are special and important to my loved ones.

For the first year or so of my diagnosis, I struggled to be present to others in my life. In fact, I was extremely self-centered as I tried to adjust to my new life paradigm. Today, I try to establish some boundaries around my experience with cancer and this is my way of reclaiming some personal power to feel like I'm in my own driver's seat. I am determined to continue to connect deeply and profoundly with my loved ones. I want the people in my life to know how much they matter to me, and cancer doesn't get to take away my ability to relate or connect with them. Lately, I feel a strong desire to give more of myself to the many people I am blessed to have in this life; perhaps this sentimentality is motivated by my fast approaching 30th birthday—a milestone we weren't sure I'd reach when I first received my diagnosis. I have found that taking periodic breaks from cancer and the cancer world/community is necessary for me. I dip into support groups when I need to, and I've gotten pretty skillful in compartmentalizing and separating my experience from other people's experiences with MBC, though it does require conscious effort.

## 5. Connecting to a deeper sense of meaning and purpose.

Viktor Frankl, Holocaust survivor and psychiatrist illustrates in his book *Man's Search for Meaning* that human beings can endure almost anything if they feel connected to a greater sense of purpose. Supporting MBC research gives meaning, shape, and purpose to my life. The lives of those of us living with MBC depends on research and development of life-prolonging treatments. Today, the overwhelming majority of money raised for breast cancer goes toward prevention and general awareness. Unfortunately, this does very little to help people in my position, whose disease has already traveled beyond the breast to other organs.

MBC research benefits everyone at every stage of the diagnosis. One-third of all people diagnosed with early-stage disease will become metastatic months or years after treatment for early-stage disease is completed. We need a CURE for ALL, and that cure will only come through funded research. We lose 116 lives every single day in the US alone to metastatic breast cancer.

This is not okay, and it does not have to be this way. Less than 7% of all money brought in for breast cancer goes toward the terminal form of the illness. Over the last 2 years, I have taken part in several opportunities to share my story. This past October, I marched on Capitol Hill with METAvivor and METUP advocating for increased funding for metastatic research. I participated in a documentary through *So Much More,* a film highlighting the grim truth of living with metastatic breast cancer. I also had the absolute privilege and pleasure to walk the runway in New York Fashion Week this past February for a collaboration between the vision of the late Champagne Joy's Project Cancerland, who lost her life to this disease in 2017, AnaOno Intimates, and METAvivor. The show brought in over $100,000 toward metastatic breast cancer research, which made taking the stage in my skivvies 20 lbs over my natural weight totally worth it. Becoming involved in advocacy has connected me to a sense of community and sisterhood which bolsters my spirits and provides me with much support. I am currently in the process of organizing a concert fundraiser for MBC research within my local community.

So, to recap:

1. Therapy and self-care
2. Movement
3. Finding creativity and joy
4. Taking time and space away from cancer
5. Connecting to a larger meaning and purpose.

Life with MBC is no cakewalk, but it can still be profoundly beautiful. I think the journey to contentment in this turbulent life starts with the gifts we give ourselves. ♦

# A FAT BALD GIFT AND OTHER OPPORTUNITIES FOR GROWTH
## JULY 3, 2019

I have never been truly happy with my physical appearance. Weight has been my biggest "issue." I've been preoccupied with it for most of my life… and it makes me sad to know that that is "normal." Not "right," but pretty normal for women today.

It's funny because seeing old pictures of myself before cancer, I see it so clearly: I was beautiful. Unhappy, yes, but beautiful. Not fat. Not in excess. Just a "healthy" young lady.

I think about what I was doing just before I was diagnosed: auditioning for grad schools and going balls-to-the-wall on an advocare diet program to try to lose that "final 15." The two "activities" were definitely related: I wanted to go to grad school feeling good about myself, confident, and worthy of the young ingénue roles that my voice type was suited for. And that meant I needed to be thin and pretty… *ridiculous*.

And yet. It isn't so ridiculous. I think about how much fear I was carrying then. I was so afraid to *live*, to be my*self*. Because I actually hated myself.

*And then came cancer.*

I can honestly say that the relationship I have with myself is more loving today than it ever has been. I don't exercise to punish myself anymore. Food still remains complicated for me, and I think it probably will for some time, but I also find it a deeply pleasurable experience (despite half-broken taste buds—thank you, Chemo!)

Today I don't look at the scale at doctors' appointments because I know I will find it upsetting. (I've been on steroids for two and a half months, and I am still quite puffy and bloated, despite currently being on the negligible dose of 1 mg for a remainder of four more days.)

And that's what self-compassion looks like today: getting on the scale backwards, and telling the tech I have no interest in knowing the number; I would, however, like to know my heart rate, temperature, and blood pressure, as those values have more "weight" in the overall picture of my health.

I wish it was that I didn't care at all, but I'm in transition around all this stuff. I can tell. Letting go. Really doing it.

I never knew that it was a luxury to have hair. Guess what! It totally is. Same with eyelashes and eyebrows (knock on wood—after six weeks of this new chemo, I still have both of those), and if I lose them, so be it. (Yes I'll be pissed—and I'll probably cry…)

If someone were to have told me that I would lose my hair twice in this lifetime I would have told them first, fuck you, and second, I'd rather die (and probably would have meant it too, sadly…).

Thankfully, a lot has changed in these last three years. Sometimes I feel like I've lived several lives in the one life I've had so far.

And sometimes I think… what a gift is that. A fat, bald, gift.

# *Postscript*

Amy was unfortunately not able to return to her blog posts or finish the book. From July 2019 on, her cancer spread beyond breast, lungs and brain, to her liver, pelvis, skull and eye. She underwent multiple treatments, including a second craniotomy, numerous targeted radiation treatments, and chemotherapies. The treatments and their side effects made for a difficult time for her and her loved ones. But there were also some wonderful, joyful times, including festive celebrations of her 30th birthday (see pictures on pages 318-322).

Amy passed away on December 21, 2019, surrounded by love. May her legacy live on.

*Judy Schnitzler*

# *Epilogue*

There is no such thing as false hope.

—Patti Davis

In the end, we're left to pick up the pieces. We miss what was. We feel the absence of what might have been. We grieve. What did it all mean? How do we make meaning from loss? Where do we possibly go from here?

Well…

What would Amy do?

She'd text her mama. She'd take a bubble bath. She'd paint. She'd curl up with a comfy blanket and watch a favorite series. Or she'd run, and put some distance between her mind and her experience. She'd write. She'd swear. She'd do yoga. She'd educate herself. She'd make a new friend. She'd advocate. But most importantly, she'd do *something*.

I like to think that all of Amy's fears, triumphs, and struggles extend beyond the pages of this book. I hope her experiences touch us in a way that helps us reclaim our own meaning and purpose. I hope her strength emboldens our own sense of determination. I hope her vulnerability helps us explore our own fears and limitations with acceptance, love, and hope. More simply, I hope we are compelled to do *something*, in recognition that this dying comes for us all.

Amy's most fervent wish was to have this book published. She wanted to share her experiences and wanted the proceeds to fund MBC research. Please help her in this goal, so that others on similar journeys may have a better ending to their stories.

*Mark Cohen*

Contributions in Amy's memory may be made to the METAvivor organization, whose mission she highly valued and spoke about with passion:

METAvivor Research and Support, Inc.
1783 Forest Drive #184
Annapolis, MD 21401

http://www.metavivor.org/take-action/memorials/

All proceeds of the sale of this book will be donated to this organization as well as to the Breast Cancer Coalition of Rochester.

Like the clamoring geese overhead
I am coming home

*Amy Schnitzler*

# Acknowledgments

Amy's family would like to give heartfelt thanks to the medical care teams, especially the following:

Brooke Alford, Receptionist, Pluta Cancer Center (Pluta)

Andrew Brandmaier M.D, Ph.D., Radiation Oncologist, New York-Presbyterian/Weill Cornell Medical Center (NYP/WC)

Lisa Choma, Nurse, Pluta

Gail Ferris Cowie, Infusion Nurse, Pluta

Jacqueline M. Doucette, NP, Pluta

Kitty Forbush, Infusion Nurse, Pluta

Robert Fortuna M.D., Primary Care Physician, Culver Medical Group

Amy R. Hayes, NP, Pluta

Robert Hebbs, Ambulatory Technologist for Computed Tomography, University of Rochester

Lesley James, M.D., Integrative M.D., Pittsford, NY

Dawn Lemanne, M.D., M.P.H., Medical Oncologist, Oregon Integrative Oncology

Michelle Shayne M.D., Oncologist, Pluta

Kenneth Usuki M.D., Radiation Oncologist, University of Rochester

Leticia Varella M.D., Oncologist, NYP/WC

Joel Yellin M.D., Surgeon, Rochester General Hospital.

<>

Our deep appreciation also goes out to:

Holly Anderson, Executive Director of the Breast Cancer Coalition of Rochester, for all her help and support.

Bob and Linda Carey, of The Tutu Project, for their generosity.

Dana Donofree, of AnaOno Intimates, for giving Amy the opportunity to participate in the Cancerland Runway Show in February 2019 and appear in the 2020 video, **NOT JUST ONE**, raising money for METAvivor.

Susan Rahn, who connected us with important resources, including the Patient Air Lift Services program, and to participating pilots who provided transportation to and from New York City for the clinical trial.

Nancy Strelau, School of Music, Nazareth College, Rochester, for the care and compassion extended to Amy long after graduation, both personally and musically.

<>

We are grateful to Merck Pharmaceuticals for allowing Amy to continue with the medication when she was no longer able to take part in the clinical trial.

<>

Many thanks to all the wonderful family members and friends who provided loving care and support along the journey. We're especially grateful to Roxanne Cocuzzi, Catharina (Ineke) and Nick Cohen, Dody Flynn, David Mancari, and Sandra Norris, who took turns spending time with Amy and taking care of her when her mother—her main caregiver—needed to return to work.

<>

Last but not least, our love and heartfelt gratitude to Amy's beloved Mark, who was at her side as she transitioned from life as we know it, and to Ineke Cohen, who worked endlessly with Amy and continued to work after Amy's death to make this book a reality.